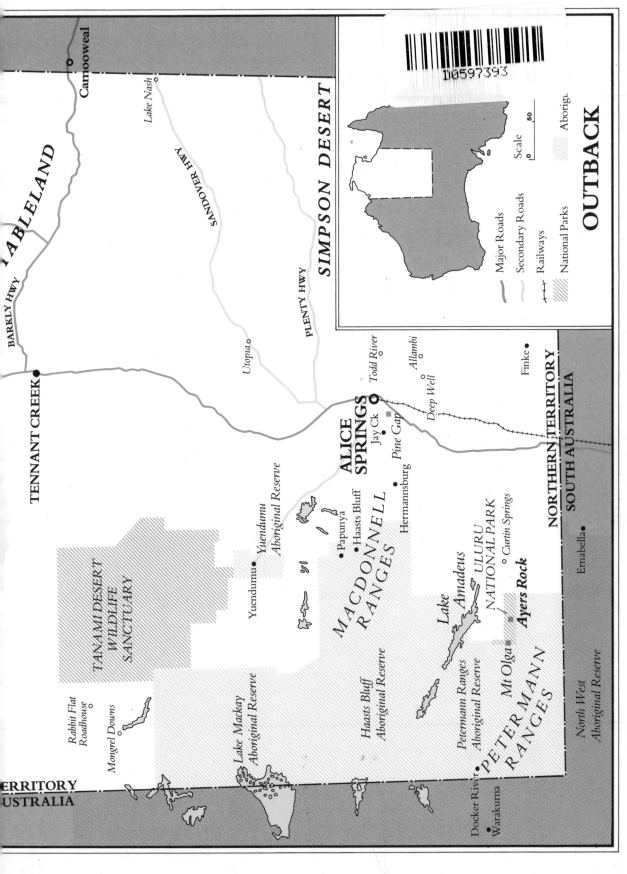

OUTBACK

Major Roads
Secondary Roads
Railways
National Parks
Aborigi.

Scale
0   50

SIMPSON DESERT

ABLELAND

BARKLY HWY

Camooweal

Lake Nash

SANDOVER HWY

PLENTY HWY

Utopia

TENNANT CREEK

ALICE SPRINGS

Todd River

Jay Ck

Pine Gap

Deep Well

Allambi

Finke

NORTHERN TERRITORY
SOUTH AUSTRALIA

Yuendumu
Aboriginal Reserve

Yuendumu

Papunya

Haasts Bluff

Hermannsburg

MACDONNELL RANGES

TANAMI DESERT
WILDLIFE SANCTUARY

Rabbit Flat
Roadhouse

Mongrel Downs

Lake Mackay
Aboriginal Reserve

Haasts Bluff
Aboriginal Reserve

Lake
Amadeus

ULURU
NATIONAL PARK

Curtin Springs

Ayers Rock

Mt Olga

Petermann Ranges
Aboriginal Reserve

PETERMANN RANGES

North West
Aboriginal Reserve

Ernabella

Docker River

Warakurna

ERRITORY
USTRALIA

OUTBACK

To Gary Hansen, Australian photographer and
cinematographer, who died in 1982

OUTBACK
THOMAS KENEALLY

With photographs by

Gary Hansen and

Mark Lang

Rand McNally & Company
Chicago · New York · San Francisco

Published in the United States of America
by Rand McNally & Company, 1984

This book was designed and produced by
The Rainbird Publishing Group Ltd
40 Park Street
London W1Y 4DE

Library of Congress Catalog Card Number: 83-43131

ISBN: 0-528-81109-6

Printed and bound in Hong Kong

Contents

List of Color
Illustrations

Foreword

Outback is of course an Australian word meaning back country. There is an implication of remoteness and sparse population, and remoteness and scarcity of people are at least an element in this book. There is also, behind the word, an implication that very little – in the human sense – happens there, and that what does happen can be slow and undramatic. This book sets itself to show that nothing could be less true. It is as if in the immensity of outback Australia people's temperaments expand like yeast to occupy and give point to the immensities of space. It is hoped therefore that in these pages you will visit an enchanting and unknown country whose customs, secrets, ironies and landscapes you could not previously have guessed at.

To return to the term *outback*: it can be applied to many regions of Australia, but the region which in the imaginations of most Australians is *outback par excellence* is the Northern Territory, and this book deals mainly with the Territory and its neighbouring areas. Among other objectives, it attempts to link the history of that astounding country to the people who live there now. It does not try to give an exhaustive chronology either of the European occupation of the Territory or of the venerable millennia of the Aboriginal Dreaming, but it looks at the frontier which still exists in the Northern Territory, at the men and women – often of a nineteenth-century-style character, certainty and toughness — who live their extraordinary lives there. This account also attempts to enter that tribal cosmos of the Aboriginals, that other Australia of the Aboriginal mind, so different from the Australia of the European as to be another continent, another planet. It tries to examine in graphic terms the points at which the two world-views – white and black – depart from each other or collide.

May the reader be diverted in this strange landscape, among the exotic people of the Territory, in the company of the sorcerers, cattlemen, uranium miners, survivors, and singers of unexpected songs.

Tom Keneally

Tom Keneally

Chapter 1

Rock

One afternoon in October 1872, a Bristol man called Ernest Giles, expiating in the wilderness his undistinguished and drunken youth, rested in the shade of some quandong trees in central Australia. It was a characteristic central Australian spring day, 43°C beneath the quandongs' sparse cover. His companions that afternoon were an English gentleman called Mr Carmichael and a young Aboriginal whose European name was Dick Kew. Dick – being a citified Aboriginal – had had nightmares about how his wild brethren of the interior would treat him. But so far, on his journey with Mr Giles into the Centre, the worst perils they had faced had been distance, thirst and natural obstacles; for example, the feature which now lay before them. It was a vast salt lake, four hundred kilometres in length. If you mounted the sand dune behind the quandong trees, you could see, beyond the blinding dazzle of the salt expanse, some weird rounded mountains to the southwest and, due south, afloat in a sea of mirage, a great red megalith, large as an island, standing by itself. Earlier that day, as well as yesterday and the day before yesterday, Giles Carmichael and Dick Kew had attempted to lead their horses across the salt lake to these mountains and the solitary red rock; but at each crossing point they tried, the horses sank through the salty surface and wallowed in hot, blue, briny mud. For in the desert, mountains were inverted catchment areas; rain ran off their slopes and lay in rock pools or sandy depositories at their base.

Now, in the shade of the low quandongs, while Carmichael mused over a map of Australia which showed the paths of other and perhaps more fortunate explorers, Giles named the vast salt lake Amadeus, after Amadeo the King of Spain, well known as an amateur geographer and a patron of explorers. (That October, Amadeo was beset by Carlist plots in the north of Spain and would not become aware of the honour for some time.) The distant rounded mountains to the southwest, which resembled giant boulders set in the desert and leaning against each other, looking not at all feminine but like a prehuman expression of the soul of this lonely, hard and unnegotiable country, he named Mount Olga after Olga, Grand Duchess of Russia. The great red megalith to the south, however, he left without a name. Thirst, fatigue and the strangeness of the thing defeated the invention of this honest, courageous, visionary young man.

His horses were exhausted by their struggles in the blue mud, so Giles took them back to the nearest waterhole at Thirsty Glen, fifty kilometres to the north. It was a characteristic Centralian watering place – the water was subsurface and a well or tank had to be dug. After each horse had drunk its fill, the tank had to be redug. The Australian wilderness kept most of its water a secret from the sun.

Further attempts to cross the salt lake towards the great unnamed rock would cause more exhaustion, thirst and boggings. Giles had left his base camp in the care of a sick South Australian boy called Robertson, and now, as the summer made travel in unknown and perhaps waterless country impossible, he returned eastwards to this depot.

Ambitious, eager to be well-spoken of in the stiflingly respectable societies of Adelaide and Melbourne, Giles would make five great journeys into the Centre, would suffer deliriums of thirst there and lose members of his party, including Gibson, a hearty illiterate Cockney who vanished on the edges of the desert which now bears his name. But in spite of his emotional investment in this country, Giles would not be the first European to reach the great red and unnamed stone. For in July 1873, William Christie Gosse, the deputy surveyor general of South Australia, following Giles's tracks from the edge of the new telegraph line at Alice Springs, slipped round the eastern shore of Lake Amadeus and arrived at the base of the rock. Gosse – with a more provincial mind than Giles's – named the megalith Ayers Rock after the Premier of South Australia, Sir Henry Ayers. With an Afghan camel driver named

In the Olgas.

10

Khamran, he climbed to the top of the Rock the following day. As any European explorer would have been, Gosse was unconscious of the fact that the Rock had a more ancient name, Uluru, and that at the point of his ascent dwelt the Sacred Water Python of the Yankuntjatjara people. He was not aware that the Rock was the responsibility of these people, who were known to the Aranda desert tribe further north as Luritja, from which the Aboriginal name of the Rock itself was taken.

Gosse called the spring at the base of his ascent Maggie Springs. And why not? It was an age in which new-world tribes were considered benighted, in which the European genius rode high, and all manner of darkness seemed to be receding.

It is now certain that Aboriginal people have occupied the continent of Australia for more than 40,000 years. They came to this ancient land mass more than two ice ages ago. It is confidently believed that, as archaeologists find more camps and burial sites, it will be proved that Aboriginal peoples have lived in northern and central Australia for more than 60,000 years or from three ice eons past. The Aboriginals have never seen themselves as immigrants, however. They look upon their lives as a re-enactment of the journeys and quests undertaken by ancestor heroes on the Australian continent in the *Tjukurapa* – the Dreamtime, before which the earth did not exist.

The tribes which are associated with the great rock of Uluru are the western desert tribes of the Pitjantjatjara and the Yankuntjatjara. These two tribes are related, and though their language is different, they call each other 'our own people'. They intermarry, partly as a means of enriching their own Dreaming, that is of augmenting each other's knowledge of their hero ancestors and of the trails – still existing – which their ancestors followed. (The Pitjantjatjara are such an important tribe in central Australia that it might help the reader to know that most whites in the Centre, like most Aboriginals, seem to pronounce the name *Pitchinjara*. This is not exactly shorthand, but at least it's short tongue.)

In a period of drought during the great European war of 1914–18, the Pitjantjatjara moved in closer to the Rock and took away from their cousins, the Yankuntjatjara, the main ownership of and responsibility for the Rock. But it would be a mistake to believe that this was an invasion in the European sense then being so strenuously exercised in France, Belgium and central Europe. It was a movement partly influenced by the desert-bred thirst and hunger of the Pitjantjatjara, but could also have arisen from a desire to take over certain ritual areas – caves, fertility stones, ceremonial sites – which had fallen into disuse with the Yankuntjatjara.

Whatever the case, in the Aboriginal camp ground at Ayers Rock today you will find both Pitjantjatjara and Yankuntjatjara who point to the Rock and say, 'This is my country.' To both of them it is not the rock of Sir Henry Ayers. It is Uluru, a sacred molar, a vast node of significance on the Dreaming trails which crisscross the Centre of Australia.

It is very hard for a European not to sense some of the sacredness and complex mystery of the Rock. For much of the day the great red

inselberg seems lit from within. Its crevices and caves are marked with ancient naïve but disturbing art. It is becoming a place of pilgrimage for European Australians, its astounding unity and indifference drawing tourists up its flank, specifically at the point known as Webo, the place where the kangaroo-rat men of antiquity crouched, ancestors with both human and animal natures, the fall of their tails creating a slope quite awesome to the European who stands at the bottom and considers the ascent. Giles himself, standing at this point and wondering whether he should make an attempt on the great rock, wrote, 'Its appearance and outline is most imposing, for it is simply a mammoth monolith that rises out of the sandy desert soil around, and stands with a perpendicular and totally inaccessible face at all points, except one slope near the northwest end, and that at least is but a precarious climbing ground . . . Mount Olga is the more wonderful and grotesque; Mount Ayers the more ancient and sublime.'

Twelve European visitors have given their lives to this sublime ascent. Four have died in falls, and eight from heart attacks, and their small memorial plaques, attached to the Rock at the base of the climb, indicate that for many Europeans as well, the place has gained a history and a ritual significance. One of the plaques commemorates a Melbourne man who died of a heart attack on the summit. 'It was one of his lifelong ambitions to climb Ayers Rock,' says his memorial.

The geodetic marker on top of Ayers Rock points north across the desert. But the mathematics of the Rock is the least of its mysteries.

In 1963 the Yankuntjatjara and Pitjantjatjara elders permitted a chain to be installed along Webo (tail), for Webo – though a site of significance – is not a major Dreaming site, not like the cave of the Mala ancestor, half a mile west of Webo. The chain has made the ascent possible for people of average daring, and Australians and foreigners come to the Rock and to the Centre itself, as to an antipodean K'aaba. Australians have always been told that a dead heart lay at the core of their continent. Since this is a demeaning image and since the Rock lies at that heart and seems living and organic, European Australians approach it now with a sense of gratitude. They are delighted to find that its habits are more akin to the living than the dead. Even in geological terms it imitates an animal, for it loses its skin evenly over its entire surface, rather like a snake. Its substance is a sedimentary sandstone called arkose, which erodes by a flaking process known as spalling. Spalling is related to rusting, but it causes an even shedding of surface layers over the entire rock area. The Rock therefore retains its form eternally, in the manner of some grand totemic animal. It is an important, affirmative, national symbol for white Australians, and for such a practical race, they approach it in an almost reverential manner.

The ranger of the Rock is a Yorkshireman called Derek Roff, a former Kenyan policeman, who sees himself as a mediator between the Europeans and the true and traditional owners of Uluru living in the Aboriginal camp near the Rock's south face. He states his task – to make sure that at the same time the sacredness of the Rock has an effect on European visitors, and the European visitors make no inroads on the sacredness of the Rock. He hopes soon to be able to hand to visitors a

In the ascent of the Rock, an enterprise of increasing symbolic importance for white Australians, over a dozen people have been killed in falls or by heart attack. The nearest plaque is to the adolescent victim of a fall from a height where nothing exists except the great red skin of the rock and an electric blue sky.

book on the Aboriginal significance of the Rock prepared by Toby Naninga, an old Yankuntjatjara man who is one of the Rock's traditional owners.

It is a fascinating but sometimes baffling exercise to try to interpret the relationship which tribal people such as Toby Naninga or the Pitjantjat-jara elder, Nipper Winmati, enjoy with the Rock. The hero ancestors in the Dreaming were themselves nomadic hunters and food gatherers and, in desert places, travelled great distances, creating and celebrating the earth as they went. The woman, Bulari, for example, an Earth-Mother figure, gave birth at the Rock after a journey which brought her eastwards from the direction of Mount Conner, a flat-topped mountain to the east of the Rock. Other totemic heroes began their journeying somewhere in the southwest or northwest and created an unchanging Dreaming trail which brought them to the Rock and then onwards to the east. Tribal and family groups still follow these tracks themselves, for there are sites along them made holy by the adventures and activities of the totem heroes.

An Aboriginal map of central Australia would therefore show a network of complex tracks and sites of enormous and sacred tribal

Before the sun spills over to the western side of the Rock, visitors climb Uluru in morning cool. The point of the ascent is known as Webo, or the place where the tails of the half-human, half-animal ancestor heroes of antiquity sloped away to ground level.

OPPOSITE:
The ranger of the Rock, Derek Roff. A Yorkshireman and former Kenyan policeman, his life is dominated by the Rock. His task is to allow white visitors to approach and climb the monolith while at the same time defending the holy significance it holds for the western desert tribes.

significance, including the extraordinary feature Uluru, the Rock. The Rock, for example, is just one point in the great travels of the hare-wallaby people, the lizard men, the carpet snakes. But it is not only for ritual reasons that the Dreaming tracks are followed. Water lies along them in waterholes and soaks, and edible cereals and roots, as well as concentrations of animals – rock wallaby, goannas, kangaroos, euros – can be culled from the country around them.

The reason why the old men of Ayers Rock, Nipper Winmati, say, and Toby Naninga, have such power in the area is because they were born in the vicinity of the Rock, rather than at some further point west or east on one of the Dreaming trails that pass through Uluru. A

Nipper Winmati, Pitjantjatjara elder and one of the traditional owners of the Rock. The house the government built for him stands behind him. Nipper organized the search for the missing infant Azaria Chamberlain in August 1980, and still believes that a dingo was responsible.

European, camping at Ayers Rock and looking over the fence at the fairly haphazard and impromptu Aboriginal shanties, would be mistaken if he saw Nipper or Toby as sad relics of the desert tribes. For these are men of amazing ritual knowledge, direct descendants of the totem heroes, holy repositories for the ritual procedures on the performance of which the continuation of the recognizable earth depends. A European looking at Nipper or Toby would be looking at desert survivors, men who can live in a landscape of widely scattered dry river beds, men who know – in country where at the height of summer a European can perish of thirst in a day – the unlikely places, rock holes or soaks or the moisture-laden roots of desert bushes, in which the ancestral and totemic heroes created or found water for their Aboriginal children. Any European, similarly, who looked on Toby's ageing wife Ada, hobbling towards the Ayers Rock store and trembling from the inroads which Parkinson's disease has made on her body, ought to see her as a woman who knows where food is in a country seemingly vacant of

The sublime sandstone conglomerate texture of Ayers Rock. The double fold of rock whose fall contradicts the slope of the other surfaces here is Kandju, a benevolent lizard who came to Ayers Rock to find his boomerang. Kandju soak, at the base of the lizard, was a very reliable waterhole to the people of the western desert.

PAGE 17:
The Olgas or Katatjuta. Pungalung, the taller of these two mounds, was a Dreamtime giant and de-flowerer of the mice totem women of Mingarri. The smaller of the two domes is Pungalung's former friend, Mudjera, the red lizard. When the de-flowered mice women turned into dingoes and attacked Pungalung, the giant unjustly used his friend the red lizard as a shield. Now the two former friends sit side by side in grand geologic enmity.

PAGE 18:
In the Olgas, near the Valley of the Winds. Every fault and erosion mark is the key to a different Aboriginal fable.

nutriment, who can find it in the seeds of the desert grasses, in the portulaca, which prevents scurvy, in yams and other edible tubers. Ada knows how to get nectar from the wild grevillea. She can make up a paste of rock figs or grass seeds, cooking it on hot stones to make it into a cake. She can live off native peaches and quandongs. She can prepare and eat the insect galls on mulga and bloodwood trees. She knows where the wood grubs can be found, and how the protein-rich witchetty grub can be extracted from the roots of an acacia bush.

She also is descended from a totemic hero, though Ayers Rock is not primarily her country. Desert Aboriginal women marry out of their clan or family group and move away from their country to that of their husbands. Sometimes she returns eastwards, towards her own country, to take part in ceremonies. She passes on to younger women of her own country a knowledge of her own Dreaming – that is, of the Dreamtime rituals associated with her own place of birth. She would also pass on a certain basic knowledge of her husband's Dreaming place, Uluru, the Rock. Nipper, Toby and Ada are – to borrow a phrase from the anthropologist A. P. Elkin – Aboriginal men and women of high degree. They are the maintainers of law and ritual. They decide when the ceremonies, on which tribal life depends for its cohesiveness and its social purpose, will be held. They see themselves not as *owners* of land and ritual but as *custodians*. They maintain the only history of which the Aboriginal is aware – the history of what the totem ancestors did here at Uluru, as distinct from what they might have done somewhere else, to the west, in the Docker River area, or far away east on the fringes of the Simpson Desert. It is the responsibility of men like Toby and Nipper, of women like Ada, to ensure that the adventures and deeds of the Dreamtime ancestors and their rites and rules are kept alive by songs and ceremonies and re-enactments of varying sacredness and secrecy.

The men and women whose country is Uluru have always been fortunate, because the Rock is a great inverted water catchment. The Rock's sporadic rainfall, an average of two hundred millimetres every year, cascades down its red flanks to make eleven waterholes. Some of them have water all the time; not necessarily surface water, but water which can be reached very easily by digging. The most famous waterhole is on the south shady side of the rock. Its name is Mutitjilda, known as Maggie Springs to Europeans. Kandju soak, further north along the flank of the Rock, is – in the terms of the Pitjantjatjara – another rich source. At the time of writing it contains a neat pool of clear water, but, even in the most arid year, water could be found there by digging. Rain falling off the great domed body of Uluru creates a rich fringe of desert grasses and trees around the base and the canny mulga wood, acacias, ancient desert oaks, all secrete the moisture safe from evaporation in their roots. For though Uluru might receive 200 millimetres of rain, the average evaporation rate is 2750 millimetres per year, and while rain is intermittent, evaporation is continuous. Surface water is therefore wasted water, and the desert Aboriginal, unlike a European, is at home with the idea of water secreted in sand or deep tunnels of rock.

Toby Naninga, Yankuntjatjara elder, stands in centralian Eden. A former stockman and ranger, Naninga takes parties of tourists out on 'bush tucker' excursions to discover food in the leaves, branches and roots of desert shrubs.

The plentiful cave system around the base of the Rock provides shelter and sites for ceremonies, and shelter for animals as well. Uluru is still a habitation for the dingo, the euro, the bandicoot, the marsupial mole and a multitude of snakes and lizards, all rich sources of protein; and before tourism girdled the Rock with a road, its watering places drew in kangaroos and emus.

If an Aboriginal is born at or in the vicinity of the north side of the Rock, he becomes a member of the Mala totem group – the Mala being the hare-wallaby ancients and heroes who, in the Dreaming, travelled from the Haast's Bluff area, north of the Tropic of Capricorn, some two hundred and eighty kilometres to Uluru so that their young men could be circumcised and subjected to the ritual of subincision. This rite is a

ceremonial cutting of the lower side of the penis and of the urethra – no doubt enormously painful, yet still practised by some of the desert peoples, including the Pitjantjatjara and Yankuntjatjara, even today.

We know about the journey undertaken by the Mala people because its history is visible in the texture and form of the Rock itself. During their visit to Uluru, the Mala or hare-wallaby women camped at an isolated stone mound at the eastern end of the Rock, a long way from the camp of the initiates and the place of the initiation ceremony. They can still be seen there today, the older women and the children, transformed into boulders. The solanum fruit they gathered and cooked up into solanum cakes are still there, changed into low ridges of rock.

The initiates and old men of the Mala camped at a location now quite visible on the northern face of Uluru. This is the place known to Europeans as the Skull, because the striations and indentations of the cliff face uncannily resemble a skull or even an Aboriginal's head. A stretch of grooves and caves on the right of the Skull is the camp of the fathers of the initiates, and the horizontal patch of striation beside that is the camp of the uncles. (In the uncles' camp an eagle chick called Kudrun was guarded, because the Mala people needed its down for ceremonial occasions, and today, the same as in the Dreaming, the Mala-group men who celebrate the ritual of the Rock decorate themselves with Kudrun's eagle feathers.) Beyond the camp of the uncles, where Kudrun was kept, are seven caves, arranged diagonally on the face of the Rock: the camps of old men not directly involved as officiants in the circumcision rite.

At a time decided by the elders, whenever the rite of the Rock is celebrated, the entire camp is laid out according to this so vastly legible map indented on the face of Uluru. During the days of the ceremony, the women keep themselves separate under the eyes of one old man, while the Mala males live in their four-part cantonment and go through the long cycle of song and re-enactments, working their way towards the act of initiation. The place of initiation for Mala boys is around the northwest corner of the Rock. It is a cave, smooth and wavelike, a typical Uluru grotto caused by differential erosion.

Recently, the Aboriginal elders at Ayers Rock asked Derek Roff to fence this cave off and to place, periodically, notices declaring that this is a sacred Aboriginal site and that Europeans should please keep out. Certainly, the cave of the Mala *is* sacred to Mala men, just as elsewhere around the great circuit of the Rock can be found a cave sacred to women's ritual and to the Earth-Mother Bulari, who, in the Dreaming, gave birth at Uluru. Women passing the cave of the Mala are forbidden even to look in its direction, just as men turn away their eyes from the holy places of women.

Dealing with the request for a fence, Roff was aware that for the Aboriginal, initiation is an astounding event. He says he has seen fathers weep with joy, speaking of their son's recent and successful initiation. He has seen old men return to the Mala cave in which they were once initiated and stand before its ancient and sacred stains, the natural rock table on which they were decorated for the ceremony, and weep with unfeigned gratitude.

Roff's sympathy for the idea of a fence was based on a frank admiration for the desert tribes. 'When I was in the police in Kenya', he says, 'I became fascinated by hunter-gatherer cultures. The Australian Aboriginal . . . look at him in the town and you say, Jesus Christ! But see him in the desert and he's the best there is. In the wilderness, he is at home, comfortable, adept. He's efficient, he's successful.' Roff likes to tell the anecdote about the airforce officer who, studying survival techniques, came into the area to investigate how the Aboriginals find water in the wilderness. 'They don't have to find it,' Roff told him, 'they know where it is.'

Hence there was no question but that Roff would give the request for a fence around the Mala cave his most sympathetic endorsement. He suggested, however, that perhaps the best defence of sacred sites, especially in a protected area like Uluru, was European ignorance. He knows that there are at least two most important women's sites in the area, neither of which the women have actually mentioned to him, and that the women depend on European ignorance, his included, for the ultimate protection of these sacred places. The proposal for the fence brought the sacredness of the Mala cave into open court and attracted hostility from some of the European locals and from Rock enthusiasts in Alice Springs, and Roff says that although this opposition did not worry him, it expressed an ill will which might ultimately lead to the harming of the site.

In the end, the cave and its environs were enclosed with a low two-strand wire fence, which was all that the elders wanted. It is not a punitive fence, it is quite easily breachable. It appeals – in a manner characteristic of the Aboriginal temperament – to European goodwill. European Australians and other tourists *do* keep out, Roff says, and the few who have illicitly visited it since the fence went up have done nothing to touch the substance of the place, have not broken stones or added their own marks to the cave paintings.

On the morning Derek took me to the cave, it was with the consent of the elders. In the geological or scenic sense it is not the most spectacular feature of Uluru, it is not even the most prolifically painted. To be astonished by the cave you would have to know its layered fables and mysteries. Once you do know the little which Europeans are permitted to, awe arises readily.

Down the back wall of the cave runs a vertical black line, on one side of which, during the ceremony, stand the initiate's grandfather, brothers and cousins. On the other side of the line gather the initiate's father, uncles, nephews. A large rock outside the entrance is the sleeping body of the Dreamtime elder who officiated at the Mala initiation. At the front of the cave is a long flat stone running about waist to chest high – it was and is the table on which the Mala group of the Dreamtime and the present painted and still paint the young initiate with various ochres – white, black, yellow and red. Around this table are smooth surfaces where the Mala men have, since before the first swamp dwellings of Europe, ground the ochre; while the young initiate, ambushed and kidnapped in the midst of his carefree and undisciplined childhood and brought to the initiation camp of Uluru, sat still and cowed awaiting the final pain and mystery of the ceremony.

The red oxides of the cave walls are the blood of the first Mala initiates and the blood also of the Mala elders, who cut their arms and let the blood flow. In modern times old men of the Mala group, whether Pitjantjatjara or Yankuntjatjara, cut their arms and spill their blood here, reaffirming their descent from the heroes. Such wounds are celebratory, are not looked upon as sadness or hardship. 'This is a plenty happy place,' an Aboriginal elder told Derek Roff.

While Derek Roff and I stood in the cave, being remotely visible from the road, we heard a man calling to us in heavily accented English. 'Hello! Is not permitted to enter. Please! Is not permitted.' The man, a tourist from Germany, is the sort of visitor upon whom the elders and Roff depend for the continuance of the Rock as both an Aboriginal and European symbol. Roff returned to the road and explained to the man that we were there with the consent of the elders. Even the fact that I am the European ranger, he said, is not the reason I am permitted in. I am permitted there only because, after fourteen years, the elders trust me. He thanked the German heartily for his concern.

The government of the Northern Territory hopes to build to the north of the Olgas a tourist complex capable of housing 6000 people a night. Will they all be as gentle towards the Rock as the German who called from the road? One hopes that the present goodwill which operates at Uluru can survive under the pressure of numbers.

Aboriginal men and women born in the vicinity of the south face of Ayers Rock are members not of the Mala or hare-wallaby group, but of the Kunia or carpet-snake totem people. The Kunia ancestors came to Uluru from the east, from a different point of departure to that of the Mala group, from the direction of Mount Conner. Before the Kunia people came to Uluru, it was merely a waterhole in a desolate plain. The present south face of the Rock was made by the very adventures the Kunia had here. For example, almost halfway between the ascent point which Giles took and the favoured spring of Mutitjilda where Gosse climbed are a series of boulders and interconnecting caves, one small and one large, associated with the Kunia heroine Bulari, who gave birth there, and whose vagina and womb were transformed into the smaller and larger caves. And, of course, imitation of Bulari continues, since Aboriginal women have always sought out the cave as a place to give birth. Bulari's cave was destined also to operate as a trigger in an extraordinary European crime, of which we will speak later.

Most of this south face of the Rock was formed in the Dreaming by a hair-raising battle between the Kunia, carpet-snake people, and the Liru, poisonous-snake people. The Liru came out of the west – the Ayers Rock people had always feared threats from that direction. They camped at the strange and massive series of mountains which Giles called Mount Olga but which the Pitjantjatjara call Katatjuta, or Many Heads. Bulari met the invading snake men and emitted a cloud of *arukwita*, the essence of death and disease. Some Liru men fell before her. At Maggie

Springs, the Liru leader and the Kunia son of another mother heroine, Ingridi, fought each other to the death, Ingridi herself inflicting the mortal wounds which killed the Liru leader. His body, his blood, the blood of Ingridi's son, the red ochre with which she painted herself in grief, and her mouth opened to keen, are all visible in the vicinity of Maggie Springs.

The Liru men were beaten off, but not before so many of the Kunia people were killed that some of the survivors committed suicide in mourning, mainly by chanting *arukwita* into stones or weapons and then swallowing the stones or inflicting wounds on themselves with the weapons. In Ingridi's cave of mourning, it has always been possible to chant an Ingridi song over a bone or some other potentially magical

A painting on the tail of a jet at Alice Springs airport promises whites an Eden at the Rock.

object which, when pointed at a victim, will give off such *arukwita* that death becomes unavoidable.

After their savage attack on the Kunia, the Liru went south, into what is now South Australia, intending to attack other non-poisonous-snake people at a place called Kundana. There they were annihilated, and vanished from the earth.

While the Kunia people were creating the south face by their struggles with the poisonous-snake men, the Mala ancestors on the north side were themselves not free of stress or the pressures of moral choice. They had set up in the midst of their initiation camp a *naldawata* pole, decorated with high colour and with sacred and secret objects hanging from it. Needless to say, such symbolic poles are commonly erected during Aboriginal ceremonies, but during the ritual of the Rock today a *naldawata* pole is never seen, and the reason for its absence is found in the events which overtook the Mala ancestors at Uluru.

While the preparatory ceremonies for the initiation were under way, a messenger arrived from the Docker River area, from the men of a magic and sacred mountain called Kik-in-gura, over two hundred kilometres west of the Rock.

Kik-in-gura is near the present Aboriginal settlement of Docker River, over by the Northern Territory–Western Australia border. Giles, the explorer, taken by Kik-in-gura's fanciful resemblance to a European castle, called it the Ruined Ramparts. But its evocations are far more powerful than that. Just as with the cave of the Mala, women avert their gaze from Kik-in-gura, though it can be seen clearly from the Docker River settlement, slotted majestically in a pass in the Petermann Ranges. In 1978, the wife of a European community adviser who visited a site in the Kik-in-gura area was fined two hundred dollars by the Aboriginal Council of Docker River and told that if she repeated the offence she would be killed. It was from this potent direction that the emissary of the Docker River men came to Uluru in the Dreaming. He invited the Mala men to leave their initiation camp and come to the ceremonies at Kik-in-gura and to bring with them as well their eagle chick Kudrun, so that the Kik-in-gura men could also decorate themselves with eagle down.

The Mala men at the Rock sent back an offensive refusal, rejecting with some contempt the idea that they should share the down of their eagle chick with the Docker River men. They despatched the emissary back to Kik-in-gura with a heap of ashes, indicating that the Kik-in-gura men could use humble fire ash to decorate their bodies, instead of the grandeur of eagle feathers.

On receiving their reply, the Kik-in-gura men were enraged, and the elders sang up a devil dingo, a mad dog, which they filled with malice by means of chant and ritual, having constructed the rudiments of his body out of mulga wood, fragments of marsupial mole and bandicoot, and the hair of women. Instilled with life, the dog travelled to Uluru and attacked the Mala camp at noon, when all but one of the tribesmen were asleep. First, it outflanked the men's camp and attacked the Mala

PAGE 27:
Maggie Springs (Mutitjilda) from which William Christie Gosse made the first European ascent of the Rock in 1873. The Sacred Serpent of Uluru inhabits the rock face of Maggie Springs. He figures in the ceremonies of many clans, and if there should be no water in the spring, he will release it from his body to those of his descendants who stand below and call, 'Kuka . . . Kuka' (Meat . . . Meat).

PAGES 28–9 ABOVE:
Uluru or Ayers Rock called to the explorer Ernest Giles from across the salt wastes of Lake Amadeus. Neither he nor many other Europeans of his day understood that besides its geological curiosity, it signifies – feature by feature – the adventures of Dreamtime ancestors.

PAGE 28 BELOW:
The white path up the holy epidermis of the Rock. Far below, a dirt road veers towards the equally mythic Olgas.

PAGE 29 BELOW:
The superb orange texture of Ayers Rock. Because of a flaking process called spalling, Uluru or Ayers Rock loses its skin of sandstone conglomerate at an even rate over its whole surface. This increases its resemblance to a vast animal, an impression which can cause giddiness and vertigo when you are half-way up its awesome flanks.

PAGES 30–31 ABOVE:
The Olgas, named by the explorer Giles after a Grand Duchess of Russia, are also Katatjuta or Many Heads. Made of a plum-pudding-like conglomerate, they were a home of giants in the Dreaming, as well as the camp-site of the poisonous-snake or Liru people on their way to attack Bulari and her tribe at Ayers Rock.

women, then it moved on to savage the initiates and old men. Some
Kunia or carpet-snake men, who were guests in the Mala camp, fled.
The Mala men themselves were put to flight by the berserk dog. Being
hare-wallaby men, they took bounds to escape eastwards along the base
of the cliff face. The frantic footprints the Mala men left in fleeing are
legible in a series of caves, and the sinuous striations of the Rock are clear
evidence of the flight of the carpet-snake men. 'You can see the panic
written across the base of the cliff,' says Derek Roff.

Some of the young Mala men snatched the *naldawata* pole out of the
mouth of the devil dingo and ran with it to the northwest corner of the
Rock. It is still there, a tall slab of stone separated from Uluru by
differential erosion and misnamed the Kangaroo Tail by Europeans.

Completing his destruction, the devil dingo of Kik-in-gura retreated
to a cave high up on the north face of Uluru, where of course he still
resides. Likewise, in that continuum in which the Dreamtime and the
present become one, the men of Docker River still use ash in their
initiation ceremonies and in their celebration of this myth, just as the
Mala men of Ayers Rock still wear the eagle down of Kudrun.

This myth of the devil dingo seems to have set up a strange reverberation
in the contemporary case of Mrs Lindy Chamberlain. Mrs Chamberlain
is the wife of a Seventh Day Adventist pastor, and with him and her
three children, one an infant named Azaria, she visited the Rock in
August 1980. Azaria in her arms, she went to the cave of Bulari the
mother, and there came face to face with a dingo of whom she said later
that 'he seemed to be casing the baby'.

That night the Chamberlains told their neighbours in the eastern
camp-site of the Rock that a dingo had entered the family's nylon tent
where Azaria and the younger of her two brothers were sleeping and
had emerged with the baby grasped in its mouth; that when Lindy
Chamberlain yelled at the dingo, it vanished into the sandhills behind
the tent.

The dingo came to Australia thousands of years ago across the land
bridges from what is now Indonesia or New Guinea. They are
scavenging dogs, the sort that come into the camp-fire late at night and
clean up the leftovers. But they are hunters as well. They have an
undeserved name as slinkers and cowards, and in Australian argot the
word *dingo* is often used as an intransitive verb to do with cowardice.
People who have a failure of nerve are said to have 'dingoed out'. To a
European Australian, the word is also evocative of cunning and sharp
teeth and the dog itself is uncritically labelled as a threat to the sheep
herds by the farmers of southeastern Australia.

Certainly, less than two weeks before Lindy Chamberlain and her
husband, strangely detached and unpanicked, notified their fellow
campers that a dingo had taken their baby, one of these dogs had
attacked a child in front of Derek Roff's ranger station at Ayers Rock.

Senior Constable Frank Morris, stationed at the Rock at the time of
Azaria's disappearance, had, as a boy from Melbourne, once seen an
advertisement for the Northern Territory Police, a force to which a

certain frontier aura is attached. In the advertisement, a policeman in an open-necked shirt and a wide hat stood by his vehicle in the midst of the desert, communicating by two-way radio with some distant and unintrusive headquarters in Alice Springs, hundreds of kilometres away. That was the image which had seduced Frank Morris to the Territory, and which kept him in outstations like the Rock. He avoided promotion because it would doom him to 'cities' – Alice Springs with its population of 9000 and its race problems, Darwin with its 40,000 people, its sprawling suburbs and its air of tropical ennui.

Morris's relationship with Nipper Winmati and with the European community of the Rock was excellent, and within an hour he had a party of three hundred beating the sandhills to the east, north and west of the Chamberlain camp-site. Nipper, though himself suffering from glaucoma, put a small army of his kinfolk into the sand dunes, and under his direction they discovered signs of a dingo and of a heavy bundle having been dragged through the low growth of the sandhills. The Chamberlains took no part in any of this and Frank Morris was surprised that Pastor Chamberlain did not turn the spotlights attached to his car into the sandhills to light the area for the searchers. He knew, however, that grief was a complex matter, and that it did not do any good to try to make judgements about it.

During the next day and the succeeding week, more senior members of the Northern Territory Police arrived. There were continual searches, but neither the child nor its remains were found. At last the baby's bloodied clothing was discovered, not in the sand dunes but over by the cave of Bulari at the southern base of the Rock. This clothing was sent to forensic experts in Darwin, whose work would later be criticized. Meanwhile, Frank Morris was given the distasteful job of camping in the Maggie Springs area, lighting a camp-fire at dusk, cooking steak and so attracting the dingoes down from the rocks. He would then shoot them and they would be opened in the expectation of finding Azaria's remains. But no trace of the child was ever found by these or any other means.

In the following year, the Chamberlains attracted both international sympathy and hard-headed suspicion. An unjust rumour was touted by the Press that the name Azaria meant 'sacrifice in the desert', and that the Chamberlains, driven by some Old Testament fervour, had sacrificed their daughter at the central feature of the Australian wilderness and then blamed it on the dingo. But in a nationally televised judgement, the Alice Springs coroner quashed this venomous interpretation of the events. His judgement was that Azaria *had* been taken by a dingo, that her body had been found, possibly by a European dingo enthusiast, who – to prevent damage to the already parlous name of the dingo species – had buried the child and left its clothes in a place where they could be readily discovered, perhaps in a misleading direction, so that the search for the child's remains would be called off.

A year after the disappearance of Azaria, Pastor Chamberlain's car was seized by the police. The seizure was a result of a number of factors – the report of a British forensic scientist on the clothing found near

One of the sheer faces of Uluru. The pock marks on its surface are the dwellings of carpet-snake women.

Bulari's cave, and transactions between the Chamberlains and a particular Mount Isa dry-cleaner in Queensland. The Northern Territory Police examined the vehicle and discovered behind its door-panelling copious amounts of blood. A further inquest was held in Alice Springs, and Lindy Chamberlain was committed to trial for the murder of her daughter Azaria. Her husband was charged with being an accessory after the fact. Because it was believed that a fair trial was impossible in Alice Springs, the trial was held in the tropical capital, Darwin. The prosecution's case was that Lindy Chamberlain slashed her daughter's throat in the front seat of the family car, emerged blaming the dingo she had encountered at Bulari's cave, and that the baby lay in the

The European camp at Ayers Rock. From this site, which adjoins the Aboriginal camp, the infant Azaria Chamberlain disappeared, supposedly taken by a dingo, in 1980.

Constable Francis Morris with a Pitjantjatjara friend, at Ayers Rock. Nipper Winmati says of Frank, 'You get married here, you get jiga-jig here, you got baby here. This is your country'.

One of the many salt lakes that proliferate in the Centre.

sedan dead even while the three hundred searchers combed the sandhills. The prosecution further claimed that the Chamberlains buried Azaria's body later in the night, and that they then doctored some of her bloodied clothing, rending it with scissors to simulate the marks of dingo teeth.

In November 1982, Lindy Chamberlain was found guilty of the infanticide of her daughter and was sentenced to life imprisonment. Her husband was found guilty of being an accessory. Though the sentences are presently under appeal, the pitiable thing is that Lindy Chamberlain may have killed her daughter to save her from the dingo in Bulari's cave.

Thirty-two kilometres to the west of the Rock are the extraordinary lumps of conglomerate known as the Olgas. They are different in appearance and texture to the Rock. While the Rock is a seamless divinity, the Olgas are many. While the Rock sloughs its skin a layer at a time, the Olgas shed their plum pudding–like substance of sandstone, granite and basalt in great lumps. But both sites are equally magical. Petroglyphs and paintings and roughly circular arrangements of stone are visible mnemonics of ritual and ancestral activities. Derek Roff says that the Aboriginals of the area do not believe that the paintings in the Olgas are the work of humans, and that this may indicate that they were painted there by the first wave of Aboriginal immigrants who had

passed southeast across the continent before the last ice age.

In April 1979, Nipper Winmati and another Aboriginal owner, Peter Bulla, claimed freehold title to Ayers Rock and Mount Olga under the Aboriginal Land Rights Act. Mr Justice Toohey agreed in his judgement that both Uluru and Katatjuta were places of enormous significance, not only to Nipper Winmati and Peter Bulla but also to a wide range of Aboriginal peoples. He stated that the attachment of all Aboriginal witnesses to both places was quite obvious, but that he could not recommend to the Minister for Aboriginal Affairs the transfer of title, because Uluru and the Olgas were features excised from the local Aboriginal reserve in 1958 and declared a national park. The Northern Territory Government has now committed itself to giving Aboriginals the title to Uluru and the Olgas, and the traditional owners, Nipper and the others, profess themselves happy that the area of the Rock and the Olgas should continue as a national park.

These visible symbols of the Centre, these manifestations of a plenteous Dreaming, first seen by Giles through a haze of thirst from beyond Amadeus, will be visited by increasing numbers of Europeans. Most of them will not be graffitists. Most of them will leave, in the strictest sense, enchanted. But how will the mythologies of the Rock, both so robust and so flimsy, stand up to the pressure of so many European eyes?

Chapter 2

Outback

'Outback Australia' say the number plates of the Northern Territory, and given the bullbars, the rollbars, the searchlights, the aggressive stickers ('Eat More Beef, You Bastards!') which decorate the vehicles of the Territory, given their patina of ochre dust, their dentedness, the emergency canisters of water they carry on their roof racks, the extra tyres and petrol strapped to their rear ends, one is not about to argue. But the outback is no monolithic state, no simple entity. Its capital, Darwin, is itself rich with contradictions. Its suburbs spread like suburbs anywhere. It sports traffic lights. The people on its streets are Greek and Chinese, Timorese, Italian, Vietnamese, and it can therefore claim to be cosmopolitan. Yet wild, sun-blasted men in the frontier mould still turn up there from ridiculously remote reaches of the Australian wilderness to spend their money as men on a binge, men from the frontier, have always spent it – on cataracts of beer and in the mercenary embrace of girls from the city's escort agencies. Nor does the city have any permanence, having been three times blown away in the last eighty years, twice by cyclone, once by bombers. Nor is it secure against intrusions from ancient Australia. During the writing of this book, two tribal *kaditja* men arrived in town to assassinate an Aboriginal who had broken the marriage laws, and officials of the Department of Aboriginal Affairs searched frantically for them so that the execution could be prevented.

The hinterland is no simple entity either. By the uranium escarpments of Arnhem Land bulldozer drivers from Croatia dig a tailings dam for a new mine, while two elders sing up the death of the Aboriginal who gave permission for a Dreaming site to be desecrated by a mineral company. In the mustering camps southwest of Katherine, horsemen, black and white, eat breakfast with a helicopter pilot who will work above their heads all day, driving cattle out of their hides in the long grass and the mulga scrub. In Tennant Creek hospital, a doctor from England and a *ngangkari* (Aboriginal physician) of the Warramunga tribe confer on the case of an Aboriginal child suffering from dehydration and a high fever. In the tropical mining town of Gove, through which no road goes, an engineer from the bauxite refinery trains little athletes, and a Macedonian husband stabs his cousin for reasons of jealousy. At Timber Creek, the manager of a cattle station of 5000 square kilometres, drives up to the pub, a seven-metre crocodile, shot and trussed, in the back of his truck. 'This is the mongrel bastard that got my stallion,' he

PAGE 43:
The Valley of the Winds in the Olgas. Here an old Aboriginal track follows a series of rock-base waterholes.

Number plates grow pitted and
rakish on the Northern
Territory's wild and dusty roads.

PAGE 44:
The Olgas or Katatjuta.
Rock peckings of simple design
in the Olgas. The local
Aboriginals do not believe that
they are the work of humans. It
is possible therefore that they are
the work of a wave of
Aboriginal migration which
passed on east-southeast across the
continent long before the present
Ayers Rock people arrived.

tells the publican. At Mongrel Downs beyond the Tanami Desert, a girl
of nine receives by two-way radio an English lesson from the School of
the Air in Alice Springs, seven hundred kilometres away along a red dust
track. At a place called Utopia, the Aboriginal Land Commissioner
listens to a Pitjantjatjara man claim, in the words of the Land Rights Act,
'primary spiritual responsibility for the site'. Above the Barkly
Tablelands, a flying doctor makes a final approach to a dirt airstrip
marked with forty-four-gallon drums painted white. By the strip, in the
back of a truck, lies a twenty-two-year-old stockman whose ankle has
been crushed by a Land-Rover which rolled while he was chasing a wild
bull. On the upper reaches of the Roper River, two elders have made a
camp and are instructing six Aboriginal adolescents who have been in
trouble with the courts. One of the turbulent boys, painted white, sits by
a camp-fire as the elders tutor him; and although the old men talk in
marvels, he still remembers the pubs of Katherine, and his mind cannot
be rid of the image of a fast red Holden sedan.

In the swamps of Humpty Doo, a middle-class English girl tends her
tomato bushes; and outside Alice Springs, an expatriate American
physicist tests a sample from his solar pond. A truck driver drags an
enormous road train – the truck itself and three 'dogs' – across the dry
river bed where, fifty years ago, the visionary gold seeker Lasseter died
of thirst, while on the Sandy Blight road, a policeman from Ayers Rock
is guided by Aboriginals to a broken-down Land-Rover in which a
European sits, three months dead of thirst and entirely mummified by
the sun. A young cattleman, making a go of it on 3000 square kilometres
at the edge of the Simpson Desert, drives northeast to Alice to take the
daughter of northern Italian immigrants to dinner at the Turner House;
and in the white casino by the Todd River they open the barely used

45

Aboriginal boy, Beswick. There is almost unavoidable pain in this child's future. For him and his contemporaries, the authority of the Dreaming will be vitiated by the appeal of the glittering and dangerous toys of white culture.

back room for some big rollers from Brunei. At Docker River, the elders waylay six adolescents and take them away through Livingstone Pass for a three-week-long initiation ceremony as ordained by the heroes and ancestors of the Dreamtime, which ended yesterday yet continues today. On the Stuart Highway a boy from Melbourne in a fast car, unaware of the irony, bleeps an old man who built the first road from Darwin to Alice Springs.

At a community dinner in Larrimah an old-fashioned politician lets his constituents into the secret that Canberra, and the effete south of Australia in general, couldn't give a damn for them. While, on a beach in Arnhem Land, twenty-three Vietnamese voyagers jump into the shallows from the gunwales of a nine-metre launch.

Chapter 3

The Discovery of
the Outback

Wearing a cheong-sam of gold and black and strolling on a Darwin beach, a Vietnamese Australian named Mi Van Tran describes the journey of the first five Vietnamese to discover Australia from the sea. It was done in this way.

A boy called Tai, the son of an import-export merchant in Cholon, the ethnic Chinese sector of Saigon, left the city to avoid conscription in the South Vietnamese army and went to help his brother, a young man called Hoang, run the family-owned ice works in the provincial town of Rach Gia on the Gulf of Thailand. After the fall of Saigon, Tai's entire family – the parents, two younger brothers and two sisters – also came to live in Rach Gia. They belonged to the class of people who felt they had most to fear from the revolution. They were bourgeoisie, they were ethnic Chinese. To Hoang, the authoritative twenty-five-year-old elder brother, the food shortages and inflation of 1975 seemed to presage greater disasters for 1976 and beyond. With a voyage in mind, he bought an eighteen-metre wooden fishing boat, KG4453, and fitted it with a good diesel engine. To run the boat as a fully registered fishing enterprise, he employed a fisherman named Han, a short robust boy. Meanwhile, Hoang himself studied the rudiments of navigation, and questioned local fishermen about the hazards of crossing the Gulf to Thailand. His main reference for distances, landmarks and currents was an American school atlas of the world, a gift of the Asia Foundation.

The greatest problem the brothers Hoang and Tai had was to convince their father to join them in the escape. A fortune-teller had once told the merchant that he would die by drowning. But once the old man's fear of predestined death had been talked down, Hoang's next task was to persuade Han, the sea-wise young fisherman, the only one who knew anything of practical navigation.

Han did not have any economic motives to escape. He belonged to the class in whose name the long struggle for a united Vietnam had been carried on. But his late father had served in the South Vietnamese army, and the possibility of denunciation by neighbours seems to have been a potent fear with him. He also felt both a fraternal and a retainer-like affection for Tai, and the idea of departing by stealth for a distant port (Hoang spoke constantly of Singapore) appealed to the small-town fisherman. Two other young Chinese Vietnamese, Son and Chau, the former an employee of the ice works and a friend of Tai, the latter a mechanic and Hoang's closest friend, also joined the enterprise.

On 28 February 1976, Han told his fishing crew to stay at home because the boat had to be registered that day. In fact the family of Hoang and Tai, together with the workers Son and Chau, boarded the boat and Han steered it out beyond territorial waters into the open main of the Gulf. Out there, everyone except Han became fiercely ill.

Mi Van Tran at the edge of the Timor Sea, the perilous stretch of water between Timor and Northern Australia crossed by so many of her fellow countrymen.

Han navigated by nose, and Hoang, who understood how to take compass readings, backed up the young fisherman's purely instinctive navigation.

When KG4453 made landfall at the port of Surat Thani in southern Thailand, the father became very excited, for he had grown up in Thailand and had a brother who was a merchant in Bangkok. Though he told the port authorities that the boat would be going on to Singapore, he did in fact mean to stay in Thailand. Therefore, after the group had had a meal of noodles in a restaurant, the father called his brother, the Bangkok merchant, and made arrangements for himself, his wife, his two younger sons and daughters to be picked up by car. He was certain that in a society as susceptible to corruption as Thailand he could, through his brother, achieve residence status.

Hoang did not agree that that was the path the family should follow. Singapore, he said, was a better and more civilized place. But the father, with his dread of the sea, went ahead with the plan, and Hoang and Tai said goodbye to their parents, their younger brothers, their sisters. Then, by force of argument and personality, Hoang convinced the remaining crew to continue with him to Singapore.

At the end of a long voyage down the Malay Peninsula, the young Vietnamese eased the boat into the port of Singapore and remained there undetected for two days. In that time Hoang spoke to various embassies. The Americans did not want to help him, the Australian High Commission offered him only an application form for an entry visa.

On the third day, the boat was boarded by Singapore police. They were, as Han says, 'fierce and angry' and he could not understand what they were saying to the brothers because the conversation was carried on in Cantonese. What was in fact said was that the voyagers and their boat would be given till dawn to leave Singapore.

The refugees and KG4453 then doubled back up the coast to Mersing in Malaysia, but the Malaysian authorities also moved them on. Hoang consulted his school atlas, adding up the distance from Malaysia to the United States. Such a voyage would take them to Borneo, along its north coast, then to the Philippines, next to Guam, and so into the limitless Pacific. A conversation between Han and Hoang at that time indicates the dilemma of the refugee. Han, nervous of the open Pacific, asked Hoang if there was some other place they could go, rather than the United States by way of Guam. Hoang said, 'Perhaps Australia. But if Australia refuses us, where do we go from there? The South Pole?'

At Kuching in Sarawak, they were greeted by the local Chinese community, but two Malaysian patrol boats nonetheless escorted them to the international maritime boundary between the Philippines and Sabah. Instead of voyaging on, however, Hoang and Han sneaked KG4453 back to a deserted beach near the port of Sandakan, where they remained for weeks, resting and exploring.

One day on the beach, Han climbed a coconut palm to fetch down the fruit and, from that height, saw a group of foreigners drinking on the sand. They called to him to fetch them a coconut, which he did. When Han reported their presence to the others, Hoang went to speak with them. They were Australian merchant seamen and told him, 'Don't try the Guam run, mate. You'll never make it.' Hoang explained that there was hardly any choice. But the seamen said that Australia had accepted refugees and might be worth a try.

During the conversation, the Australians found out that KG4453 had no proper charts, and they lifted some from their own ship, leaving them under a stone by a palm tree. Han later claimed that the charts made it all easy, but the others remember that they encountered great seas in the Straits of Makassar and in the Celebes Sea. Beyond Timor, they sailed for sixteen days without seeing land. The detailed charts the Australian seamen had given them covered their journey only as far as the eastern tip of Timor. They were back to the much-handled school atlas for the run across the Timor Sea itself. On the sixteenth day, however, they sighted Bathurst Island. Slipping down the Beagle Gulf, they anchored one evening at dusk off the Darwin suburb of Nightcliffe. They saw Australians strolling on the beach, and by the wall of Lim's restaurant, the property of an earlier voyager from Asia, a crowd was drinking beer and watching the sunset. For this was a bibulous landfall which KG4453 had made.

Next morning, having worked round to the Stokes Hill wharf in Darwin Harbour, Hoang came ashore in a makeshift dinghy and asked an Australian fisherman where the police station was. Like the Chinese, the Portuguese, the Dutch, the Macassans, and the British before them, KG4453 had discovered Australia's wildest coast.

Perhaps it is fanciful to describe Hoang, Tai and the others as discoverers of the Territory, though subjectively they were that. And it was as if they set a precedent, for the five-man crew of KG4453 were only the first of a stream of such travellers.

Mi Van Tran, who was a Vietnamese student in Canberra at the time of the fall of Saigon and who lives in Darwin now with her English husband, has met thirty-two boatloads of refugees. The motives behind their arrival on the coast of the Northern Territory have been akin to Hoang's – hunger, fear, a sense of the nullity of the future, deprivation of educational opportunities. Political and economic motivations were intermingled. 'I think you have to say', said Mi Van, 'that they were in equal measure political *and* economic refugees.'

The smallest refugee craft to pitch up on Australia's northern coast was only eight metres long. Others were eleven to eighteen metres. There was an occasional trawler, hijacked from a Vietnamese fishing fleet or else stolen by its crew. One boatload of over twenty people arrived in Darwin overnight and were found wandering down Smith Street at about store-opening time the next morning. Another of over fifty made landfall in the Wessel Islands of Arnhem Land, and the first Australians they encountered were a group of tribal Aboriginals.

All of them, says Mi Van Tran, ask the question Hoang first posed, 'If the Australians don't take us, where do we go from here?' Most of the later comers have had the benefit of resettlement centres and of an increasing sensitivity from immigration officials. Hoang, Tai, Han,

Chau and Son could fall back only on the goodwill of the St Vincent de Paul Society and of the small Darwin Vietnamese community. Han and Tai successfully took on labouring jobs in Darwin – it was a city which had been devastated only the year before by a cyclone named Tracy. Tai would eventually marry a Timorese Chinese girl, Han would get his mother and his family out of Vietnam – they live now in the suburbs of Darwin. But within eighteen months Hoang and Chau would die in an automobile crash in Queensland, having left Darwin after becoming dispirited by failures in a succession of jobs. Only Hoang's family and, of course, Mi Van Tran, understand what a seafarer had perished when Hoang was killed! She still retains the small school atlas which was the major tool for their journey of 3500 kilometres.

Mi Van Tran herself believes there will be fewer boat people in the future – once it was possible to bribe Vietnamese officials to let people out, but it is not as easy now. She holds four entry visas – for her mother, her sister, her brother, who has recently concluded six years in a labour camp, and for her brother-in-law, who is still interned.

It is hard to get the Vietnamese government, however, to give exit visas to these people. Without being sentimental about it, it is possible to say that for Mi Van, the school atlas is a tangible symbol of what can be achieved.

If Hoang and the others were driven by political and economic motives to seek this fantastically remote coast, what of earlier travellers?

It is believed that the Aboriginal peoples of Australia reached the continent across land bridges either from the direction of Timor or else from New Guinea by way of what are now the Aru Islands off West Irian. If they had come from the Timor direction, they would have had to take canoes across what were known in ancient geography as the Timor Narrows. Whether they came by both routes or either, their many languages and their genetic origins are a mystery. The land bridges were finally washed away some 5000 to 10,000 years ago, enclosing and isolating the race and rendering them immune from outside influence. The people brought with them and further developed on the mainland of Australia a range of tribal structures, each celebrated in its own language. Though in that long occupation of the continent there were interior migrations, the expansion of one tribe's territory, the diminution of another's (as happened in the early twentieth century when the Pitjantjatjara people of the western desert expanded their territory to include the great monolith of Ayers Rock), these movements never occurred in response to any European- or Asian-style concept of conquest. In any case, the expanding tribe would quickly take over the myths and ritual responsibilities of the one that was diminishing. So the ancestors who made the earth, and the rites of renewal which they had initiated, continued in all areas of the continent.

The Aboriginal tribes of Australia, in their long geological isolation, saw the earth as eternal and perfectly constructed by the ancestor heroes. Every aboriginal, male or female, born in Australia during that long isolation, was born through the power of a particular totem ancestor which had both human and animal qualities. Every Aboriginal, male

and female, grew up with a responsibility for the area of his of her birth – whether it be a dry river bed in the western desert or a rocky outcrop in Arnhem Land. His task was to celebrate and maintain that site, to preserve the rituals attached to it by performing them himself, all over again, year by year, with his kinsmen. When the woman gathered food, or the man hunted, the trail he or she followed was not just a hunting trail. It was a Dreaming trail, a trail which one or many ancestors travelled, hunted animals or gathered food on. Life was therefore unchanging, there was no history except the history of the Dreaming, no earth outside the earth made holy by the ancestors, and so no impetus to anyone to become an Aboriginal Genghis Khan. The normal human hunger for power was expressed instead in the acquisition of ritual and magical knowledge. In Arnhem Land today, as on the fringes of the western desert, magic is still more powerful than battalions.

In what is now called the Top End, where monsoonal rains fall from December to March, Aboriginals live, within the tribe, in a clan group. This may consist of seventy people or more. Their clan area will abound in swamps and watercourses, and the earth will be rich with fruit and edible roots. In the desert areas, the basic tribal group will be a single descent line – an old man and his wife, for example, their son and his wife, their children, and the children's unmarried uncles and aunts. Only occasionally, in places where there is plenty of water and food, can an entire desert tribe meet up. When they do, it is always for major ceremonial events. In between these occasional gatherings, contacts between the various groups of the tribe are often kept through marriage – in the desert tribes, the men always marry women from another family group. The new wife brings with her, as a sort of dowry, knowledge of her own family's Dreaming, of her own birthland. There are some areas of knowledge about which she cannot speak, even to her husband. But she presents her husband's family or clan group not just with a new face, not simply with new blood, but with an augmenting of the family's picture of the world. She endows her new husband and his family with a second-class but very real association with her own country, a country of which they may have had, given the extent of the land over which desert tribes are spread, very little real or mythic knowledge.

It all sounds so well arranged, so fundamentally rational that there has always been a temptation to see these tribes who crossed the land bridges to northern Australia as noble though savage saints. Sometimes men would kidnap another tribe's women. There were many ways a man or woman could break the laws of marriage or sexual association, and therefore many ways in which intra- or extra-tribal groups could find themselves lined up, facing each other and armed with spears. And in a society where most deaths and mishaps are believed to stem from sorcery, there have always been retributive spearings of supposed sorcerers from another clan or another tribe. But the truth is that neither in their attitude towards the earth, towards possessions, nor towards history would these sparsely scattered tribes have anything in common with the races they would begin to meet in the second millennium of the Christian era.

Married couple, Bamyili. In the billy can is sugar bag, a wild beehive knocked down out of a tree with a tomahawk. The husband is probably twenty-five years older than his wife, and indicates a tribal tradition by which older men are given young women. As the tribal fabric breaks down, this practice leads to much unrest among the young men; to attempted escapes by young lovers to either Darwin or Alice; and to frequent reprisals by *kaditja* men.

Chapter 4

Early Comers.
Late Comers

A Ming figurine of the God of Longevity was discovered in the roots of a banyan tree at Doctor's Gully in Darwin in 1879. When examined in this century, it raised the possibility that ships of the great Ming fleets of the eunuch admiral, Cheng Ho, which had been operating along the chain of Indonesian islands between 1405 and 1431, might have been the first to intrude on the long isolation of the northern Australian Aboriginal. Certainly the Chinese 'discovered' Timor, and the likelihood that they would go seeking beyond Timor is strong, especially since their ships were so commodious and seaworthy and, for their day, such marvels of modern transport.

A strong lobby of historians seeks to give the credit for the *European* discovery of Australia to the Portuguese, who settled in Timor from 1516 onwards. The claim rests heavily on a map produced by the Dieppe school of mapmakers in the sixteenth century of a coastline marked Jave-la-grande, supposedly based on the charts of Captain de Mendonca. It is plausible that the Portuguese, in Timor for ninety years even before the Dutch had turned up, and being acquisitive and enquiring, would have reconnoitred south of Timor looking for the Southland whose existence the Greek geographers of Alexandria had predicted.

It is the Dutch visitors to northern Australia whose names we know. By the early seventeenth century, the Netherlanders were in residence in the spice islands of the Flores and Celebes. Governors and officials of rugged soul administered the Dutch trading stations. The names of the captains the Dutch governors sent out to look at the rumoured Southland are probably forgotten in modern Holland. They are flung peremptorily at Australian schoolchildren in the first, pre-British chapter of history textbooks, staring out from grainy engravings, remote and barely identifiable in lacy collars and strange-fashioned beards. In fact they were robust men; the moral and spiritual resources of their firmly Protestant souls were enormous, even if there was sometimes a callousness, a narrowness there. They sailed in pinnaces and small ships of generally less than eighty tonnes. They were prodigious navigators. Fever and high seas did not make them quail. They knew that trade was next to Godliness, and that any natives they met were the spawn of Satan. For any Aboriginals they encountered, they represented fair warning of what would come later.

The first Dutchman to visit what is now the Territory was a captain called Willem Jansz, who, in 1605, was given command of a small survey vessel called *Deufken*. Jan Verschoon, the official in charge of the Dutch port and trading station at Bantam, ordered him to explore the coast of New Guinea and other unknown land masses to the south and east. He lost nine men in the enterprise – to man-eaters, he says in his report. (These man-eaters were almost certainly Papuans, since cannibalism – though it has occasionally occurred among Aboriginals, as among Europeans – has no established place in Aboriginal culture.)

After the massacre of his men, Jansz tracked down the Carpentaria coast of northern Australia, but probably believed that too was part of New Guinea. He landed, however, before returning to Bantam with negative reports.

Seventeen years later the governor of Ambon sent out two pinnaces, the *Pera* and the *Arnhem*, on a similar expedition. Jan Carstensz led the party in the *Pera*, but when Captain Meliszoon of the *Arnhem* was murdered with nine of his men on the New Guinea coast, command of the *Arnhem* passed to Willem van Colster. The ships followed the same stretch of coast as the *Deufken* had. But van Colster became rebellious because the voyage was yielding nothing, because he believed the hull of the *Arnhem* was not seaworthy and because its sails and rigging were in such poor condition. One night he steered the *Arnhem* away from the *Pera* and sailed back towards Ambon. At the end of April 1623, he encountered a coast which he named Arnhem Land, after his ship. Arnhem Land, rich in tribes, Dreamings and uranium, did nothing for the Renaissance soul of van Colster.

The reports which van Colster, Carstensz and, later, the great Tasman brought back to their Dutch principals did nothing to encourage any commercial exploitation of Australia's northern coast. For neither van Colster nor Tasman enquired into the world view of the Aboriginal, but judged them instead from the angle of interest of the Dutch East Indies Company, that is, as potential trading partners. From this aspect, the tribesmen were 'indigent and miserable' and had nothing to negotiate, 'having absolutely no knowledge of gold, silver, tin, iron, lead or copper, and also of nutmegs, cloves and pepper'. There is no doubt that the Aboriginals, if told of the indifference of the Dutch, would have been delighted by it.

In this vacuum created by Dutch uninterest, double-ruddered praus from the great ports of Macassar began to visit the Arnhem Land coast, and would do so for the next three hundred years to collect *bêche-de-mer* or trepang, an edible sea slug, popular in chinese food and famed as an aphrodisiac, from the shallow waters of the Arafura Sea. The coastal natives of Arnhem Land still call white men 'balanda', which is believed to be a corruption of Hollander, the name they called the Macassan trepangers. A fleet of up to 1000 persons might spend a season dragging trepang from the shallow sea bed of northern Australia, drinking with the coastal Aboriginals, making alliances with their women, and introducing venereal disease. For the tribes of the interior, the Dreaming continued. But for the Tiwis of Bathurst Island, the Murngin and Gunwinggu of Arnhem Land, the Larrakeyah of what would be the Darwin area or the tribes of the Cobourg peninsula, the ancient *stasis* of the world took its first shock. Some Aboriginals became so popular with the trepangers that they sailed with them up the Indonesian peninsula and as far as Singapore. It is hard to imagine what sort of shock the Singapore of say the 1820s was to an Aboriginal's picture of himself, his ancestors, his clan and tribe. But these transcultural refugees can serve as a symbol of the relentless toll of shocks which have occurred since.

On a more benign level, it is believed that the Aboriginals of Arnhem Land might have got their taste for wearing pointed beards from the Macassan trepangers, who themselves acquired it from the Dutch. Van Dyke, it seems, cast a long shadow.

You would think that the best way for a European to discover the Australian Aboriginals is through the word of anthropologists. Some modern anthropologists, however, deny that this is absolutely true.

Mark de Graaf, a Dutch-born Australian anthropologist living and teaching in Darwin, says there have been too many European presumptions in the attitudes scholars have taken towards the Australian Aboriginals — especially towards the desert Aboriginals. Yet, he announces, the only way you will ever find that out is to spend months at a time in the desert, as he does himself. He has lived and travelled on foot with family groups in the Gibson, in the Great Sandy Desert to the north of the Gibson, and in the Tanami. He is involved as a ceremonial member in three descent groups. He avoids the application of the word 'clan' to the desert Aboriginals because in the desert it can take four hundred to five hundred square kilometres to support one patriarch, his wives and children. Yet although up until the middle of the 1960s the anthropological view of these people was that they lived always on the edge of misery, he says that if he had to find an epithet for his experiences – always taking account of the fact, of course, that at the end he would be getting out and going home – he would use without apology the term 'the Good Life'. De Graaf took up his interest in anthropology while a young schoolteacher in the Warburton Ranges mission in Western Australia. In those days, he says, the missionaries would try to prevent tribal ceremonies by driving Land-Rovers through the midst of them. After some years of travel in the Gibson Desert area, he went off to the University of Perth, on the grounds that if he had discovered so much as merely an observant schoolteacher, how much more must the anthropologists in the major universities know. He claims to have been disappointed.

It is true that many of the older anthropologists worked in the manner of Margaret Mead, interviewing subjects not in their own milieu but in a European one, on the verandah of a mission house, say, at a table covered with texts and notebooks. One aspect in particular of what de Graaf was taught in the cities distressed him. It was taken for granted that Aboriginal women had no important ceremonial functions. They were involved purely with love magic, with seduction rituals. It has always been known that women are powerfully engaged in love magic. In Arnhem Land, for example, they sing love chants from a distance at the men they desire, often invoking the help of animals, the elements and so

Mark de Graaf, rebel anthropologist, has been granted membership of three Aboriginal descent groups in the western desert. Though he says that older anthropologists have tended to pity the desert Aboriginal, if he himself had to think of a term to summarize the life of the desert Aboriginal, he would choose 'the Good Life'.

on, often singing *djarada* (or love magic) into weapons or other objects which belong to the man, or into something he has thrown away, or else into his excreta. But apart from the power of *djarada*, and a certain basic and childlike knowledge of Dreamtime history, it was assumed the women have no secrets and no knowledge. Yet de Graaf had been impressed by a Warburton woman who had said to him, 'We women got our Dreaming too.' She explained to him that those white professors were never told about it, partly because they were men, partly because they took it for granted that women were powerless.

It has taken the arrival of female anthropologists, their coming to mature womanhood and hence to an age when they can be acquainted with some of the truth of the earth, to adjust the traditional picture of the Aboriginal woman as a mere seductress excluded from the true mysteries.

Men have more time for ceremonial, but the men and women together own parts of the one Dreaming. In some Dreaming ceremonies, men and women take part. In others men only, or at least elders, including those promoted ahead of age because of their knowledge covering long distances of the Dreaming trails.

De Graaf's form of in-the-desert anthropology has its dangers. He has got into critical conditions as regards water five times in his career, but only once when travelling with an Aboriginal. However, they can die too, says de Graaf. The absolutely reliable waterholes are very far from each other. You can get into a situation where your way back is barred by waterholes you've discovered to be dry, and the way forward might offer no hope either.

The sort of anthropology in which De Graaf believes is called advocacy anthropology. He has made submissions to the Law Reform Commission, he has spoken to the police, he has advised on Land Rights. There is no denying, he says, how important and immediate the Dreaming and the land are to the tribal Aboriginals. Everything comes from the Dreaming. The languages were delivered to the people by the Dreamtime being. Every implement used in daily life has its origins in the Dreamtime, from the food basket to the stone axe. The land is such that it is eternal, and life is endless. But a site, a spirit centre destroyed, can destroy all life. Knowing that, says de Graaf, one has no choice than to be an advocate.

The British founded a convict settlement in southeast Australia, in a spacious harbour where Sydney now stands, in 1788. Throughout the early years of the nineteenth century, a succession of brilliant navigators, operating with the goodwill and support of the British administration in Sydney, drew the map of the complex coastline of Australia. There was, first, Mathew Flinders, very young, prodigiously gifted, doomed to grow ill during a French internment on Mauritius and to die too young, having first popularized *Australia* as the name of the southern continent which up to then had been commonly called New Holland. There was Phillip Parker King, who spent nearly four years surveying the northern, most remote coasts of Australia, two of them from the deck of an eighty-four-tonne cutter called *Mermaid*, which was little more than thirty metres in length. Then, from 1837 onwards, the renowned brig *Beagle*, particularly under the charming John Lort Stokes, finished off the survey, discovering the great tidal estuaries of the Adelaide and Victoria Rivers and entering a harbour which Stokes named after a young and as yet unknown naturalist who had sailed on the *Beagle* earlier in that decade – Charles Darwin.

These three navigators were the first of a string of people stricken too readily with enthusiasm for the northern coast. Seen under the right sun, during the tolerable days of the dry season, it is a country of many if shallow anchorages, of fine beaches with palm and pandanus behind them, of mangrove swamps and rivers plentiful in sea food. Of Port Essington, a harbour on the Cobourg Peninsula which he named after a British admiral, King wrote that 'it must, at no very distant period, become a place of great trade, and of very considerable importance'.

This sort of talk seemed to please the Admiralty, who were nervous of French intentions in the area. It also reflected a complaint by Sir Stanford Raffles that the Dutch possessed the only straits through which ships might pass into the Malay archipelago – the Sunda Straits or the Straits of Malacca – and that British ships penetrating these waters had not 'a single friendly port at which they can water and obtain refreshments'. In the end the British Secretary of State for the Colonies, Lord Bathurst, authorized the establishment of European ports in this much-praised territory.

Flinders, King and Stokes had all been wrong, however. The lives people led in those ports would be piteous. There is next to nothing left now of any of these great tropic projects; at two of the ports even the graves are hard to find. At Port Essington, some stonework done by convicts is the only remaining structure. Jungle grass has grown over the burial mounds, and only the cities of ants proliferate there, the tall ant mounds which mimic gravestones.

In 1824, a little more than fifty men – marines fresh from Britain and soldiers of the Buffs previously stationed in Sydney, together with their nameless women and children and forty-four volunteer convicts, who had been promised a remission of sentence for taking part in this enterprise – landed deep in the shoal-ridden harbour of Port Essington on the Cobourg Peninsula and ran up the flag. Within three days their leader, Captain Gordon Bremer, had doubts about the accessibility of the place, the water supply, the rather swampy air. He packed everyone back into his convoy of three ships and took them to the northwest coast of Melville Island, where he built a stockade named Fort Dundas, facing north towards the expected trade from Asia. Bremer himself departed a few months later, after declaring the site excellent and the settlement flourishing. But with the arrival of the wet monsoon, despair became palpable. The Tiwis, having an ancestral recollection of Portuguese slaving raids against Melville Island, kept their distance but occasionally struck out. Malaria, dysentery and loneliness caused more widespread harm. A Lieutenant Hicks lost his wife and two children. In the wet season of 1826–27 the Commandant, Captain Campbell, wrote, 'Our little colony became very sickly.' He had lost six men that month from fever. Alan Powell, a historian of the Territory,[*] listed some of Fort Dundas's more pathetic case histories. One pities Mrs Walker, wife of the captain of the supply ship *Amity*, put ashore there with her children and a girl convict as her servant because 'their presence aboard was to the detriment of the Public Service.' One pities the wife of the gardener Richardson, who was granted a free passage to Sydney for the benefit of her young children, but whose permission to leave the place was cancelled because of an argument her husband had with a marine. The soldiers and convicts did not always behave with delicacy towards the Tiwis, and so in the wet season of 1827 the surgeon and the storekeeper, out for a walk, looking for a breeze, were speared to death.

[*] *Far Country*, Alan Powell, Melbourne University Press, 1982.

In 1827, a further settlement was authorized and founded at Raffles Bay on the mainland, specifically on the Cobourg Peninsula. There too it was a story of treacherous climate, bad rations, malaria, dysentery, hepatitis and madness. A soldier of the 39th Regiment wandered away into the wilderness. His wife went mad, dressing in his uniform, slipping away continuously to search for him, being brought back raving by the soldiers. The Commandant, Captain Smythe, ended by putting prices on the heads of 'thieving natives' and armed his convicts to go and hunt for them. An Aboriginal woman and her children were slaughtered, one child surviving and being adopted by a soldier's wife.

But under a new Commandant, this second settlement, Raffles Bay, began to attract the Macassans. A fleet of thirty-four praus visited Raffles Bay in 1829, and although they could not trade their trepang – it was already spoken for by Indonesian merchants – still they gave the place the semblance of a trading port. But such evil reports of both places, Fort Dundas and Raffles Bay, had reached Britain that in 1829 both encampments were abandoned. The French explorer D'Urville visited Raffles Bay ten years later and recorded that nothing was standing, that all European oddments of equipment had been taken by the Aboriginals, even the nails from the coffins of the pestilential dead.

The very fact that D'Urville and other French voyagers visited this coastline was taken in London as evidence of firm French intentions. To forestall these, the final and most pitiable attempt to build a great British seaport in the north was undertaken. Captain Gordon Bremer again convoyed unknowing souls from London to Port Essington, and in October 1838 landed them at the place he had himself occupied for three days fourteen years before. The Commandant, John McArthur, named the place Victoria after the new Queen. He built his Government House on piles, to thwart the relentless white ants. He erected a church, and John Lort Stokes, captain of the *Beagle*, visiting this new Singapore in its first months, reflected that whereas for most nations the first buildings to appear in a new city were the tavern, the theatre and the dancing-house, where Englishmen are concerned 'the church is first thought of'. Yet in a great cyclone a year after the settlement began, Government House was blown off its piers and the church and all the flimsy houses of the marines and convicts were torn apart. The naturalist of the *Beagle*, T. H. Huxley, called McArthur 'a most pragmatical old fogey', but his relationship with the local natives was excellent, and McArthur set to building a second and a third Government House with a firm Britannic will, and observed in the garden of his residence all the niceties which were part of the European Dreaming – Government House tea parties, formal balls, and receptions; while his eighteen-pounder cannon faced across the harbour towards an enemy who would never deign to intrude.

The first garrison was relieved in 1844, and by that time malaria had already achieved a high casualty rate. It would be worse still for the replacements and their wives and children. Lieutenant George Lambrick, a young man of enormous charm, had brought with him from Somerset his wife Emma and his three children. Emma had enquired in Sydney about Port Essington, and had heard pleasant reports of it. She

Port Essington, founded on the Cobourg Peninsula as the new Singapore in 1838, had an eleven-year history marked in equal measure by madness, fever, brutality and futile moral courage. Now all that remains are these convict-built stone ruins and a number of pitiable graves.

and two of her three children would die of malarial fever there. This 'quite agreeable little woman is the only lady and, with the exception of the men's wives, the only Englishwoman in Port Essington', wrote a visiting English officer from H.M.S. *Bramble*. 'She said she was very happy, but I could not fancy it.' She shares the graveyard now with nearly fifty others. These include Surgeon Tilston, twenty-six marines, a Mrs Norman and her newborn daughter, and an Italian priest, survivor of the wreck of the supply ship *Heroine* in Torres Strait in 1846.

Infectious fevers from Port Essington spread to the Aboriginals of the area, but they had their own means of disposal of the dead, all to do with the return of the soul of the departed to its spirit place. The Aboriginals knew that, if the proper rites were performed, the dead could live on happily in their spirit places and return to fleshly form when called on by the totem ancestor. But Emma and her children would never return to green pastures or soft rain.

Rumours that come from Essington are of McArthur, in the tatters of his uniform, conducting Government House levees for ragged, fevered, scarecrow guests; of a querulous convict, Squires, who had escaped from Sydney to Singapore but been returned to Essington, there to stir up the rich discontent among the other convicts; of the Italian Benedictine monk Angelo Confalonieri, who, eager to preach to the Aboriginals, enquired into their language and unwittingly delivered to them sermons full of broad obscenities. One Sergeant Masland arrested three Aboriginals for theft and shot one who tried to escape. McArthur feared general reprisals, but the Aboriginals taught him something of their system of retribution by attacking not the Europeans but a young tribesman, called Neinmil, who had sailed on the survey ships *Fly* and *Bramble* and was much loved in the settlement.

Early in the town's history, there had been theatrical performances – Lieutenant Owen Stanley of the *Beagle*, who would give his name to the great central divide of Papua, produced a play called 'Cheap Living', in which the marines acted and sang the parts. All singing ceased at Essington from the mid-1840s onwards. All but the most formidable of the citizens of Port Essington fell into lethargy.

However, Confalonieri, the remarkable monk, found the energy to map the peninsula, showing the location of the tribes. His efforts to compile a lexicon of the Aboriginal tongue were thwarted by the fact that in the surrounding countryside there were seven Aboriginal languages. He was attracted by the black people's openness and charm, but repelled by their hedonism. He was still working on his dictionary and attempting to translate the Bible into Iwaidja when malarial fever killed him in 1848.

A few days after his death, a supply ship arrived carrying a large crate addressed to him with the words POSA PIANO* painted on it! The marines, starved for music and entertainment, tore the crate apart to find that it contained vestments and a Roman missal for the saying of Mass.

---

*Handle with care.

Perhaps the only Europeans delighted to spend time at Port Essington were the members of the Leichhardt expedition in 1845. Ludwig Leichhardt was a Prussian, ambitious and demonic, who explored most of the hinterland of Queensland and then headed across the Carpentaria area northwest for McArthur's northern capital. He would later disappear in central Australia and inspire Patrick White to cast him as an antipodean Messiah in his great novel *Voss*. When he and his men reached Essington, they were suffering from malnutrition. They had had to eat the dried meat of their own horses and to fall back on various edible tubers which the Aboriginals had pointed out to them. They had even been reduced to eating flying fox, the fruit bat which fills the sky at dusk in the Top End and whose flesh if eaten causes the body to give off a foul smell from the pores of the skin. They were carrying too one of their party, John Roper, who had been struck with six spears during an Aboriginal raid on their camp in the Cape York area and whose eye had been beaten out with a club. On arrival in Port Essington, they would eat Christmas dinner gratefully with McArthur, but leave as soon as a ship arrived with places for them.

At last the British government decided to deliver the survivors of Essington. The India and Australia Steam Packet Company had finally refused to make use of the place as a port, and neither the Americans nor French nor Dutch had shown any imperialist fervour towards the Australian north. McArthur, Lambrick and the others were taken away at the beginning of the wet season of 1849. What remains there now is a lime kiln, a hospital wall cut and erected by convict masons in 1845, a few chimneys and foundations.

Essington's major input towards the future of the territory was an unwitting one. Indonesian buffalo had been imported as a meat source for the garrison, but the herds had been hard to confine and in the later years of the town had wandered south down the peninsula. Now they are prolific right across the Top End, and the buff hunters, operating still on the fringes of Kakadu and on the Marrakai plains south of Darwin, are figures to whom the Territory attaches a mythology. They are nineteenth-century individualists who cull by licence the progeny of benighted Captain McArthur's Indonesian herds.

There may be something gained by contrast from looking at the destiny of a modern Englishwoman living in the Top End. The name of the woman is Dee Hay. Her father is a gentleman farmer from Frome in Somerset, and she grew up in a late Cromwellian manor house there. Her background, that is, is akin to the background of Emma Lambrick, who was buried at Port Essington. In some ways, the passage of time makes the comparison between Emma Lambrick and Dee Hay ludicrous. Dee Hay, for example, can work in a bikini, whereas Mrs Lambrick was forced to dress up to her stature of being – as the officer of the *Bramble* had put it – 'the only lady and, with the exception of the men's wives, the only Englishwoman in Port Essington'. It is also unlikely that Dee Hay will be suddenly and fatally stricken with malarial fever, although the Northern Territory can still be an unhealthy milieu.

What does apply is that for both women there were the same problems of adaptation to a grotesque environment. Of the two women, Dee Hay is probably the more adaptive, though, once again, it is hard to speak for nineteenth-century women, for the admirable Emma Lambrick herself, who was forced to live according to the opinions of her officer husband and the demands of her children.

Dee Hay's father announced to her when she was young that England had had it; he intended therefore that, unlike most other Englishwomen, she should learn languages. He sent her, after Cheltenham Girls Grammar, to a finishing school in Switzerland, where she learned French, German and the unwritten Swiss German. He then enrolled her in a further and rather eccentric finishing school at Alassio on the Gulf of Genoa, where a Mrs Brown kept an Italian language academy on the first storey of a *pensione*.

A great termite mound dwarfs a buffalo. These beasts, introduced by the British settlers of the Cobourg Peninsula, have run wild throughout the Top End.

OPPOSITE:
Dee Skewes, girl from Somerset and product of two finishing schools, farms tomatoes at Humpty Doo. She flourishes in a climate which, in the nineteenth century, took the lives of many English girls.

In 1976, she arrived in Darwin for a six-week holiday, fell in love with an Austrian called Rudi, and agreed to his suggestion that they should go into business together farming tomatoes on a small acreage Rudi owned in a place called Humpty Doo, some fifty kilometres from Darwin.

She now laughs at the naïvety she initially brought to her farming career in the backblocks of Australia. She called a friend in England who was an agriculturist to ask him what sort of tomatoes to plant in Humpty Doo. It was a mistake which historically all colonists have made – seeking advice from another hemisphere on problems that are purely local. Rudi and Dee found that fungus disorders spread with dazzling speed in their tropical garden. A barely visible fungus on two potatoes growing in a pot by the back door of their shanty spread to the entire crop of tomatoes. They began to consult the agriculturist at the experimental farm down the road and produced their first bumper crop at a time when there was a glut of tomatoes on the Darwin market. They adapted quickly, operating on a trade basis which would probably be possible only in a remote town like Darwin, paying their dental and grocery bills with boxes of their produce. They worked themselves fiercely, labouring part-time in a chicken-feed plant at Humpty Doo – Dee sometimes waitressing in Darwin. They were learning every season and determined to organize their smallholding on a scientific basis to yield the best possible crop.

Rudi died suddenly, at the age of thirty-eight, of an asthma paroxysm. The death failed to drive Dee off the allotment. She built an ornamental pool in Rudi's memory to the south of their small house. Then, desperate for finance, she took a job as a barmaid in the Humpty Doo pub.

The pub stands on the Arnhem Highway, which goes east to the uranium mine at Jabaru and then ends. Its clientele can be eccentric, rowdy, brutal. On her first night serving at the bar, Dee saw an Aboriginal woman brained with a wrought-iron chair. Later in the evening, a white woman who owned a local cattle station and for whom the Aboriginal woman had worked turned up in the bar, two revolvers strapped to her waist, screaming to know who'd 'hurt her Bessie'?

Dee had time, though, to speak to the publican's son, Patrick Skewes, a large, genial Australian boy, and to agree in the end to marry him. Mrs Dee Skewes lives now in her house on her allotment with her husband Patrick. The property is threatened by a legal dispute, but Dee is hanging on, and the banana trees and palms which she has grown to shade the house bring in the kingfishers and magpie geese and all the plentiful bird life in the Adelaide River area. The house is airy, constructed of mesh wire, fibro, iron. The walls of the living areas are open to the air, except that blinds can be brought down during the monsoonal downpours to provide shelter. Dee dresses for the climate, and her son, grandson on his mother's side of the captain of *Hood*, which was sunk with all hands by the *Bismarck*, wavers most unnautically around the house dressed in nothing but a napkin. There is in the home of Dee Skewes none of the doom-laden air which hung over the household of poor Mrs Emma Lambrick in the fever port of Essington.

Chapter 5

The Un-Lasting City

The South Australians acquired control of the Territory by Letters Patent in 1863. The South Australian government was sure it had been given a zone of unlimited European possibilities, and like the British government before it, wanted as a matter of priority to found a great northern capital. They appointed a Territory Resident called Boyle Travers Finniss to locate a site for a capital. Ten kilometres down the estuary of the Adelaide River he founded a town at Escape Cliffs. Like loyal Britons in exile, the South Australians required that the new settlement be called Palmerston in honour of the British prime minister. But the ominous resonances of a name like Escape Cliffs fitted the new town better. Its short history mimicked that of Essington itself. Fever, quarrelling, murder and a sense of unreality dominated the settlement's short history. The place was given up after a few years and Finniss was taken to Adelaide and disciplined by a board of enquiry. When Surveyor Goyder laid down the foundations of a new town in a bay earlier named Port Darwin, the resounding name of Lord Palmerston was simply moved west and attached to the new location. It was only after the young Australian government took over management of the Territory from the disappointed South Australians in 1911, that Palmerston vanished and Darwin became the town's official label.

Whatever its name, Darwin has always had a transient air. Despite its large hotels and the regional patriotism of its Australian/ English/ Greek/ Chinese/ Timorese/ Lebanese/ Vietnamese/ Yugoslav/ Italian residents, it has always looked, and still looks, like a temporary cantonment for exiles.

In Smith Street, Darwin, stands the Legislative Assembly of the Northern Territory. In some ways, its system is the Westminster system of Great Britain. The Speaker, a cattleman from Katherine called Les McFarlane, wears a parliamentary wig and black alpaca robes. His rugged and sun-tanned face sits a little oddly in their midst. The members of both parties, the National Party and the Labor Party, face each other across elegant hardwood desks. They wear short-sleeved white shirts and ties and look young and healthy and confident. The five women members wear floral dresses, and emanate good health in a manner that was never seen in tragic Essington. Pound for pound, it is the most muscular parliament in the world. Its king, the Chief Minister, is a husky Irish Australian called Paul Everingham. He is an immensely

OUTBACK

successful politician – the Opposition are outfoxed and rather cowed by comparison. Though the total constituency of the Territory is only 100,000 people, a grotesquely small number, the area over which they are spread gives some plausibility to a Territory government. It costs as much to bring education and health to a child in the Tanami Desert as it does for a whole village in more closely settled and older cultures.

The Northern Territory Legislative Assembly is partly a national government, for the Territorians see themselves as a nation. Not even in Texas do you see a regional flag flown so fervently, and the Northern Territory flag, with its black, its ochre, its Southern Cross, its Sturt's Desert Rose, resembles more a national flag than does the flag of the Commonwealth of Australia itself with its hybrid of Union Jack and Southern Cross. At question time, Everingham and his Ministers refer to 'southerners' – any other Australians apart from themselves – as if they were members of a separate federation.

Paul Everingham, with two Greek constituents, stands before the flag of the Northern Territory. Greeks from such islands as Kalimnos came to Darwin as sponge divers soon after the war, but quickly saw that there were less traditional ways to make their fortune. Now Kalimnos is supported from Darwin.

68

The people to whom Everingham is most kindly disposed on the floor of the Legislative Assembly are the people of South East Asia, for like the British planners of the 1820s he looks to Asian trade to vivify the outback. He invites the Sultan of Brunei to open the Darwin Show. He sends trade delegations to the Philippines and keeps a Northern Territory stall at the Singapore Trade Fair each year. His Immigration Minister, a member of Darwin's large Greek community, travels to the cities of Asia promoting the idea of 'entrepreneurial immigration' to the Northern Territory. Among other zones of interest, he visits Hong Kong looking for Chinese industrialists who might be jumpy about the impending lapse of the British lease on the Crown Colony and who might like an assisted transfer to the stable yet climatically similar purlieus of Darwin.

To further honour the Asian connection a new casino is being built at Mindil Beach to attract big betters and investors from Asia, while, facing a fine coastline dotted with signs that warn that sea wasp bites are fatal and will kill within two minutes, a large international hotel is going up for a consortium called Burgundy Royale from oil-rich Sabah. An American or a European, checking into a hotel like that, may well be alarmed by the explicit information about what to do in case of cyclone. But an Asian would accept such conspicuous counsel without a tremor.

When the Chinese tycoons from Singapore, Hong Kong or Borneo come to Darwin, they go to the back room of the present casino. The manager says he has seen them play for three days solid at baccarat, risking $2000 a time on the turn of a card. Since Everingham and his government have imposed quite remarkable restrictions on the casino owners in matters of how the money is handled and counted, a vast part of these Asian gambling stakes goes straight into the revenue of the Northern Territory. The night I went into the back room there were some local Greeks and third-generation Darwin Chinese there, conspicuously wealthy, yet not quite up to the $2000-a-throw level. Perhaps this is merely an echo of Port Essington – like Captain Gordon Bremer and Captain McArthur, Everingham has prepared a party, but whether Asia will come to it is another matter.

There are great plans, however, to ship live cattle out to the populous Muslim states of South East Asia, to run a joint prawn-trawling venture with the People's Republic of China, to export demountable buildings, suitable for emergency housing or for mining towns, to the booming oil principalities along the coast of North Borneo. The Filipinos also want to enter into partnership with the government of the Northern Territory and grow rice for export to the whole western Pacific area. The average Darwinian is gripped by this Asian expectation, the hope of a strong Asian connection. If he has four days off, he will fly to Bali or to the island of Ambon in the Celebes rather than to Adelaide or Melbourne.

But expectation has always flowered well in Darwin's exotic climate. From the ruins of Port Essington on the Cobourg Peninsula to the deserted rice blocks of Humpty Doo, to the abandoned workings of Rum Jungle and the devastated homesteads north of the Victoria River, the north is littered with the detritus of great hopes, and Darwin is still an outpost. It has now, and always has had, however, a sense of destiny that would have done Athens credit.

Its history has in fact encouraged a sense of impermanence. For Darwin has known three near-total destructions. The first was in the new year of 1897, when a cyclone circled in from the northwest across the town. In those days Darwin was a polyglot place – it had its Chinamen, its Japanese pearlers and prostitutes, its Filipinos, Indonesians, Malays, as well as its Europeans. On all of them indiscriminately, even on the fringe-dwelling Aboriginals of the Larakia tribe, the Wongar spirit, the Thunder Man, descended with catholic indifference. Chinatown was destroyed, the Catholic and the Anglican churches exploded. Roofs sailed south, but the greatest loss of life was

suffered by the eighteen pearling luggers, which were shattered on the rocks or overturned at anchor.

The second destruction of Darwin derived from a different sort of thunder. On the morning of 19 February 1942, a Father McGrath, missionary on Bathurst Island and provided with a military radio so that he could act as a coast-watcher, called Darwin to say that a large fleet of aircraft had just passed over heading south at great speed. Due to tropic lethargy, rivalry between the services and simple rawness, no alarm was sounded in Darwin. The air fleet flying south was Japanese, and had been launched from four Japanese carriers, which had sneaked through the Banda Straits the night before. Its strength has been variously estimated, but it seems to have consisted of some seventy bombers and three dozen fighters and dive-bombers. A second wave of fifty-four medium bombers had taken off from Ambon in the Celebes to support the carrier-based force. The Darwin sirens were not heard until the Australian anti-aircraft gunners on Stokes Hill were firing at the first low-flying dive-bombers. Most bombs dropped in the harbour, but many hit the town, one of them killing the postmaster, his wife, his Aboriginal servant, the telephone operators at their switchboards. The harbour was quickly a shambles. 'The wharf was burning near its inner end,' wrote the Chief Medical Officer of the hospital ship *Manunda*. In fact the wharf locomotive and a number of wharf labourers had been hurled into the sea. '*Barossa* and *Neptuna* at the wharf both appeared to have been hit, and *Neptuna* appeared to be on fire.' *Neptuna* was a liner carrying explosives. Its final detonation would kill forty-five people. 'The *Lambia*, about five hundred yards away, was on fire. *British Motorist* was sinking by the head. *Meigs* was on fire and sinking aft. *Mauna Loa* was down by the stern with her back broken.' The catalogue of wrecked shipping continues. 'An American destroyer, ablaze aft, went dashing across our bows, missing us by inches and steering with her engines. Another American destroyer was on our port side, a solid mass of flames with burning oil around her, and what was left of the crew jumping into the burning oil.' This destroyer was in fact the USS *Peary*, which had recently been turned back from the approaches of Timor by Japanese air attack.

There were ten American Kittyhawks in Darwin that day. They too had been intended for Timor, but had turned back because of bad weather. Five of them had actually landed in Darwin that morning and were refuelling when the attack came in. The other five were providing cover at a considerable height. All of them were under the command of Major Floyd J. Pell, whose craft was among the five refuelling. He ordered these to attempt a take-off, but they were all destroyed, either on the ground or close to it. Pell himself parachuted from twenty-four metres; remarkably, he landed safely but was then shot to death on the airstrip. Another pilot, having crashed, was dragged from his cockpit and into a slit trench by an Australian soldier. Of the five aircraft that had been providing cover, four were shot down; in the remaining aircraft, Lieutenant Oestreicher shot down two of the bombers from the cover of cloud and was able to land safely at the end of the raid.

Chinese coolies were first brought to the Territory in 1874 to work on the Darwin–Pine Creek railway. 'This place welly good,' said one of them. 'By and by all China come, Emperor too.' Here Australian girls pose outside the Chinese joss-house in Pine Creek.

The raiders departed at about 10.30, leaving a shattered town and a ruined hospital. Within ten minutes the second wave from Ambon was in. They did further damage to the Australian airfield and the ships in the harbour. And then they too went.

There was immediate panic among the forces that had not been directly engaged in dealing with the Japanese and among the civilian population. People swept out of town on the road to Adelaide River. An Australian airforce officer noticed a Chinaman on a bicycle-driven ice-cream cart. 'Where are you going?' he asked the Chinaman. 'Melbourne,' the Chinaman told him genially. In fact one Australian airforce serviceman did flee as far as that, a distance of 4000 kilometres.

Ultimately, it was decreed that all civilians should leave town, and all women except the army nurses. There would be further attacks on a more organized and militant Darwin. General MacArthur, escaping from the Philippines in a B-17 and approaching the northern Australian shore, would be diverted from Darwin to Batchelor Field because Mitsubishi fighters and various Japanese reconnaissance planes were active in the Darwin area. But the bombing of Darwin was not, as most Australians feared at the time, a sign of an inevitable intent to attack the Australian mainland. It did serve to give Darwin a symbolic importance, now that most Australians had twigged the fact that Australia was not moored off Kent in England but was in fact geographically and strategically part of Asia. People began to use the phrase, 'Australia's northern gateway'. Prime Minister John Curtin gave it a priority as regards garrisoning. But once the Japanese were turned back outside Port Moresby in New Guinea later in the year, Darwin became a languid backwater of the war in the South-West Pacific Zone. It nonetheless had acquired an added holiness in the minds of Australians as the only Australian town of any size which had suffered obliteration at the hands of an enemy. In fact, nearly three hundred people had died in that first raid of 19 February, and four hundred had been wounded and maimed. At the time, the Australian government considered these statistics to be so startling that they doctored the report, and Australian newspapers stated that only seventeen had perished.

Many of the human and moral failings that had contributed to the Japanese destruction of Darwin contributed even more strongly to Darwin's most recent devastation on Christmas Day 1974.

In most public places in Darwin, in all hotel rooms, at the front of every telephone directory, Cyclone Action Warnings are posted. They counsel you to ensure your transistor radio is working with fresh spare batteries, to check that you are under a secure roof, to know your nearest safe high area in case of storm tide warning, to collect tinned food, water containers and so forth. You are also advised to board or tape windows, to fuel your vehicle and put it under cover. When the cyclone comes you are to stay inside in the strongest part of whatever structure you occupy. You should anchor yourself to a strong fixture, such as water pipes, and protect yourself with mattresses and blankets. What you must beware of is the calm Eye. You should wait till you hear on your transistor, or until you are officially advised, that the cyclone has passed. This sort of wise advice, now almost unavoidable in the Top End, was not offered so regularly or in such codified form before the great disaster of Christmas Day 1974, when Cyclone Tracy brought about Darwin's third destruction. As on the day the Japanese attacked, official rivalries and tropical lassitude delayed the raising of the alarm and departmental and municipal officials stumbled in a pre-Christmas fug of humidity showing the sort of administrative impotence which characterizes the bewildered officials in Camus's *The Plague*, itself a novel of a great natural disaster striking a humid city – in Camus's case the city of Oran in Algeria.

Three weeks before Darwin was destroyed, a cyclone the meteorologists called Selma had swung away north when only fifty kilometres from Darwin, the citizens of the city were therefore unimpressed by the mere high winds which resulted from Selma, and may have presumed that the new cyclone forecast on Christmas Eve and labelled with the banal name Tracy would be no worse than Selma. Major General Alan Stretton, a retired soldier who was Director General of the Natural Disasters Organization in Canberra, and who would be put in charge of the destroyed Darwin on Christmas Day, found this wishful thinking of the Darwin populace quite understandable. In the humidity of the Wet, the mid-winter feast of Christmas is celebrated as energetically and as riotously in the Top End as in any European community. People did not want to have to be bothered with the concept of a cyclone on Christmas Eve, and that was fair enough. According to General Stretton, what was less than forgivable was the torpor in which the senior officials of Darwin seemed to spend that day. The Tropical Cyclone Warning Centre in Darwin had been plotting Tracy, which had begun weakly 1000 kilometres to the northwest, for four days. By 9 a.m. on Christmas Eve, it was obvious that Tracy was making directly for Darwin. Weather officers began contacting local officials from mid-morning. In those days the Northern Territory was subject to federal authority and administered by a Department of the Northern Territory, whose headquarters were in Canberra. Paul Everingham's glorious state had not yet been founded; the Territory flag of Sturt's Desert Rose and Southern Cross had not yet been designed or flown. On Christmas Eve 1974, the officials of this Federal government department, after consulting with the weather bureau, decided that a taped cyclone warning would be given every half hour over the two Darwin radio stations and on television. The message was full of solid advice. After beginning benignly, declaring itself a 'warning from the Darwin Weather Bureau and Northern Territory Emergency Services Organization as a community service for Top End listeners', it declared that a cyclone was imminent and suggested the storing of water and advised people to find a substantial shelter. It closed with a warning that after the calm Eye of the cyclone passed, the winds would return from a different direction but with equal ferocity.

One of the officials of the Department of the Northern Territory, Ray McHenry, tried to get together members of the local Emergency

Committee for a meeting, but found it almost impossible to reach them. Most of them could not be found. They were travelling round from department to department, enjoying the long, convivial party circuit on which Australian public servants have always departed by noon on Christmas Eve. Stretton would later comment, 'One would have expected that with thirty-minute warnings coming over the radio, responsible officers would have contacted McHenry . . . or that in some way authorities in Darwin could have arranged a meeting of the Emergency Committee.' More incredibly still, in all those air-conditioned offices, among all that minor sibilance of cans of Fosters and Carlton and Four-X being opened, no official took the trouble to notify the federal government in Canberra. There had also been a dispute, settled only on the eve of the cyclone and still rankling at a departmental level, between the Commissioner of Police and the Department of the Northern Territory over who would have ultimate management of the Disaster Plan. 'It was thus', wrote Stretton later, 'the unhappy circumstances of switching responsibility in the middle of the disaster season that could have had a bearing on the lack of initiative shown by the local officials on Christmas Eve.'

The public therefore had no sense of urgency because the bureaucrats had none, and the efficient officers of the Bureau of Meteorology went on issuing warnings into the boozy, sultry vacuum, until the last warning given at 2.30 a.m. on Christmas morning which said that the Eye of the cyclone was now only eighteen kilometres from Darwin and would move over the city soon.

Australia's darling of country and western music, Slim Dusty, would write in 1975 a popular and sentimental song called 'Santa Didn't Make it into Darwin'. Shortly after midnight, children who should have been sleeping that febrile Christmas Eve sleep which is likely to bring them awake, howling with joy, by 5 a.m., were clinging to their parents in the last remnants of their devastated houses. The survivors speak of the enormous noise of the wind, which would break the anemometer at Darwin Airport at three o'clock in the morning when the instrument was registering a two-hundred-and-seventy-kilometre per hour fury. The destruction was amazing. Families sheltered in cupboards, in laundries, their roofs gone, horizontal sheets of rain lashing at them from every crevice. Some parents who, early in the cyclone, tried to carry their children to vehicles had them plucked from their arms. Many sheltered in bathrooms as the rest of the house was blown apart around them. Many of those who made for vehicles, trying to escape the clutter of household wreckage, and the decapitating sheets of iron scything about on the wind, were killed when the gusts lifted their vehicles bodily and crashed them into other, parked cars.

Some time after 4 a.m. the wind dropped, and despite the reiterated warnings about the calm Eye, many went outdoors. People called congratulations to each other on their survival. A man in the suburb of Nightcliffe put a ladder against the side of his house and went up to repair his roof. When the wind returned with a sudden but prodigious roar, the rest of his roof rose, decapitating him. This second fearsome

Wreckage in the suburbs of Darwin following Cyclone Tracy on Christmas Day 1974. The cost of rebuilding Darwin would be one billion dollars.

spate lasted till 7 a.m. In the end, Tracy left sixty-five dead, one hundred
and fifty injured. It wrecked twenty-five of the thirty ships in the
harbour. It devastated ninety per cent of all buildings. The people who
crawled out of Darwin in the first light had been tyrannized for hours by
the raging wind, had had no sleep yet could not now rest. They had
suffered the trauma of the cyclone's disregard for them and their
possessions, and sleep was unthinkable.

Gough Whitlam's government acted very deftly that Christmas Day. Gough was out of the country, but his deputy, Jim Cairns, appointed Stretton the Administrator of Darwin and immediately ordered the evacuation of the city and pledged that it would be rebuilt. As in 1942, people took to the road to Adelaide River, Alice Springs and Adelaide. The urge to flee Darwin was primal and totally understandable but it took no account of the pressure such a stampede would put on fuel and food supplies in the small communities to the south.

People who lived on the Stuart Highway running south of Darwin showed astounding open-handedness to the panic-stricken refugees. The service station at Adelaide River gave petrol and tyres on credit, on the fairly remote chance of being repaid someday by these wide-eyed travellers. In Alice, a relief operations organization was set up under the chairmanship of Reg Harris, a man who had first come to the Territory as an electrician in 1947. His organization had gathered seven and a half tonnes of clothing, food, canvas sheets and cooking gear by ten o'clock on Christmas night itself. By the following night, they had collected $72,000 worth of relief funds. By noon on 27 December, cars began arriving from Darwin. The people in them were in desperate need of napkins for babies, of such humane gestures as gifts of comics and colouring-in books for kids. The trauma of the cyclone had brought women's periods on all at the same time, and there was a desperate need for sanitary pads. Eleven hundred vehicles would be repaired by Reg Harris's organization, and of all these less than ten broke down on the rough one-thousand-three-hundred-kilometre stretch of dirt road from Alice Springs to Port Augusta in South Australia. From 28 December, orders were sent from Harris's organization to all road houses up the track to supply all goods required by refugees, and to charge these transactions to the Alice Springs fund. Alice also sent a plane-load of tyres to Adelaide River. By New Year's Eve, cyclone relief donations in Alice had reached $133,000, nearly $20 for every resident in the town. 'These white fellers stick together,' an old Aboriginal told Harris.

In fact some Aboriginals saw the disaster at Darwin as a late – perhaps too late – assertion of the authority of the Thunder Man, Djangawul. The Aboriginal writer B. Wongar, whose collection of short stories *The Track to Bralgu* won international acceptance, wrote in a short story based on the Darwin disaster, 'The whites are coming back, pouring in from the sky by plane, by helicopter, even by parachute. Soon the whole mob will be back and even more eager than they were before . . . No, there's no way to outwit the whites; but the night before last Jambawal – Cyclone, the whites call him – had a pretty good try. One sweep this way and another there, and now in the whole town there's hardly a tree or a pole left standing . . . I'm glad he made it at last. . . . After the night of the storm even the whites must have learned that Jambawal is stronger than any of us, that to harm him or his people is to risk his anger.'

Darwin was rebuilt, perhaps too hastily, a straggle of tropic suburbs draped uneconomically about a vast airport area. 'The houses are stronger,' says Vin Keneally, a young architect who came up from South Australia in the wake of Tracy to build some of the larger structures in town, including – as supervising architect – the new hotel for Burgundy Royale, 'even though they're not as good for tropic living. There's a new wind code – it's a problem for the structural engineers rather than the architects. We just build in what the structural engineers call for.' The whole city re-grew too quickly, he says, without any plan for rapid transit. It is on the face of it ridiculous to have a tropic and remote port like Darwin which suffers traffic jams daily. Meanwhile Keneally works, as only a young architect can, in a recently devastated city. He built a large city mall for a Greek family called Paspalis, besides being supervising architect on the five-star Esplanade Hotel costing $40 million; and as supervising architect of the Performing Arts Centre attached to the Esplanade, he is responsible for banks, plazas, carparks. Djangawul rather brutally cleared the decks in Darwin, and although the architectural opportunities were there, the chance to make an ideal capital was missed. The unexpected rapid return of the Darwin people forced the town to become what it has always been, a town with a sense of transience, a city of a certain flat and frank ugliness, an assertive town which nonetheless looks ephemeral beneath the high sun.

And there is no denying that Djangawul will be back. Besides the 1897 cyclone and Tracy, there were other storms of 'unusual force' in the cyclone seasons of 1878, 1882, 1917, 1937. As General Stretton says, 'Statistics show that Darwin can expect that about every two years a cyclone will pass within a hundred and fifty kilometres of the city, while every three years a cyclone will pass within a hundred kilometres. It is only every six years that a cyclone can be expected to pass within fifty kilometres of Darwin.'

But for a city that would prefer to be thought of as permanent, a six-year cycle of threat is perhaps too regular.

End Note

June de Rosario is a young town planner, born in India, and a member of the opposition in the Northern Territory Assembly. She says that the reason there are so many women in the Territory's parliament is that the preselection processes are less ramified in the Territory than they are in the major southern cities. There are no recognizable factions, and that makes it easier for women to become candidates. But the electoral prospects of the Labor Party, so high elsewhere in Australia, are not good in the Territory. The accomplished fact of uranium mining assures that Everingham's coalition will remain in power. The Labor Party is more ambiguous about mining, and already there are too many jobs tied up with mining and mining services for any anti-mining party to get far.

June says as well that the Land Rights Act is unpopular with a solid core of whites, who believe that at least Everingham's government puts up a fight against it, often entering Land Rights claim cases as a party opposing the claim.

On the Saturday I met her, the Labor Party was expecting political heavies from down south – Bob Hawke, who at that stage was not yet Prime Minister of Australia or even leader of his party, but already had enormous political weight, and Chris Hurford, a Federal shadow minister. The heavies had not materialized. Instead, a few hacks from Adelaide had turned up. De Rosario was visibly disappointed, spoke passionately about the ironies of the Territory, and put forward something like a log of complaints about the way the Territory was run. The Territory government, she says, fights on behalf of foreign and absentee owners of Territory land against Land Rights excision appeals brought by Aboriginals. That is, it fights against the interests of its own constituents. Is that fair?

'Ministerial propriety isn't an issue in the Territory', she said. 'Ministerial impropriety might be a regular phenomenon in the Westminster system, but in the Territory it wasn't even a matter of debate.' And then Darwin itself. It was degenerating from a promising port into a social wasteland where the adults stupefied themselves with booze and the kids sniffed glue.

In a way, of course, her depressed recital, provoked by the non-arrival of big-timers from the south, was itself a testimony to the marked political talents of Paul Everingham and the difficulties associated with unseating such a skilled frontier campaigner.

June de Rosario, member of the opposition, Northern Territory Legislative Assembly. A town planner and member of a frontier version of the Westminster system of Parliament, she claims that ministerial propriety is not an issue in the Territory.

The Pub Owner's Wife
A Narrative

The pub owner's wife was in her mid-forties, her husband a little older. Together they ran a pub on one of the roads in the Top End, southeast of Darwin. Among clumps of pandanus and palms, it sat under a vast sky and catered to a thirsty clientele. Their customers were truck drivers, Aboriginal and white stockmen, miners passing to and from Darwin, illicit tropical bird smugglers, bull catchers, buffalo shooters, aerial musterers. Since it was a noisy pub, the pub owner and his wife lived in a house some distance off, and the wife would walk down to the pub from the house every evening to help out in the bar. It was a dark walk through a sparsely populated landscape, and her husband considered it a dangerous one. He could not say specifically who it was he feared would attack her, but he was aware of the violence and madness which always seemed close to realization in the humidity and endemic drunkenness of the Top End. He therefore pressed her to carry a .25 Biretta with her whenever she walked down to the pub at night. 'I'm not worried about the blackfellers,' he told her, 'it's the mad white bastards that worry me.'

His fears had reasonable statistical grounds. The annual average for murders in the Territory is fourteen times the Australian national mean; the prevalence of fire-arms, geographic remoteness, grievances germinating richly beneath the humid sun and fed on liquor, the high rate of individual eccentricity, the mysterious business of Aboriginal retribution – all that helped the figures along and made it wise for a woman walking at night through a concentration of drinkers to go armed.

It became a habitual matter for the publican's wife to carry the small revolver, though the pub owner himself may well have forgotten that he had pressed the weapon on her.

Lately she approached the pub in the evenings with a certain sense of grievance. Among the regulars were a number of hard-drinking women. She was aware that intimate signals passed across the bar between some of them and her husband. She hoped it was all just a bit of social byplay. She had never seen anything more than that.

As well as her minor sexual suspicions, she hated the rowdiness of the pub, the aggravation that prevailed there, the racial insults, the struggle to get the aggressor and the drunk out of the door at closing time, the turning from an eventually closed and locked front door to see the swill, the vomit, the sometimes overturned furniture.

One night in 1980, carrying her bag, the Biretta half-remembered inside it, she strolled down as usual from the house to the pub. She passed through the screen of battered four-wheel-drives in front of the place, familiar vehicles, each of them matched to the face of some regular boozer already inside and settled down to an evening of hectic drinking. She went to the back of the pub and came into the bar through the office. From the office door she could not see her husband serving the customers. She presumed he was in the storeroom. She went out into the night again and saw the heavy door of the storeroom ajar, a little light spilling through it. Opening the door further, she saw her husband in there with one of the women customers.

The pub owner was of course astounded. He dragged his trousers up, belted them and walked towards her, beginning to speak. He discovered, before she did, that the Biretta was in her hand. As he reached the door she shot him through the wrist. The bullet passed through and hit his buckle. 'Bloody surprised he had his buckle done up,' some of the local people would say later.

Bleeding, he turned away from her and ran away into the open night. She shot him twice in the buttocks. It did not occur to her to take any vengeance on the woman. The pub owner travelled in a wide circle, then stumbled into the pub and collapsed. The pub owner's wife went into the office and wept, while the barmaid called the local police station.

The pub owner was rushed to Darwin by ambulance. The pub owner's wife was put in the caged back of a police van and also driven to Darwin. She was appalled by her murderous impulse, yet at the same time too angry to be repentant. When the Darwin magistrate released her on bail, she went to visit her husband in hospital.

It is the sort of crime which in the Old Testament atmosphere of the Northern Territory attracted a light sentence, a mere fifteen months, to be served in the new Fannie Bay prison. Fannie Bay has been, historically, a foul and tragic place, though the new wing is air-conditioned and the regimen more humane than it has previously been. But to go to prison was, she found, still a shocking business. 'If I'd killed him and got twenty years,' she said, 'I'd be better off dead.' But reading got her through – 'She's a great reader,' her husband used to boast to people before the shooting.

The pub owner himself might have suffered the worst punishment. As soon as his wounds began to heal, he found that they were considered undignified injuries. According to the contradictory morality of a frontier town, a man is permitted to liaise with strange women, but he is not permitted to be caught by his wife nor to be shot in the buttocks. The first night he hobbled back behind the bar of his pub, the locals were merciless. 'Here's Ray again,' one of them yelled. 'Half-shot as always.' He proved very paranoid about shooting jokes, and about the possibility of further attacks. He bought new weapons – Magnum revolvers, shot guns. The jokes continued for a time, but there was a limit to them.

The pub owner's wife was paroled after nine months. She met her husband again. They were old-fashioned people, it was unlikely that, having both survived the shoot-out, they would separate and seek a divorce. The passionate shooting probably added something – a spice, a brio – to the middle reaches of their marriage.

They decided that the pub was not good for their marriage, and put it on the market, selling it easily. For, although it was what Australians call 'a blood house', a rough boozer, it was a gold mine. The former pub owner and his wife bought the local store, and can be found there behind that more prosaic counter today. When people come in and ask the wife to witness documents for them, she tells them with the pride appropriate to a survivor, 'No use asking me. I've got a criminal record.'

Chapter 6

The Dreaming of Cattle

Jeanie Gunn, a slight girl from Melbourne and, at the turn of the century, newly wed to Mr Aeneas Gunn, may not have been the first white woman to live on a station in the Territory. Mrs Giles, whose husband Alfred had driven sheep north from South Australia in 1872 to sell to the men working on the Overland Telegraph line and had then became manager of Springvale, one of the earliest Northern Territory cattle stations situated near Katherine, has the honour of being the first woman to reach and reside at a northern homestead. By the end of the century, European women were not quite an oddity in the settlements. There were three of them in Katherine. But when Jeanie Gunn arrived in Darwin in 1902 to accompany her new husband on a journey to the Elsey cattle station and to live there with him, it was still a strange enough ambition to attract a lot of opposition from the European womenfolk of Darwin. During her brief stay in Darwin, Jeanie was visited by knots of two and three who told her that the idea of a woman going bush was sheer madness, that no woman travelled in the Wet. That even if she reached the homestead, she would die of boredom. 'You don't understand,' they hastened to explain. 'He'll be camping out most of his time, miles away from the homestead,' and 'I said, "So will I."'

There was opposition also from the chief stockman of the Elsey, a Scot who galloped one hundred and fifty kilometres from Elsey to the telegraph station in Katherine to send preventive telegrams to Aeneas Gunn in Darwin. 'Wife coming, secure buggy,' Aeneas Gunn had already telegraphed. 'No buggy obtainable,' the Scotsman now fired back. 'Wife can ride, secure suitable mount,' replied Aeneas Gunn. 'No side-saddle obtainable,' the Scotsman answered, 'stockhorses all flash.' 'Wife determined, coming Tuesday's train,' replied Aeneas Gunn. This telegram, says Jeanie, 'was followed by a complete breakdown at the Katherine.'

Jeanie was not insensitive to the worries that lay behind this barrage of telegrams from the Scot. 'Although a woman in a settlement only rules her husband's home, the wife of a station manager holds the peace and comfort of the stockmen in the hollow of her hand.'

Jeanie's travels in the Top End began with a train journey on the narrow-gauge line from Darwin to Pine Creek, where the Scot was waiting with horses. After Pine Creek and as they rode south, the rain began. The Ferguson River, quite empty in the Dry, was raging, and little Jeanie had to be winched across the torrent in a flying fox, the landborne equivalent of a bosun's chair. Travelling through the long grass south of Katherine, among boulders and the millions of termite mounds taller than a horse, Jeanie remarked that the going was rough and that it might be better to find a track if they could. 'We're on the track,' the Scot told her. 'We're on the main transcontinental route from Adelaide to Port Darwin.' And so, following the track which only the Scot could see, they disappeared into hundreds of square kilometres of grass three metres tall and taller. 'This is what we call long grass,' the Scot told her. When they emerged from it they arrived at the Elsey, a cattle station of 6000 square kilometres.

Reflective linemen on the Overland Telegraph in 1908. Thirst, disease, loneliness and aggrieved Aboriginals still threatened life and sanity.

The Overland Telegraph,
completed in 1872, became the
only safe transcontinental route
for the overlander to follow. In
1902, Jeanie Gunn visited the line
and listened in to the cable traffic
flashing north and south.

There she encountered the curiosity of the 'station blacks', the already dispossessed members of the Upper Roper River tribes who lived in a fringe settlement on the edge of the homestead paddock and supplied cheap labour for the running of the place. The response from the Chinese cook, however, and especially from the stockmen, was a less genial one. They were at the best of times suspicious and sometimes hostile. Jeanie was – once more – bright enough to understand the causes behind this resistance by the stockmen. She writes of Mack, who was head stockman at the Elsey, 'Year by year as the bush had shrunk before the railways, he had receded with it, keeping always just behind the Back of Beyond, droving, bullock-punching, stock-keeping and unconsciously opening up the way for that very civilization that was driving him further and further back.' Gradually however, because she was good with horses and settled in without being plaintive about the condition of the homestead – a half-finished structure put together out of the materials of its predecessor which had been wrecked in a cyclone, and 'mostly verandahs and promises' – they began to respect her and to call her by nicknames, since they were so heavily nicknamed themselves. To the Dandy and the Quiet Stockman, to Fizzer Pelham and Mack she was always 'the Little-un' or the 'Goer'. A goer she was. She settled blithely to the business of leading the life of a gallant Edwardian Briton, dressing as if for a summer picnic in Hyde Park throughout the steaming Wet and on into the torrid Dry.

Hard travelling in the Territory, early twentieth century.

Jeanie had the usual Edwardian sense of the inevitability of British progress in desert places (she quotes the old Kaffir woman who says that the British-born can conquer anything but death). And although she took it for granted that her culture had precedence over the tribal Dreaming, she gives a fascinating picture of the destiny of those tribes whose earth was taken for the pasturing of cattle. Aboriginals on stations were supposed to camp either in the homesteads, where by tradition they received rations of flour and tobacco, or else right out beyond the boundaries. They travelled in and out of the station, but they had to keep to the main travellers' tracks. 'Blacks among the cattle have a scattering effect on the herd, apart from the fact that "niggers in" generally means cattle killing.' No one can hope to keep blacks totally obedient to the rule, she says. But the wise cattle-station manager gives the occasional bullock, especially at tribal-ceremony times, and he does not worry too much about cattle that are killed on the boundary of the station, 'where cattle scaring is not all disadvantage'. If his kindness fails he should give hints of harsher treatment, but he should not be too demanding of the Aboriginals. 'The white man has taken the country from the blackfellow, and with it his right to travel where he will for pleasure or food, and until he is willing to make recompense by granting fair liberty of travel, and a fair percentage of cattle or their equivalent in fair payment, cattle killing, and at times even man killing, by blacks will not be an offence against the white folk.' She refers darkly to the clashes between cattlemen and Aboriginals, small, tragic, often unrecorded skirmishes which, given the firepower of the Europeans, could end only one way. Europeans 'forget to ask who of us would go hungry if the situation were reversed, but condemn the blackfellow as a vile thief (if he spears cattle), piously quoting – now it suits them – from those same commandments, that man "must not steal", referring in the same breath to the "white man's crime" (when it finds them out) as to "getting into trouble over some shooting affair with blacks"'.

The station was yearly supplied by bullock waggons. What you ordered in one Dry turned up the next Dry on the back of a bullock waggon punched inland from the coast. The waggoners were men with a taste for solitude who spent the entire season bringing desperately yearned-for commodities to places like the Elsey. The craft of waggoner was dominated by the question of water.

Further south the use of bullocks was impossible, and Afghans delivered goods from South Australia using camels. Their life too was one of loneliness, interspersed with the bouts of jubilation and statements of gratitude which greeted their arrival at a homestead. Both in the Centre and the Top End, however, given that each cart could carry only five tonnes of stores and given the slowness of the business of delivery, cartage on goods could sometimes cost up to sixty pounds a tonne, in those days perhaps the most expensive freightage in the world.

Mack the Scot became a waggoner and described to Jeanie the way to get a bullock team over a 'fifty-mile dry', a stretch of eighty kilometres without water. You pulled the waggons out sixteen kilometres from the last waterhole in the cool of late afternoon. Then you unyoked the bullocks and brought them back to the waterhole, letting them drink and rest the night and most of the next day. Late on the following afternoon, you gave them their last drink, took them back to the waggons sixteen kilometres out by sundown, yoked them up and travelled all night and as much of the next day as was necessary. When you were sixteen kilometres out of the next waterhole, you unyoked the bullocks from the waggons, took them forwards to the water and let them drink again and rest a night and a day. Then in the cool of the next evening, you pushed them back to where the waggons had been left, yoked up once more, and brought the waggons to the new waterhole during the night.

As well as waggoners, Jeanie received some two hundred and fifty guests during her year at the Elsey. One was a telegraph worker, who took everyone on an excursion to the telegraph line, attached clamps to it and allowed the others to listen to the cable traffic between Darwin and Adelaide. This was an excursion which impressed Jeanie. The line was one of those symbols of British mastery. It was also a route across the continent, since any traveller following the line and getting into trouble had only to cut the wires and he would, within a day or so, be found by a repair crew.

Another visitor to the Elsey was a line-maintenance man called Dan, who complained to Jeanie that the Territory wasn't what it used to be. 'Can't travel a hundred miles nowadays without running into somebody!' he asserted. A further visitor was Fizzer Pelham, a former bullock puncher who brought the mail from Darwin. Fizzer had not only to deliver the mail. Often he had to find the addressee by gathering clues as he went. Some of the letters he showed Jeanie were addressed fairly indefinitely.

> F. Brown Esq.,
> In charge of stud bulls going west,
> Via Northern Territory.

Another address:

> Jones,
> Travelling with cattle for Wave Hill.

Camel trains, under the management of Afghan camel-drivers, delivered mail and stores to the Centre. This photograph shows the arrival of a camel train at Alice Springs telegraph station in the 1920s, a decade when the camel was still more reliable in the desert than the automobile.

Occasionally there was a woman traveller. The wife of one of the telegraph station masters, travelling to Queensland by horseback with her baby son and her husband, confided to Jeanie that, 'it was nearly two years since she had seen a woman.' She meant of course a woman of her own culture, a European.

On a rise not far from the homestead were buried those travellers who arrived too late or else died before reaching the Elsey. 'In Memory of Hughes, a Traveller, Died 1898,' reads one headstone. 'In Memory of an Unknown,' reads another placed over a travelling man who carried no letters, no marks, and was either dead or comatose when the Elsey

people found him. The Chinese cook Lee Ken lies there too, and William Neaves, who, journeying with his mate from Queensland, caught malarial dysentery at Warloch Ponds to the east of the Elsey.

The story of William Neaves's sickness and death encapsulated for Jeanie the whole business of *mateship* among men, its rituals, its etiquette, the strange impenetrability it presents to women. William Neaves's mate turned up at the Elsey one morning saying that the man he was travelling with was sick, had a touch of fever, and was camped back there at Warloch Ponds. 'I've had a bit of a job to get him as far as this.' Jeanie knew at once what the touch of fever was – the traveller had

In the absence of any official monument to all those bush travellers who died of fever and whose bodies were found innocent of any means of identification, this grave stone on the Elsey does service not only to the bushman who lies there but also to the tradition of the travelling stockman.

caught malarial dysentery from the questionable water of the Warlochs, which lay at the end of an eighty-kilometre dry stretch. But when Jeanie offered to go out in the station buckboard to tend to the sick man, Neaves's friend refused. 'If you please, ma'am. If the boss'll excuse me, me mate's dead set against a woman doing things for him . . . he'd rather have me. Me and him's been mates for seven years.'

When Jeanie's husband, the *Maluka* (in Roper River dialect the *Boss*), rode out to visit William Neaves, Neaves – shivering beneath a blanket – told the *Maluka* that his mate was worth 'ten women fussing round . . . a good mate's harder to find than a good wife.' But in the end he had to

A genial notice to employees on the Elsey station.

be moved to the homestead, and accepted Jeanie's last nursing gratefully. He did not get through the final crisis of his fever and died at the Elsey homestead at dawn. After the funeral, Neaves's mate approached the *Maluka* and held out two sovereigns to him. 'If that won't pay for all me mate's had, there's another where they came from. He was always independent, and would never take charity.' When the *Maluka* refused to take the money, Neaves's mate made a speech of gratitude and rode out towards the Overland Telegraph to look for work on a maintenance crew. He'd been travelling with Neaves for seven years – they must have set out from the south together when they were both seventeen. If he found another mate at the Telegraph Line, if he steered clear of foul water, his travelling career might stretch for years yet.

It has become fashionable in later years to look upon mateship in the 'Neaves and his mate' sense as a form of homosexuality. To believe that is to misunderstand what mateship was. It was a response to the twin mysteries of the wilderness and of women. A mate could help you through the wilderness, he was easier to talk to than a woman. The best response to the phenomenon of woman was to decide she didn't matter as much as a mate. As old Dan from the Telegraph Line explained to Jeanie, an unmarried bushman was like a 'tailless tyke'. Man was the essential entity in desert places. 'Dogs seem able to wrestle through without a tail, but I reckon a tail 'ud have a bit of a job getting along without a dog.' Jeanie seems to have accepted these demeaning figures of speech in good spirit. Jack, the Quiet Stockman, didn't really dislike women, someone explained to Jeanie. 'He only draws the line at conversations.' And the more she camped and mustered with the stockmen, the more they paid her their strange inverted complements. 'Most of the other women I've struck seem too good for rough chaps like us. Of course that's not saying you're not as good as 'em. You ain't a freezer on a pedestal, that's all.'

Jeanie's second wet season was also marked by the arrival of men suffering from fever. A seventy-year-old traveller survived malarial dysentery at the homestead and rode on westwards. None of it affected Jeanie's Edwardian faith. 'Full of bright hopes, we rested in that Land of Wait-a-While, speaking of the years to come, when the bushfolk will have conquered the Never-Never and laid it at the feet of great cities.' Unfortunately the 'scourge of the Wet' was about to attack her own marriage. The *Maluka* was stricken and died, as Neaves had, at the height of the fever. Having buried him in the same hard soil where all those other travellers who had died in the environs of the Elsey were laid, she returned to Melbourne and exercised her grief on the writing of a memoir. Her *We of the Never-Never* was published in 1907, and for generations of Australian schoolchildren became a primary document on the nature of the frontier and on the lives of frontier people.

Mrs Aeneas Gunn's life at the Elsey was no more remarkable than that of a modern Territory woman, Tookie Gill. Tookie is a small girl of great mental toughness and varied background. She is Eurasian – a Thai mother, a New Zealand father. Until she was fourteen her parents ran a

Successor to Aeneas Gunn, John Davis, manager of the Elsey, hangs carcasses in the Elsey meat room. At the time of this photograph, the 6000-square-kilometre station was owned by Californian and Hong Kong interests who were considering abandoning the lease because of the fluctuating price of cattle. John was awaiting their arrival and the chance to convince them he could make a go of it.

restaurant in the northern Thai city of Chiang Mai, in that salient part of Thailand which lies between Burma and Laos and which, during the years of the Vietnam War, was something of a crossroads. Ten years ago, her parents sent her to school in the safer though less racy environment of the South Island of New Zealand. When her schooling was finished, she set off on a grand tour of the kind which so many young Australians and New Zealanders take as a sort of ritual preparation for a life in the duller reaches of Antipodean adulthood. In Brisbane she applied for a job as governess on a Northern Territory cattle station – a place called Bradshaw's Run, north of the Victoria River, though she had no idea of its exact geographic location.

The trade of governess, a vanished one in most of the English-speaking world, flourishes in the Northern Territory. One reason is that the station children do not disappear from the house at 8.30 each morning, but instead have to be directed to and supervised in a classroom on the premises, one equipped with two-way radio suitable for picking up the broadcasts of the School of the Air.

The Bradshaw manager's two small girls had been democratically permitted by their parents to come to Brisbane and participate in the selection of a governess, and when Tookie had been chosen, she flew with the family to Darwin. There the assistant manager of Bradshaw's, Dick Gill, was waiting at the airline counter to fly them in his Cessna four hundred kilometres south-southwest. Even sloped languidly across the counter, with his hat held slackly on the back of his head, Gill was an enormous man. To signify his impenetrable privacy of soul, he chewed meditatively on a stick and stared straight ahead. At that moment Supatra – she had not yet submerged her Thai name beneath an Aussie soubriquet – felt a powerful and terrifying fatalism. Her mother had been Buddhist and had given her an appropriate sense of destiny. It had been luggage she had carried quite lightly up to now, but here, at an airport which was meant to be just one stop on a world tour, an old-fashioned sense of ordained events arose and claimed her. Her panic had more to do with evading destiny than evading a relationship. 'I wanted to go straight back – on the next flight – because I knew this was as far as I would go if I stayed.'

Dick Gill's courting of the governess consisted more of warning off the few other European males on Bradshaw's than of any positive statements to the woman herself. She spent some time flying with him – he was and is an extraordinary flyer, spending much of his day flying and banking lower than treetop level, just above the tops of the grass, spotting cattle and frightening them out of concealment, generally working with one door off, a shotgun on his lap, his cattle dogs leaning out the door and barking furiously despite the noise of the engine and of the cattle below.

Aeneas Gunn himself had once run Bradshaw's – in the 1890s – for his cousin Captain Joe Bradshaw, a visionary and speculator, member of the Melbourne Stock Exchange and the Royal Melbourne Yacht Club, who had been trying to raise sheep and cattle in the Kimberleys and had fallen out with the Western Australian government over taxes. Bradshaw commissioned Gunn to find a new place in the Territory, and Gunn did in fact find it far up the tidal reaches of the Victoria River on the Whirlwind Plains. The sheep did not survive there – the grass was too long, and great numbers of them were speared. The Aboriginals of the tall saltwater tribes stole the sheep shears and turned them into murderous shovelnose spears. Under Aeneas Gunn, Bradshaw's Run carried 40,000 cattle, a stable of blood horses. Chinese coolies worked there on acreages of cotton and rice, and, as a result of such endeavours, you can still encounter cotton growing wild – not only on the Victoria River, but throughout the Top End. Besides Bradshaw's Run, Captain Joe leased Hodgson Downs on the Roper River, Wollogorang over near the Queensland border, and a great square mileage of country in Eastern Arnhem Land near the mouth of the Glyde River, country now long since an Aboriginal reserve and presently owned by Aboriginals. Joe Bradshaw's fleet of yachts and steam launches delivered mail and supplies all up and down the coast of northwestern Australia from Port Darwin to Wyndham. He had contracts for delivering cattle to the Eastern African and Cold Storage Company. Regularly he visited England and Scotland to raise capital for his northern Australian enterprises, but would also travel up the Victoria to Timber Creek to act as a magistrate. He is described as holding court seated on a beer case, a bottle of scotch at one elbow, in his right hand a loaded twenty-five-centimetre revolver which he used as a gavel.

Aeneas Gunn would leave the employ of his cousin, marry Jeanie, and die at Elsey Station nearly three years before affairs at Bradshaw's reached crisis point. One of those contributing to the crisis at Bradshaw's Run was a Russian named Ivan Egoriffe. One day in 1904, Ivan was found adrift off the mouth of the Daly River in a dinghy. He told police that during the night a party of Aboriginals had boarded the Bradshaw launch *Wunwulla*, crewed by himself, a stockman named Old Larsen and a crew of three saltwater Aboriginals. When two constables from Darwin asked questions around the Daly River Jesuit mission station, two young Daly men named Kammipur and Mungkum came forward and confessed to the murder of Larsen and the three saltwater blacks of *Wunwulla*'s crew.

It is a curious comment on the unreality of European law in the eyes of Aboriginals that the two young men from Daly River, though committed for trial at the Supreme Court in Darwin, were found to have made up the story merely to tease one of the constables, Stott, because, as they explained, Stott reckoned he knew everything about everything, and they wanted to make a fool of him.

In fact it was the crew of three saltwater blacks who had knocked Egoriffe overboard and then killed Larsen.

The police hunted the criminals down in the ridge behind Bradshaw's Run. One of the three they shot, the other two stood trial, and one of them was condemned to be hanged on Bradshaw's Run itself, a cautionary hanging which was meant to be witnessed by all the station blacks. In fact, on the eve of the execution, all the saltwater people vanished. Aboriginal black trackers of other tribes were sent out to find them, and either had no success or pretended not to have found a trace. In the end the condemned man was hung in the station yard while 'Ivan the Terrible' Egoriffe and the police ate breakfast.

Even during the time that Supatra and Dick Gill were governess and deputy manager respectively on Bradshaw's Run, the stockmen of the saltwater tribes remembered Ivan, remembered the ill-advised severity of the Bradshaw family.

Captain Joe Bradshaw intended to spend Christmas 1905 at Bradshaw's Run, having just returned from Europe. Fred Bradshaw, the Captain's brother, together with Ivan Egoriffe and one of the stockmen, set out from Bradshaw's on 12 November 1905 to run up to Darwin and fetch the Captain. The great tidal outflow of the Victoria was capable of sweeping them out into Queen's Channel and Joseph Bonaparte Gulf (named by the French explorer D'Urville) at a great pace, but they turned aside up the Baines River to the cattle station of Auvergne to see if there was anything the Auvergne people needed in Darwin. The great station of Auvergne had existed longer than Bradshaw's Run, but its history had been equally marked by frontier courage, pitiable fevered death and racial savagery. Frontier skirmishes go without their chroniclers, but it is certain that conflict between Aboriginals and cattle men continued well into the 1920s and probably later on Auvergne, and within the memory of the three white men on the *Bolwarra*, two stockmen called Mulligan and Ligar had been ambushed in a gully near a baobab tree. Both men, though critically wounded, survived the ambush, and a trooper and seventeen stockmen rode about Auvergne looking for the culprits and exacting largely unrecorded vengeance at Aboriginal camp-sites.

The men on the *Bolwarra* that November remembered one of the ambushers, Ligar, as a character. Speared through the cartilage of the nose with a glass-tipped spear, his wound had never healed over, and he could make bushmen hoot, or else affright young ladies staying at bush pubs, by passing their hat pins backwards and forwards through the spear hole.

So a certain rough tenderness and nostalgia sent Fred Bradshaw and Ivan out of their way to Auvergne. There they found out that Jerry Skeehan, the head stockman, had broken his arm that morning and had ridden off towards Wyndham looking for a doctor, a ride of three hundred and twenty kilometres with the bone projecting from the flesh of his arm. Aboriginals were sent to fetch him back, and so Jerry Skeehan joined the *Bolwarra*.

A few nights later, all four Europeans were killed with clubs and stone axes. Among the victims was, of course, the unfortunate Skeehan, bludgeoned while nursing his broken arm beneath a mosquito net in the bowels of *Bolwarra*. He left a wife and child on Auvergne. The crime against him and the other white men had not been without motive. At Port Keats, the crew of saltwater blacks had deserted – the head of aggression which the Port Keats Aboriginals had built up against a government water-boring team temporarily working in Port Keats had communicated itself to the saltwater blacks too. Fred Bradshaw and Ivan simply went ashore then and press-ganged five Port Keats boys, bringing them back on board the launch in irons. The party which killed Fred and Ivan, Skeehan and the stockman, also liberated the black crew.

The victims' bodies were retrieved and buried by Captain Joe on a high point on the ridge behind the homestead at Bradshaw's Run. The coffins were basic, made out of crates and butter-boxes. Saltwater blacks who had not been involved in the crime carried the dead up onto that red and very stony ridge. They are still there – in unmarked graves. A nearby rock-pecking depicts a boat with sails, probably a representation of one of Captain Bradshaw's yachts, or else of the explorer Gregory's home-made cutter, the *Tom Tough*. There is even a chance that the pecking may have been provoked by D'Urville's ship, or even by the sails of some still earlier visitor. Yet, in its way, it offers some explanation.

As well as the victims of *Bolwarra*, there are other Europeans buried on the Run – one of them, Palmer, a bank clerk turned stockman in the 1890s and dead of a mauling by a Victoria River crocodile. A woman who rode all the way from Queensland to work on the Run with her husband and who died there of fever, also lies at Bradshaw's. Malaria killed Hughie Young, who until the turn of the century was renowned in the Territory as the piano-playing stockman. He would ride seven hundred kilometres into Katherine for occasional recreation, and could compel music out of the hulk of a piano at the pub, the instrument itself being the survivor of a shipwreck and brought inland to moulder in a Katherine bar. Wheeling above these and other graves, banking low over the mangrove banks of the Victoria – which Aeneas Gunn had described as 'a jungle cathedral conceived in delirium' – Dick Gill got on with his understated courtship of the governess.

The foreign owners of Bradshaw's, said to be Israelis, ultimately let the lease lapse. MacBean of Innesvale took it up, but there is little doing on Bradshaw's now. This is not the first time Bradshaw's was abandoned. Falling cattle prices prior to World War I forced Joe Bradshaw out. One of his managers, Biers, built a homestead on a framework of pipes from Ivan's irrigation system. Such a structure was white-ant proof. But during the Wet, frogs boomed away inside the hollow pipes and drove Biers and his wife close to dementia. Some saltwater blacks believed the noise was the foul spirit of Ivan complaining there, and so fled from the homestead. Biers himself caught fever in the saddle, sent his stockman on ahead of him while he himself rested under a tree. When the stockman came back, Biers had disappeared. His body was never found.

The tragic history of places like Bradshaw's Run, their cyclical abandonment by European cattlemen, has done nothing to sap Dick Gill's faith in the final validity of cattle. The dream of cattle – a characteristic Scottish, Irish, North Country dream – runs powerfully in men like Gill. He and his wife Tookie now live fourteen kilometres east of Katherine near the fringes of bush country which stretches away to Katherine Gorge and beyond that to infinity. They are still in the cattle business. At the beginning of 1982, worried by a decline in the beef industry in the Katherine area and a lack of employment for himself and his Cessna, Dick Gill took the risk of flying over the Northern Territory border to the Kimberleys in Western Australia. His journey was a variation on that of the old style itinerant bush worker. Dick did not arrive on foot, a swag on his shoulder, but instead dropped out of the sun in his Cessna. This reconnaissance took hours of flying and cost Gill something close to $2000, but on one of the stations – Napier Downs – he got the mustering contract.

There were many rogue cattle in that country sheltering in scrub or in the rough country which backed onto the King Leopold Range. The contract was that Gill would clear the Napier Downs country of these cattle so that the station could be properly restocked.

To work on this enterprise he subcontracted two helicopter pilots and their machines, some four or five bull-catchers, a number of stockmen, white and Aboriginal, a cook and a mechanic. He moved his personnel into this remote stretch of country by plane or four-wheel-drive, the bull-catchers driving their own vehicles in, machines fortified with rollbars and massive bumpers and intended to go anywhere a wild bull would lead them.

There is a pattern to mustering operations. After initial reconnaissance by the aircraft has shown the area where a large mob of cattle can be found, and after observation of the way the cattle in question move towards available water, you direct your stockmen, vehicles and cook into the area you intend to work in.

From 4000 feet above the countryside, Dick Gill chooses the best site for the setting up of a portable mustering yard into which the mob will be driven. The cattle have some sense of landscape too, so that the boss of a mustering camp has to decide, given the contours of the earth, the way the mob will choose to run. 'Sometimes,' says Dick Gill, 'it is best to run cattle off flats into the river bed, or vice versa. Siting is absolutely crucial.' From 4000 feet he says, you can see the regular paths and pads the mob takes, and it is in terms of these that you will begin your mustering.

It takes one and a half days to set up the portable mustering yard. If you have had to disassemble it somewhere else and move it to the new site, that will take a day and a half as well. By the time it is set up on new ground, it is quite immense, very like the permanent stockyards attached to a cattle station. It has separate paddocks, and races for loading cattle onto road trains. For that is another thing to be taken into account – the road train has to be able to get in to take the cattle away.

From the mouth of the mustering yard, the stockmen and labourers erect two great walls of hessian running out eight hundred metres down country to make a funnel six hundred metres across at the mouth, into which the cattle will be herded. The hessian is flimsy, it flaps in the wind, it shows clear daylight beneath its edges. Somehow the cattle will never attempt to break through it or duck under its hem. But the funnel of hessian will only work if the country you drive the cattle over makes its contribution as well, itself exercising a funnelling effect on the mob.

From the river bank, where the herd might be drinking, you can begin to exert gentle pressure using the Cessna and the helicopters. It *should* be gentle pressure at first; you do not want the young bulls breaking loose from the rest.

Perhaps you drive them round the blind side of a hill, for you do not want them to sight the great flapping walls of the hessian funnel yet. When you have them following the contours of land you have chosen, you increase the pressure, dropping lower. The stockmen ride in on the tail of the mob. The noise of aircraft, the protest of the mob, the roaring and whistling and whip-cracking of the stockmen create a tremendous rage of sound, and the dust is prodigious. The helicopters and the Cessna are now very low. It is accepted aviation wisdom that fixed-wing aircraft and choppers should not operate close to each other. But here are three aircraft, all as low as six metres, all having to concentrate not only on the cattle but on their distance from the ground and from each other, helicopters hovering, the aircraft banking, circling, returning within the same dusty and restricted volume of sky. By the time the cattle are near the funnel, you have not eaten since 5 a.m., the sun is high, your mouth is full of red dust. And you do not know whether it will all work.

When wild bulls leave the herd and make a break, the bull catchers will run them down. Sometimes the helicopters will assist in this. The most macho way of dealing with cattle is for a stockman to jump from the struts of a helicopter and roll the exhausted bull over by the tail, holding him down and strapping the beast's hind legs. It's well paid, the craft of bull catching, and so is mustering. But the hours are prodigiously long. Once you have the herd in the mustering yard, you have to draught them, brand those which, up to now, have never carried a brand, and ship them aboard the road trains.

There are also few comforts in the camp, though one of the greatest of them must be the bushman's swag in which you sleep. It is a weatherproof roll, which, when opened up, offers a thick rubberized mattress and blankets, and heavy waterproof flaps which can be pulled across the whole thing if rain comes down. The cooking is probably less of a comfort. In mustering camps it is traditional to complain about the cook. He is often a loner and sometimes a drunk. Mustering bosses like Dick Gill make sure that their cooks do not order in too much lemon essence, since lemon essence is traditionally used by pastoral cooks as a cheap form of booze. The cooking itself can be very rudimentary, but most cooks will be respected if they can make good bread. Tookie Gill has in emergencies sometimes been brought into mustering camps as a cook – her husband says she is one of the best. But she prefers to work on the mustering as a stockman. (The more artificial aspects of feminism have not reached the Territory, and to call a woman a stockperson would be considered grotesque.)

But most of the time Tookie is in Katherine, and the journey home to visit her involves four hours' flying and an expense of hundreds of dollars. Until she got a litter, Dick's favourite cattle dog Djunga would fly with him. 'When I'm coming home I take the Cessna up to 9000 feet and have a bit of a snooze. As soon as the plane gets out of

attitude, Djunga rouses me. Anyhow, even asleep, I've got my ear out for the motor. A slight change in the engine note will wake me.'

After Bradshaw's closed down for them, Dick and Tookie came to Katherine specifically because it seemed to offer lots of work for aerial musterers. In fact Katherine was an area which appeared to be hard hit by the fall in cattle prices, and Dick took the Napier Downs job in the hope that in the meantime the Territory industry would revive. 'The Territory is nothing but cattle, and cattle's dead.'

The Territory cattle business – like the Australian industry in general – is dependent not only on rises and falls in world prices, but on the quotas of beef America, Japan, and other countries will take from Australia. It is, of course, little consolation to the cattleman who sells his beef on the hoof for a few hundred dollars to know that in Japan a good lump of sirloin, of the type that is thrown down by the dozen on Northern Territory barbecues every weekend, may cost about ninety dollars a kilo.

Once he started the mustering contract, Dick Gill could see that the west Kimberley area included some of the best open range country in Australia. He and Tookie would like in the end to take up a lease in that region. But even in that ambition there is a component of struggle. Struggle is inherent in the way Tookie describes the Kimberley country. 'The best grazing country in Australia for someone to build up.'

If the Kimberley plan falls through, the Gills will revert to their original schedule, Dick finding mustering contracts closer to Katherine and ultimately taking out his own pastoral lease in the Territory.

Meanwhile, for Tookie Gill, life near Katherine is in part a repetition of the homestead loneliness of that other small and impermeable Territory woman, Mrs Jeanie Gunn. Dick is away six weeks at a stretch. She rises at 5 a.m. for the extraordinary Territory dawn.

The Wet season will be time to sleep and, above all, time to read. 'A good book for the Wet,' is one of the standard phrases of the Gill household. The house itself is in the bush about fourteen kilometres from Katherine in one direction, about one kilometre from Katherine airport in the other. Large sharp conical rocks surround it and screen it from the Stuart Highway. It stands on a cement slab – white-ant proof – and the corner posts and uprights of the house are held at their base in small steel brackets, again intended to defeat the prodigious hunger of termites. The walls of the living areas are of thick gauge wire and have waterproof blinds which can be let down in the Wet. The rest of the house is corrugated iron. It is the primal Australian house, a modern variation of the house in Patrick White's novel of Australian Eden, *The Tree of Man*. It is very deftly planned, serviceable, comfortable, little. The first thing you notice about this household is that there is an admirable order to it. It has been lovingly planned by both the Gills. It has all the marks of a bush homestead – a water bag hangs from the wire walls, a one-hundred-and-nine-litre drum is suspended from the treetop by a chain. A diesel generator hums in its own shed, sharing its space with a telescope and a saddle, both signifying Dick Gill's passionate interest in the stars, and in horses. There is a vegetable plot tended by

Djunga, waiting to fly off with Dick Gill to muster cattle in the Kimberleys, sits on the transfer case of a four-wheel-drive used in the hard business of bull-catching. Dick and Djunga, door off the Cessna, will spot wild bulls from the air, and the bull-catchers on the ground will run them down wherever they go.

Tookie Gill, who keeps chickens and an eccentric rooster named Sebastian Roost. The treetops are full of genial and beautiful apostle birds, and behind the largest conical rock in the garden, a bower bird is building its tubular nest of snail shells, fragments of glass and pottery and ring-pull beer-can tops which the Territory's population strews so prolifically over its immense spaces.

Tookie's main companion during Dick Gill's six-week absence is a sturdy but unconfident cattle dog called O. J. Nab. He is named whimsically after his father, Banjo. O. J. Nab and his sister Djunga have both worked with Dick Gill at mustering and in the cattle yards, but O.J. lacked Djunga's timing and has paid for this lack. If you are going to harry cattle along over open country or down races by nipping at their ankles – that is, if you are to know one of the great challenges and joys of being a cattle dog – you have to strike in the instant when the beast's hoof is flat in the dust, otherwise you will be savagely injured. O. J. Nab, when young and over-zealous, struck at the wrong moment and had his teeth kicked out by a hoof on the rise. Now that his only use is as a

Tookie Gill and her husband Dick on their smallholding near Katherine. It costs Dick hundreds of dollars a time to fly home in his Cessna from the remote mustering camps he runs in the northwest. They are both sure that the loneliness will pay off in a future of cattle.

companion and a household dog, there is an indirectness in his gaze;
he has the air of a man whom destiny chose to destroy by a decimal point
of a second. When Djunga is home, a visitor can see the difference
between them. Her manner is exactly that of a sharp and intelligent sister
being attentive to a brother who will never amount to anything. Her
eyes are alert, her approach confident. Her brother's line will not be
regarded, but she will be prized and will produce litters of sought-after
dogs. The right timing is written into her DNA; she is Dick Gill's
colleague and peer, and she knows it. But if O. J. Nab is a failure
professionally, he is a gentle and genial presence in Tookie Gill's small
home in the scrub. And though toothless, he is a brave barker.

The house stands in some sixty hectares of scrub which, before the
arrival of whites in the Katherine area and probably for some time after,
supplied spearheads and cutting stones from the large boulders of
crystalline rock scattered about. The girl from Chiang Mai wanders in a
palaeolithic quarry when she walks in her back yard. Stone chippings,
spearheads worked on with great patience and then flawed at the last

moment by a careless or unlucky stroke of the fashioning tool are strewn everywhere. To create this much industrial debris, Aboriginals must have worked for centuries at this site of special rock, precious because hard. Tools and weapons from this area would have been traded away over a great distance to other tribes, and on the underside of one rock, an ancient painting of the rainbow serpent suggests that the site might have been turning out palaeoliths, cutting and fashioning instruments in the Old Stone Age manner, for a thousand years or even longer. At night the moon shines on these flinty stones and Tookie shares the absolute black and the sharp stars with the residual presence of Aboriginal quarries and fashioners of instruments.

Of course, Tookie Gill's isolation is not absolute, any more than Jeanie Gunn's was. She works as a dental therapist for the Northern Territory government, in a primary school in Katherine under the supervision of a government dentist. She goes on bush trips in a mobile unit – up to Pine Creek, down to Bamilyi Aboriginal settlement. She can take X-rays, clean scale, surface-fill, and extract first teeth. The rest is done by the dentist. There is back-up from the Aerial Medical Service, which has a Navajo set up as a dental surgery for emergency cases. Tookie has noticed the high-pain tolerance among Aboriginals as compared to either white or Asian patients, a phenomenon which has been widely remarked on by other medical aides and practitioners in the Northern Territory. For one thing, most Aboriginal children in the Territory have not been exposed at a young age to the traumatizing experience of a dental surgery, as most whites and Asians have been. 'If an Aboriginal child complains of pain,' says Tookie, 'then you look at him pronto.'

Dick Gill's cattle dogs. Mere dogs? In the cattle business, dogs are colleagues, and the brightest can talk. Of Djunga, the bitch on the right, aerial musterer Dick Gill says, 'If ever I snooze off at the controls of the Cessna, she nudges me as soon as the plane gets out of attitude.' Her brother, O. J. Nab, however, lost his teeth by striking at the heel of a bullock at the wrong instant. He has become a house dog, and his line will not be regarded. The relationship between the two of them is like that of clever and successful sister and failed and embarrassing brother.

Tookie Gill's house, in the centre bottom of the picture, standing in an immensity of scrub, termite mounds, and monoliths once much favoured by local tribes as a source of spear heads, axes and tools. Katherine Gorge is in the far distance.

The rest of Tookie's professional life is taken up with doing the books for Dick's mustering company. It would be wrong however to think of Tookie as merely a dutiful wife keeping the office straight. There is a ruggedness of purpose in this small twenty-four-year-old. There are projects that fall beyond the ambience of Dick Gill's ambitions.

It is ironic, Dick Gill thinks, that most of the cattle heroically and arduously mustered in the Northern Territory and the Kimberleys, once slaughtered and packed in cartons, go to the making of beefburgers in America and elsewhere. The idea of beefburger eaters in Washington

This photograph, taken at Pine Creek in 1917, has the flavour of the nineteenth century about it. But in the Northern Territory the nineteenth-century-style frontier ran late and is not yet dead.

and Chicago swallowing down all the valour of the mustering camp is one that must tease any cattleman. But it is also one which illuminates the problem the Territory cattle industry has had since it first started – the problem of getting the cattle to market over those great thirsty distances before they have lost their condition. Dick Gill himself is much taken by a proposal of Sir William Gunn, a spokesman for the cattle industry and, yes, a member of *that* family. Gunn's suggestion is that young healthy cattle be shipped live to Asia, where they can be slaughtered under Muslim supervision. The sort of slaughtering that is

Tookie Gill will travel 1500 kilometres at a time to bring dental hygiene to the wilderness. Aboriginal tolerance of pain, she says, is enormously higher than that of European children.

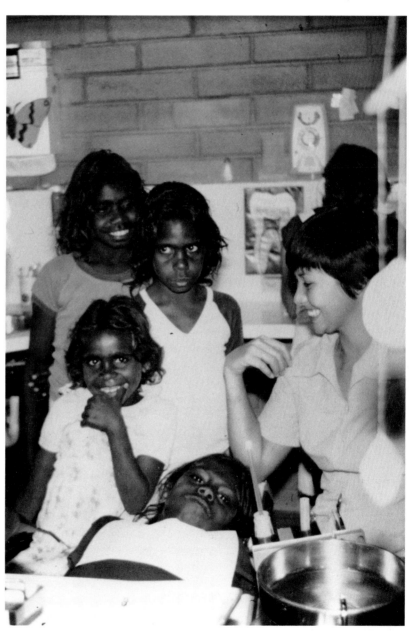

done in Northern Territory abattoirs makes the beef unsuitable for consumption by orthodox Muslims in populous Indonesia and in the rich oil sultanates of North Borneo. If the cattle were shipped young and robust and by fast transporters, the Muslims could look after their own requirements as regards slaughter.

Again we see that old hope – that the sparsely peopled but favoured Territory might prosper by connecting itself to the enormous markets of Asia. It occurred to the South Australians when they ran the Territory, it occurred to the people who tried to grow cotton and rice on the Daly River and in Arnhem Land, it occurred to Captain Joe Bradshaw and his Eastern and African Cold Storage Company. As early as 1884 two South Australians, M. Lyons and C. B. Fisher shipped their cattle from the Marrakai Plains southeast of Darwin to the markets of Hong Kong, Java and Singapore. Other cattlemen took up the same outlet. But again the problem was the condition of the cattle, combined with the effects of drought and of red-water fever, which led in the end to the closure of most Asian markets to beef from the Territory. Red water or tick fever no longer exists in the Territory, and Asia is still there, beguiling the gleam of hope which shows in the eyes of William Gunn, even in those of the hard-headed Paul Everingham. The vision operates in the Gills too. It is palpable how willingly they would give themselves to a hard cattle run, how willingly they would bet their young lives and prodigious energies against the chance of getting into the great markets. The frontier favours demonic hope – that is why it is the frontier, and that is why people like the Gills live there.

End Note

The author must preface this small footnote by saying that even as a child he detested the bogus sentimentality of dog stories. But cattle dogs are different – they are real dogs because, as is said above, they are real colleagues. In 1982 Djunga was mated with a champion cattle dog sire and during the later stages of her pregnancy stayed in Katherine with Tookie and O. J. Nab. She would sometimes wander down to the airport to see if Dick Gill's Cessna was in. Having delivered a litter of nine pups which were bought by cattlemen from Queensland to Western Australia, she was on her way to the airport one day during her convalescence, when she was knocked down and killed by a truck on the Stuart Highway. Through her progeny, of course, her sharp timing survives. The cattle will be running before her for years to come.

Chapter 7

The Two Healths

In August 1927, a miner called Tom O'Brien, standing in a bucket and being winched to the surface of the Black Star Mine near Mount Isa, slipped and fell to the bottom of the shaft. Once the shock of the impact had passed, O'Brien moved his limbs experimentally and called to the surface that he was 'devilishly sore'.

The mine radioed to Cloncurry, asking Qantas to send a plane to ship O'Brien out. On impulse, a Dr George Simpson, a Melbourne surgeon who happened to be in Cloncurry, flew along in the De Havilland 50. 'The return trip was not pleasant, and I almost disgraced myself by being air-sick. The vibration rather upset our patient, so I gave him Morphia $\frac{1}{4}$ g. and some brandy, which he promptly vomited. Evans (the pilot) made a beautiful landing and the aerial medical service was an accomplished fact.'

In fact, the business of organizing an aerial medical service in the wilderness was undertaken not by Simpson himself but by a friend of his, the Reverend John Flynn, a Presbyterian minister from Adelaide. Flynn was a zealot for the aeroplane and the wireless transmitter, and in his efforts to provide the outback with what he called a 'mantle of safety', he encountered and recruited another gentle and altruistic self-improver, a farmer's son and radio expert called Alf Traeger. Traeger had had a passionate interest in wireless since childhood and, while still at primary school, had connected a receiver with a transmitter along a line between his father's implement shed and the homestead. The magnet for this device was the prong of a pitchfork, the diaphragms of the receiver were cut out of tobacco tins, and charcoal was used for the carbon granules of the microphone. In his twenties, Alf Traeger had produced a small generator, that could power a Morse transmitter. Now Flynn set him to work to make a portable transmitter, something which could be put in distant homesteads, and in the end Traeger delivered a wireless set connected to bicycle pedals. The operator cycled, and so generated the power necessary to send Morse messages. In 1929 Traeger at Alice Springs and Flynn at Hermannsburg sent and received messages using pedal wireless.

Flynn had already employed a Flying Doctor – a Sydney surgeon called Dr Kenyon Welch, who was fed up with the urban practice of medicine. Welch himself did not fly, a Qantas pilot was seconded for that purpose; and the Flying Doctor Service's first aircraft was a De Havilland biplane with room for four passengers and a pilot. Alf

Traeger and Dr Welch had already made their first flight – one hundred and thirty-six kilometres to Julia Creek, where Welch performed two operations at the Bush Nursing Home. That was all very well. The nursing home had radio contact. But there was no radio network for outback Queensland, the Northern Territory, Western Australia or South Australia. The people who needed Welch most were unable to contact him.

Traeger therefore spent six months of every year travelling to the most remote European residences in the world installing and then reconditioning his pedal wireless sets. He put in the first six in 1929, but white ants ate the wooden cabinets. He had ten metal replacements ready in 1930. To enable bushmen to use the sets, Alf invented a Morse typewriter, a machine which translated messages punched out in English into Morse signals. In 1935, he began to replace the Morse sets with radio telephony. He developed sets that could be carried on camels, or on the trays of trucks. By the beginning of World War II, he had a model which did away with the bicycle pedals altogether, thus dispensing with the sweaty business of bicycle-based transmission.

The founders of the Flying Doctor Service were, of course, men of their day, men with a sense of empire and of the ineluctable European conquest of remote places. Dr Simpson, in a speech in 1927, saw the new service as a benefit to Europeans, 'removing that area which is the greatest hindrance to present-day family life in the bush'. If its founders did not see it as a service to Aboriginals as well, it was in large part because Aboriginals rarely sought European medical advice. The Flying Doctors themselves were captivated by the demands and spiritual rewards of frontier medicine for whites. The Europeans they treated had desperate and unambiguous need of them. Aboriginal cases were sometimes more complex because they were based on causes outside the European doctor's ken, that is, on potent sorcery.

Now that the Flying Doctor Service connects not only with remote cattle stations but with Aboriginal settlements as well, the Flying Doctors, like physicians in the Northern Territory generally, are frequently confronted with and work parallel to the alternate medicine of the *ngangkari*, or Aboriginal physician.

Today the Royal Flying Doctor Service still saves lives in the classic Flynn manner, and under conditions which could prevail only on a frontier. An old stockman called Ted MacFarlane lived on Mallapunyah Station in the Barkly Tablelands, equidistant from Darwin and Alice Springs. Many miles from the homestead, he bred horses and boasted to the occasional visitor that he had not been to a town or in a shop for fifteen years. Nearly every morning, the station owner's wife would call him and ask after his health. The homestead people also left their radio switched on, so that it could receive immediate transmissions from Ted. On the day of his severest asthma attack, however, they had gone away early and forgotten to switch on the radio. There was therefore no chance that a stockman, passing the radio room, would hear the sick man's transmissions. The rest of Ted's account has – despite its references to radio and aircraft – the aura of deeds of an earlier age, the sort of endeavours which in the cautionary boys' stories of our childhood attracted terms such as 'plucky' and 'British grit'.

'Luckily Mrs Murphy, wife of the manager of Walhallow Station, fifty miles away, heard me calling. I had the oxygen bottle near the radio, and between gulps of oxygen told her the situation. Like a true bush woman Mrs Murphy took command and . . . rang Darwin on the radio telephone. Darwin arranged with Katherine to send a plane to Mallapunyah airstrip to pick me up. All the men were away from Mallapunyah with the four-wheel-drive vehicles, which meant (for me) nine miles of rocky road in the station utility, wading the creek with the oxygen bottle and on to the airstrip for take-off to Katherine Hospital.' At the time of writing, Ted is still living with his horses, his four favourite butcher-birds and his water goannas, which he feeds with banana and pawpaw.

In one day in 1982, the Alice Springs base of the Flying Doctor Service evacuated to the base hospital an Aboriginal boy who suffered a broken leg and internal injuries while playing Australian Rules football on a mission, a seventy-two-year-old who slipped a disc while loading petrol on trucks at a cattle station; a boy who had received massive head injuries in a fall from a horse and who was under observation in Alice Springs Hospital only four hours after the injury, and a four-year-old who was found floating in a wading pool in the garden of a homestead.

To enterprises such as these so much romance is attached that John Hepworth, a radio expert from Yorkshire who runs the Alice Springs Flying Doctor base, and Dr Kerry Kirke, the local health administrator who supplies the doctors for the services, are continually pestered by German, Japanese, American and British television crews and journalists who want to observe and film a mercy flight, especially a desperate and juicy one.

But as well as flying to emergencies, the three Navajos of the Alice Springs Flying Doctor base also service outstations and clinics maintained by the Northern Territory government in remote settlements. Every morning between ten and eleven and every afternoon at three, these outstations and clinics call in for medical advice from Dr Kirke or one of his colleagues. On a given morning in 1982, the first radio call was from Finke River, an abandoned stop on the Ghan line. The health sister sought advice in the case of an elderly Aboriginal's urinary tract infection. From Docker River, on the edge of the Gibson Desert – hundreds of kilometres from Finke on the edge of the Simpson – a government sister called Patricia Kemp rang about a fifty-two-year-old Pitjantjatjara male who had long-term back pain, now crippling. Kemp wanted advice about further analgesia. From Ernabella in South Australia, there were two enquiries – one about a thirteen-year-old boy whose eye had been severely damaged by a stick. Fragments of wood were still embedded. There had been a motor accident as well. A middle-aged woman, also Pitjantjatjara, had a severe lumbar injury. Dr Kirke decided to despatch an aircraft at once and bring both cases to Alice Springs. Kirke explained that the air ambulance would be at Ernabella in

a little over an hour and would be already offering treatment. 'This is a faster service than anyone can expect in these dubious times in a metropolis.' From Ayers Rock came two enquiries – one concerning a European child from the tourist camp who had severe croup. Treatment was prescribed, and the sister at Ayers Rock was to call back at the 3 p.m. session with a progress report. Similarly an eighteen-year-old Aboriginal resident had been hit in the eye with a rubber band. The eye was occluded and vision was blurred. Kirke suggested that he be evacuated to hospital by vehicle.

This session, which deals with diagnosis and further treatment, is always followed by a relatives' talk-back. At Docker River, Yuendemu,

Flying Doctor bases, in whatever part of Australia, always present the same façade to the world as this one at the base in Alice Springs. But although the design may be worthy of an officers' mess in a Biggles novel, there is no gainsaying the extraordinary medical rescues carried on by this fabled service.

A young Arunta captures the ball during an Australian Rules football match at Hermannsburg.

Finke, people whose relatives are under treatment in Alice Springs Hospital come to the settlement radio transceiver to get news of the condition of patients.

In the 1970s, the health authorities began to train Aboriginal health workers to work in the settlements. It was believed that Aboriginals could communicate their distress more honestly and directly to a health worker who happened to be a kinsman. There are problems of communication of course if the Aboriginal who comes to the clinic, and the health worker he faces, are inside forbidden degrees of relationship and cannot look at each other, let alone talk to each other. But a nursing sister from Jay Creek says that these forbidden bounds of kinship are not a major problem. There are generally two Aboriginal health workers at each clinic, so that if one is within the prohibited area of relationship for dealing with a certain patient, the other is free to take the case. As well as that, she says, one of the Jay Creek workers lives a strange bifurcated existence. He can speak to his mother-in-law, one of his forbidden personages, when she comes to the clinic as a patient; she can speak to him. But back in the camp in the evening, they observe the ancient prohibitions on contact, ocular or conversational.

The Central Australian Aboriginal Congress desires to remove health services for Aboriginals from the control of Mr Everingham's government. The Congress employs appositely named 'Congress doctors', Europeans who work under the control of the Aboriginal community where they are stationed. There is no denying that for traditional people this local control is important. From the Congress doctors, it is proposed, Aboriginals will receive more 'culturally appropriate treatments'. For Aboriginals in the Centre therefore there are now two alternate health systems – that provided by the government in some communities, and that provided by Congress in others.

Aboriginal Congress health workers are trained at the same centre in Alice Springs as the Health Department's people. In the field, however, there is not always the same open feeling. In some desert settlements where the elders are making up their minds to accept a Congress doctor or sister, the government nurse will confess to being slightly hurt. She has worked hard, she will tell you, and professionally; and now she finds her territory invaded by Congress workers, black and white, whom she considers, generally, to be very ideological. Because of the costs of providing medical care to remote groups, it is unlikely that Congress will quickly take over the entire system of Aboriginal health. At Utopia, one hundred and fifty kilometres from Alice Springs, a Congress doctor operates, but at Lake Nash, seven hundred and fifty kilometres east of the Alice, European medicine is still represented by a Department of Health sister.

The existence of Congress doctors does not mean that government doctors are necessarily insensible to traditional Aboriginal medicine. Many of them work regularly with *ngangkaris*. A young government doctor called Robert Hall describes a case he treated while working at Tennant Creek Hospital, of a child with fever which would not ease. The parents believed that the illness was due to the influence of spirits and asked that a *ngangkari* of the Warramunga tribe attend its bedside. Robert Hall gave permission and observed the treatment. The *ngangkari* chanted and then began sucking the child's forehead. From it, without producing any lesion, he took out a piece of wood which was then disposed of in the traditional manner, being put into water and carried away from the hospital, out into the bush. Once this ritual of the sacrement of withdrawal of spirits had been completed, the parents suggested to Hall that an injection of antibiotics might work. It was time for the 'white feller medicine' to attack the symptoms left over from the animist misfortune their child had been stricken with.

Pat Kemp, English nurse at Docker River. She works with Aboriginal health aides and radio connects her with the Flying Doctor. She is aware that an alternate medicine, an alternate law, operates side by side with the one she practises in her clinic. Most commonly, her clinic treats runny ears in children, mild malnutrition as well as the occasional cases of snake bite, broken limbs, injuries resulting from fights.

The reason why Western physicians should co-operate with *ngang-karis*, says Hall, is that the Aboriginal perception of illness is very different from ours. They do not use the term 'sick' very much. 'I'm weak,' is the most common assertion of the ailing Aboriginal. Because they know that illness is often caused by sorcery, it is when they believe they have been sung that they will describe themselves as ill, even though no symptoms of illness are present. Some diseases they look upon as entirely the *ngangkari*'s concern, others they believe can be cured only by a European doctor and a *ngangkari* working in tandem, complementing each other. Other diseases are considered entirely the preserve of European doctors. There is, for example, in the armoury of the *ngangkari* no traditional means for dealing with alcoholism and venereal disease. But children with severe diarrhoea, admitted to Alice Springs Hospital, have numerous bite marks on their abdomens where the *ngangkari* has sucked out the evil influence of the spirits which have assaulted the children. The territorian doctor, these days, takes these bruises for granted, as also the fact that payback wounds, ritually inflicted, should not be instantly dressed – the premature treatment by Western medical workers of such injuries will only mean that the wounds must be inflicted all over again.

Robert Hall describes the body of wisdom which a Western doctor collects in such circumstances as 'remote area medicine'. It is as distinct from the usual wisdom of the European physician as one can imagine. It imposes, of course, a wisdom and a tolerance not always found in big-town physicians.

In every distant homestead and settlement which does not have a nurse, the Flying Doctor Service provides basic medical charts and a kit of drugs. The blue charts hang on the walls of every radio hut. They show the human body, front and back. Frontally, the human trunk is divided into segments which are numbered. Back, it is divided into segments to which a letter of the alphabet is attached. 'When describing region of pain quote corresponding number or letter on chart,' the printed caption advises. 'Note: Where pain starts. Course of pain. Severity of duration. Type of pain – state if sharp, dull, throbbing, constant or irregular.' A plaintive sub-text is in a way a tribute to the mental toughness of frontier people. 'If you receive advice over the air, it is always appreciated if you report back progress. Thank you.'

The drug kits the Flying Doctor installs in homesteads consist of a series of trays, and in each tray the drugs are numbered. If the physician at the base in Alice Springs or Darwin, Mount Isa or Oodnadatta prescribes drug No. 23A on tray C, he is prescribing decicaine. If he prescribes drug No. 98 on tray A, he is prescribing powerful ampoules of morphine sulphate. There is also a surgical tray with numbered instruments and bandages. If, as happened recently at a station on the Barkly Tablelands, a highly-honed kitchen knife slips in the hand of the cook and slices the radial artery in his wrist, a bystander can prevent his bleeding to death by following instructions over the radio and by the use of bandages and instruments from the surgical tray. The owner of the

The Finke, the world's most ancient river, is named after a patron of the explorer Stuart. It takes its present shape from the kilometre-wide bankers which run down it in time of rain, but mostly it flows empty 1600 kilometres to the southeast, losing itself in dry creek beds at the edge of the Simpson Desert.

most remote roadhouse on earth, the Rabbit Flat roadhouse on the dirt track through the Tanami Desert, delivered his wife of twins by following instructions on a Traeger two-way radio and having recourse to the drug and instrument set. This is the mantle of safety of which Simpson and Flynn spoke continuously in their fund-raising visits to southern cities, and which the Flying Doctor and the inventive Traeger between them provided.

The Flying Doctor and Alf Traeger, however, can provide no mantle of safety for the Territory's greatest medical problem, alcoholism and booze-related disease. In 1980, the Northern Territory Minister for Health amazed the southern states by announcing that fifty-five per cent of beds in Northern Territory hospitals were occupied by people suffering diseases deriving from alcoholic excess. Stupefying quantities of beer are drunk by Northern Territory Europeans. Ports, sherries, flagon wines are downed by Aboriginals. With Europeans, the pretext is the climate, especially in the Top End, where, at the height of the wet season, even the most moderate social drinker needs half a dozen cans of strong Australian lager to get his thirst out of the way so that he can then settle to the more positive business of achieving booze-euphoria. Apart from climatic aspects, Bacchus has always ridden high on the frontier. An old Australian tradition which connects size of thirst with manly fibre is beginning to diminish in the southern cities, but is much honoured in the Territory and turns morbid around the barbecue pits in the undistinguished suburbs of Darwin.

As for the Aboriginals, in a history which may be 50,000 years old, they have been exposed to fermented liquor for only one hundred.

In the Centre, the characteristic desert fluctuations of temperature occur. On superb 'winter' days when the temperature does not drop below 30°C, the nights can bring thick frosts.

PAGE 117:
Sunset on the Elsey. Such scenes, available at a short walk from the homestead, must have soothed Jeanie Gunn's sense of isolation.

Before European settlement their only narcotic was *pituri*, the treated leaves and roots of a shrub known to botanists as *Duboisia hopwoodie*. Untreated, the leaves of the *pituri* shrub are toxic, but after a drying and refining process they can be reduced to a fibrous, gummy black ball. Anywhere in the settlements you see men and women rolling a ball of *pituri* around their mouths as they speak to you. It is a mild drug; it is not hallucinogenic. Unlike the much-touted magic mushrooms of Mexico, it does not bring about trances, at least not on its own.

The reason why Aboriginals, like the tribes of North America, took so energetically to liquor is still debated. Some experts believe it is due to a different and congenital level of zinc in the Aboriginal's liver. The man on the street in Alice Springs, as well as – once more – some experts, believes that the damage liquor does to the Aboriginals is explained by the millennia of isolation which passed before the Aboriginal saw his first bottle. 'We come from generations of pisspots,' says old Ly Underdown, former proprietor of Telford's Hotel in Alice Springs. 'They've knocked our livers into shape. But the poor bloody blackfella, he's got no resistance to the stuff.' Certainly, you'll hear from whites in Alice the same judgement that is made of Indians in remote towns in British Columbia, or on the edge of the Sioux reservation in South Dakota – 'With liquor in them, they're violent as hell!'

In the early days of the Territory and up until 1966, when an Australian referendum gave the Aboriginal complete civil rights, the Aboriginals were excluded from pubs and it was an offence to sell them liquor. This edict was partly racist but largely motivated by paternalism. It grew out of a European supposition that liquor was more ruinous for Aboriginals than it was for whites. The Aboriginals of course acquired liquor, often from unscrupulous and overcharging whites. For large sums, Europeans might even sell methylated spirits (white lady) mixed with rosehip syrup.

Until recently, right in the centre of Alice, the dry bed of the Todd – one of the world's most ancient rivers – was peopled by Aboriginal alcoholics and their families, as well, of course, as by people in from the settlements on a temporary binge. A recent ordinance forbidding public consumption of liquor within a two-kilometre radius of Alice has moved the river-bed dwellers either north or south of town. It is an improbable life that is led there between the banks of the river. 'If you had to define hell,' said a Northern Territory cop, 'it would be the existence of an Aboriginal kid living with his parents in the Todd bed.'

Everywhere in the Territory you encounter a poster designed by Aboriginals and addressed to Aboriginals. 'Don't let booze destroy our culture!' It is perhaps a better rallying call than the one addressed to the European drinker, 'Boozers are losers!' Certainly the revival of Aboriginal culture deliberately undertaken in the last ten years and the founding of the outstation movement, described elsewhere in this book, have helped temper the Aboriginal thirst. On top of that, a fundamentalist movement originating in Western Australia and sweeping across the desert – the desert being no bar to ideas for the Aboriginal – has caused many Aboriginals to abstain from booze. 'I'm a Christian man,' is

PAGES 118–19 ABOVE:
A Scottish family ran cattle here in the pre-Flying Doctor days of the early 1920s.

PAGES 118–19 BELOW:
By 1872, a telegraph line ran north to south across the Australian continent.
This Telegraph station, part fortress, part home, was the beginning of Alice Springs. The springs themselves, named after the wife of the builder of the Overland Telegraph, Postmaster-General of South Australia, Charles Todd, lie beyond the low hillock to the left of the picture.

PAGE 120:
This cattle station stands in an immensity of unpromising territory near the Queensland–Northern Territory border.

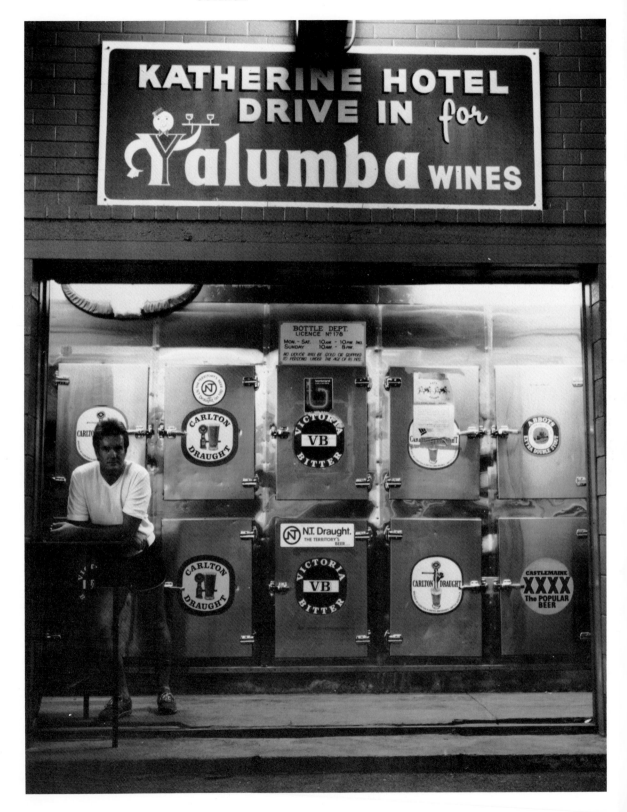

The pub at Mataranka, close to the hot springs which have been favoured by travelling stockmen, American and Australian servicemen in World War II, and now by the Southern Australian out to see the Territory.

OPPOSITE:
The ten doors of a Katherine liquor drive-in offer a selection of Australia's best beers in the tropic night. The Territorian thirst is so fierce that, for white and black, it constitutes a major human and social threat.

a reason an Aboriginal can give for not joining in a binge, a reason which will be accepted without trouble by those who do drink.

But the threat of liquor to the old culture is a desperate one. Though many settlements, such as Hermannsburg and Docker River, have a complete ban on the introduction and consumption of liquor; though this ban has been sought and imposed by the tribal councils and backed up with liquor legislation; though at the border of the Petermann Aboriginal Reserve and the Hermannsburg Aboriginal area large notices threaten large fines for the introduction of liquor and declare that cars and aircraft containing liquor will be subject to confiscation; wine and beer *are* brought in, sometimes by the younger Aboriginals in defiance of their elders, sometimes by Alice Springs whites who, short of money, pile up the boots of their cars with three-dollar flagons of Red Ned, drive an hour and a half, and sell them for thirty to forty dollars each inside the boundaries of Hermannsburg.

From the European side the worst aspect of the sometimes aggressive, sometimes defeated drinkers in the Todd bed is that these are the only Northern Territory Aboriginals the southerner, on trek from Port Augusta to Darwin, sees. He is too quick to presume that the entire race is represented by these river-bed drifters. In fact, many of them are rejects from their own settlements. It is not unknown for elders in some distant settlement to hitch a troublemaker a ride on a small agricultural aircraft or the back of a truck back into Darwin or Alice Springs. In one settlement recently the elders passed the hat around to collect enough money for a fare to send one of the wilder young men away.

The threat of liquor is one of the main concerns of Aboriginal leaders. And lest the Europeans be too self-righteous about it, an elder from

Having travelled hundreds of kilometres for a binge in the Alice, this man had lit a camp-fire in a parking lot. He would leave town the following morning after release from the Alice Springs cells.

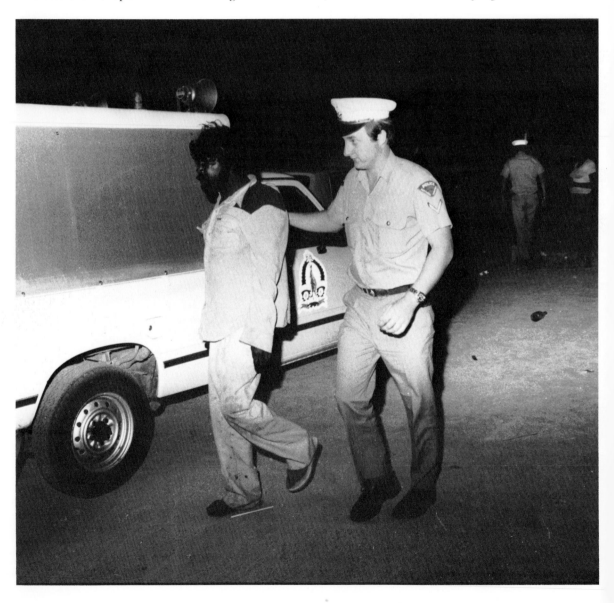

Arnhem Land proclaims, 'If you take our land, you take our soul. And now our soul is gone, why shouldn't we have a drink?'

The term *medicine man* is not only old-fashioned, it carries with it a freight of prejudice. In the films of our childhood the medicine man emits meaningless chants. He has a bone through his nose. He binds the people to him by fakery, and in the last reel Tarzan or Jungle Jim breaks his hold over the people. But to make up for the prejudice of popular culture and to call the medicine man a black physician is equally misleading. A further problem is that since there are so many tribal languages, no one Aboriginal word can be used as a substitute for medicine man. For convenience we can use the central Australian word

Docker River is, by democratic choice of its members and by force of law, a dry community. But the Liquor Act is hard to police and is often satirized by passing travellers, both Aboriginal and white.

Aboriginal burial sites are places of intense spirit activity. It is sometimes within their environs that the fledgling medicine men undergo their trance experience, being eviscerated and killed by the spirits but restored to life again, new men with new and powerful insides. Many such burial places are secret or beyond the normal tracks followed by Europeans, but this more accessible one in Kakadu requires protection by the law.

ngangkari to cover the class of Aboriginal men who have been inducted, either by their elders or by an experience of spirits, into this special order of Aboriginal expertise.

The *ngangkari* is a man who has been through the fire. He is often chosen from the time of his initiation – if people are impressed by the attitudes he takes as he goes through the strenuous experiences of being made a man, of being illuminated and transformed into a tribal being, then when he reaches young manhood it will be time for him to be transformed into a *ngangkari*. He may be taken to live for days in a place so spirit-ridden that a normal person would never approach it. It may be a powerful graveyard, a waterhole where a potent snake spirit lives, a swallower of souls. The anthropologist Elkin tells of a cave only fifteen kilometres from Ayers Rock where Aranda postulants for the high order are taken. They must sleep at the mouth of this cavern seething with spirits. The boy postulant would never in his life have been anywhere near this place. The peril to him is as great as an approach to the naked core of a nuclear reactor would be to us. The risk is absolute. The risk is the risk of annihilation. During the night, and often in dreams, the spirits will come out and take the postulant into the deeps of the cave, where there is always sunshine and where water runs. They will kill and disembowel the boy, will replace his viscera with new and powerful ones, will revivify him and take him on long journeys through the spirit world. In his trance he will encounter the totemic animals who will be his messengers and familiars, who will travel for him, endow him with power, assist him.

It may be that in ceremonies after his ritual death the elders will rub stones into his body, making them vanish without inflicting any wounds. In some tribes, older medicine men put the postulant through his ritual death by inserting invisible spears ear to ear, across his throat, frontways through his body. In the Warburton area of Western Australia, older medicine men will rub the postulant's body with shells from the Indian Ocean, materials which have travelled hundreds of miles from the coast and are the equivalent of magic stones. In the Daly River area the aspirant is sent out to meet and fight Wolgara, the spirit who judges and guards the dead. Wolgara fells him, kills him and cuts up his body. Hawks whom Wolgara calls on breathe life back into the novice, and he already has the healing power when he returns to camp. His capacities will increase, however, with further instruction from the elderly medicine men and with further trance experiences.

The *ngangkari* is a priest – he knows what people's ritual crimes are, and he can bind and loose them. He can absolve, taking an evil word off a person. Elkin describes a case of this nature that occurred in 1976. While out hunting, a young Aboriginal stockman sighted what he thought was a *kaditja*, a tribal executioner endowed with magical powers. The young stockman kept to the bush in terror for his life, and an Aboriginal who happened to be a medicine man as well as a community health worker went out to find him. The health worker sang and called on spirits of the stockman's ancestors to come and help him against the invisible spears of the *kaditja* man. Ultimately the stockman spent some time in hospital recovering from his terror, and while a Western doctor saw his condition as depression induced by recent deaths in his family, the man's relatives believed that it was entirely the influence of the *kaditja* man, and thought of bringing into the case a very powerful medicine man from the Port Hedland area.

The medicine men can also restore people's spirits and physical health. In the Kakadu area, a woman who leans over to drink water from a deep waterhole, or eats fish from it, can let her child's spirit run out into the water, where it is eaten up by a totemic snake. The medicine man, because of his association with the snake, can bring the spirit up out of the mud, can grab it and – by pressure – replace it in the mother's head. When next she suckles the baby (who by now will have been showing signs of illness, hence the mother's desire to consult the medicine man in the first place), the child will get its soul back through its mother's breast.

Though in the 1960s it seemed as if the medicine men were passing, there has been a resurgence in their numbers. Wherever a man cannot be taught, he can at least go through mystical and trancelike experiences at the end of which, through ancestor and totemic spirits, he finds himself endowed with power. Again Elkin instances a medicine man from Haasts Bluff, who says that, while lying all day in the sun, naked on the stony earth, he received three spirit familiars from his dead father. Medicine men of the Jigalong Aboriginals, on the eastern side of the Gibson Desert, keep in contact with their powerful ancestors by making trance-journeys to the bottom of Lake Disappointment, where the ancestor spirits dwell.

As for the medicine man's impact on physical health, European doctors, even European patients, have seen the *ngangkaris* withdraw quantities of blood, serous matter, foreign bodies, by sucking on an infected limb or stomach and without making any wound. The removal and bearing away of foreign objects supposedly sucked from wounds may seem like faking to us. But it has its sacramental aspect. It is a symbolic enactment of what the medicine man hopes will happen to his patient. He is no more faking than our ministers of religion are when they purport to wash away the sins of a candidate for baptism by pouring the symbol of water. He is no more faking than is the Catholic Church when it indicates that one of the results of the Last Rites is frequently an improvement in the patient's health. The medicine man loosens the curse which binds the organism, the patient's certainty of being foredoomed. Whether he has a direct physical effect on top of that is a question that is argued.

To the Aboriginals themselves, to the medicine man, there is no sense in which this body of ritual and curing can be considered false. The tribal doctors are men who have been through terrible dream deaths, who have journeyed with the spirits of the ancestors, with totemic familiars, with the great Rainbow Serpent, across the constellations of the night. They have been purified by terror and by mystical experience. The ancestors have destroyed and then remade them. Beside what they can do, the mere injection of two hundred millilitres of Penicillin seems a very ordinary business indeed.

End Note

The School of the Air began in Alice Springs and with the help of the Flying Doctor. The 'Air' of the title did not refer to education by flying teachers, but rather to the use of radio to teach children who live beyond the reach of conventional education. An Adelaide woman, Adelaide Miethke, conceived the idea – it grew out of a journey she made into the interior with a British Parliamentary Delegation in June 1944. Though she has since died, she left a record of the experience which gave rise to her notion. During its journey north, the Parliamentary Delegation touched down at a station called Mount Eber. 'I looked round at the hard brown gibbers . . . at the scanty trees and the distant bush country. What a lonely spot. Noticed a hen searching for food among the hard gibbers, and the thought came, "people *live* here." Then I caught sight of two sober little faces peaking round the corner of a building. . . . The picture of those two children, too shy to meet any stranger outside their own limited world, stayed with me.'

Experimental transmission of lessons from the Alice Springs Flying Doctor base to homesteads set up with the Traeger two-way radio began in September 1950. There were early problems – transmitting on a wavelength of thirty-four metres, the teachers found that radio reception within four hundred kilometres of Alice was not as good as it was in more distant places. The director of the base therefore transmitted on two wavelengths, fifty-five and thirty-four metres simultaneously, and the transmissions of the School of the Air in Alice still go out, over an area of 2.2 million square kilometres, on these two wavelengths.

The School has its own buildings and its own radio transmission studios today – they are on the north side of Alice. The teachers transmit in the morning to junior high school students, in the afternoon to primary school children. They speak simultaneously, over two channels, to children at Kirkimbi, over near the Western Australia border, at Wollogorang in the Carpentaria country a few kilometres from Queensland, to the kids of Noel Fullerton, a camel farmer and conductor of camel safaris west of Alice Springs, to the children of Allambi station on the edge of the Simpson Desert. Families with children and living in remote places are supplied with video and television equipment – educational video can be shown even where television transmissions are not received. And then there is the two-way radio, by which the child communicates with its teachers in Alice, by which it shares a simultaneous lesson with children who live as far from them as Lisbon is from Warsaw.

Given these preposterous distances, lessons take the form of classes anywhere. The teacher asks a question, the kids hit their button if they

OVERLEAF:
Beswick school, air-conditioned to combat tropic lethargy. Schooling may be intermittent for Aboriginal boys like the ones in this picture. Troublesome adolescents can be taken away by elders for four months of 'ceremonies' in the wilderness.

know it. A smart child from Deep Well, that is, competes with a girl from Auvergne in the Victoria River country, a remove of 1700 kilometres, to get his answer into the ether. Classes sound like an extended version of this:

Teacher: Now, what is the Ghan?

A number of lights come up on the teacher's console, a number of children are pressing their buttons. The teacher switches into one of these lights.

Teacher: Yes, Peter.
Peter: A train, over.
Teacher: That's right. Now true or false, Alice Springs was founded because the Ghan came off the tracks and people had nowhere else to live.

Again the glitter of lights.

Teacher: Yes, Warren.
Warren: True, miss, over.
Teacher: Do you agree with that? Susan?
Susan: I think it's false, over.
Teacher: That's right.

Peter uses the momentary absence of traffic to switch himself back in.

Peter: I think it's false now miss too, over.

A girl from Rabbit Flat in the Tanami Desert switches in to say that she cannot hear the teacher on Channel Two, but the teacher cannot hear her unless she transmits on Two. 'Listen on Channel One then,' the teacher suggests, 'and answer on Two.'
Maths goes the same way.

Teacher: What is three times zero? Elaine?
Elaine: Zero, miss, over.

A boy comes on and says that he couldn't transmit last week because the radio packed up. It's all right now though.

Once a year, largely at the expense of the School of the Air, the children meet with the teachers in some central place. If it is possible, the high school kids go to some southern city – in 1982 it was Canberra. The primary school children meet in Alice, see the sights, have barbecues at the teachers' places, see the faces they share the air waves with. Then, when they return to their mothers and governesses in the schoolroom at the cattle station, in the air-conditioned caravan at the mine site and sit down again to their Traeger two-way transmitters, they will have the benefit of having faces to match with the air traffic of the maths lesson, the mêlée of the true and false sessions.

The Pintubi Man
A Narrative

There was a Pintubi man who lived with his wife in a desert settlement in South Australia, just over the southern limits of the Northern Territory. His tribe was the one inveigled in out of the Gibson Desert over the past twenty years by Federal government officials who believed them to be perishing of malnutrition. As evidence of the wisdom of this paternal action, photographs of Pintubi children suffering from yaws were published. Just the same, it is still argued whether there was any necessity, other than the European psychological need to pity all desert-dwellers, to uproot the Pintubi from the desert and bring them to the settlements.

Now the Pintubi can be discovered living among alien tribes in places as widely scattered as Papunya and Docker River in the Northern Territory, Giles in Western Australia and Amata and Ernabella in South Australia. Pitjantjatjara people sometimes look on them as a threat – not for economic or social reasons, but for the reasons which have always prevailed between strangers in Aboriginal society, the risk of sorcery or incantatory malice. The Pintubi are less worldly in the European sense than the Pitjantjatjara, who may have had a fairly brief exposure to European values but a longer one than the Pintubi have experienced. The Pintubis are not as political. In the settlements they live in what amounts to a Pintubi quarter. Their housing is of traditional design – a low arched wurley, open at both ends, constructed largely of mulga wood branches. It is a design which the hero ancestors consecrated in the Dreaming and which is found, with variations, throughout Australia. If the Pitjantjatjara have made some concessions to ideas of European housing, the Pintubi have made fewer. Flooring is unthinkable for them. But they are happy to incorporate in their design elements of European material – roofing iron, doors taken from abandoned Fords and Holdens. In brisk dawns on the reservations you see the Pintubi, standing taller than their low, mounded houses, talking and laughing into a revivified camp-fire, and you can tell – in spite of their disinheritance – how sharply they savour the morning.

One night, the Pintubi man with whom we are concerned was accused by his wife of looking at another woman. The Pintubis, like other Aboriginals, have no inhibitions about arguing in public. The marital argument is at the same time entertainment and a form of social control, since the complaining party is in effect calling on the whole clan or family group to put pressure on the wrong-doer, it is even warning the husband of the other woman to keep his eyes open.

There is no evidence to tell whether the woman was justified in screaming at her husband that night. The question would soon be transcended by another. The husband picked up a hunting boomerang and tried to skim it off the ground against his wife's ankles – a customary means of expressing marital anger. He missed her ankles the first time, and the boomerang hit something off to one side and fell in the dust. The wife's accusations became more high-pitched still. The Pintubi man searched around with his hands in the dark and found the weapon again. There was not enough light for him to see that the shorter, broader-bladed end of the boomerang had shattered and was now sharp-pointed. He walked back into the zone of firelight, faced her, and hurled the thing again. The sharp point penetrated her knee, severing an artery. She fell sideways, wailing. Her blood fountained from her knee. Her husband tried to cover the puncture hole with his hands. Someone, perhaps an elder, ran to the Ernabella police station and found a constable. Elders will often call in the police in cases of serious blood crimes. It is not so much a gesture of respect for European authority, but rather that old men fear that such a crime might provoke an instant chain of reprisals, and so lead to an even greater and severe European involvement in the end.

The constable arrived at the Pintubi camp while the wife was still warm. There were no vital signs however. Women wailed in the dark, grieving for the wife's unhappy and frightened spirit. The man's three adolescent children, who had been sleeping some distance away at their maternal uncle's camp, arrived wailing and threw handfuls of dust into the air. Their father was forfeit, they would not even look at him. He was arrested at once by the police, charged with murder, and placed in the demountable cells of Ernabella to await the arrival of the South Australian magistrate.

For a European, a prison is – however unpleasantly – an extension of his home. It has a roof, floor, walls, a window and a door. It is at the window and door that the idea of imprisonment is vividly signified by bars, and the bars are the central symbol of imprisonment for any European. But at least the cell, even the demountable cells of Ernabella, are in a mode the European can identify.

For a Pintubi, who has never lived indoors and has always slept in immediate contact with the earth, there are no terms of reference by which prison can be understood. It is the cement floor, contained by the walls, which most baffled and appalled the Pintubi man, removing him from the earth's breast he had known since boyhood. Added to this was the knowledge that his wife's baffled spirit lingered in the camp, looking for familiar faces and objects, while her body, bagged in green plastic and loaded into the back of a police van, travelled open-eyed towards the futile European ritual of the autopsy slab.

The Pintubi had a tobacco tin with him. Either he had hidden it during the search, or else the constable had let him keep his tobacco and papers out of pity. The Pintubi flattened the lid of the tin and worked it to a fine edge on the cement floor. When it was sharp enough, the Pintubi cut his throat with it. The constable could hear him gurgling in his cell and unlocked the door to find him sitting against the wall gasping. The constable was able to stop the seepage from the jugular vein while his wife radioed the doctor.

A young Aboriginal Legal Aid lawyer from Alice Springs came down to defend the Pintubi at the inquest. He found that his client had little to say. To talk with the Pintubi about the hope that the magistrate might commit for manslaughter rather than murder was a meaningless exercise. Above the white swathes of bandages around his throat, the Pintubi's features were locked in a private uncommunicating grief. Manslaughter was not a Pintubi concept. Most deaths were intended, either through sorcery or malice. If the Pintubi wondered whether someone had 'sung' the boomerang to make it shatter, to turn it lethal, he did not discuss the matter with the Legal Aid lawyer. The young lawyer himself developed a powerful sense that the next day's inquest would be a futile business.

In court the next morning the shattered boomerang was produced, the pathologist's report read. Witnesses were questioned, and the lawyer from Legal Aid argued for a finding of accidental death. The magistrate would not have it though. He claimed the law required him to remand the Pintubi man on homicide charges. Not hoping for much, the lawyer asked the magistrate to release the Pintubi man on bail. The elders could be talked to, he said. They would prevent the man from disappearing. The magistrate's answer, however, astonished the lawyer. The Pintubi man could be released on his own recognizances. But the condition was that the lawyer was to accompany him back to the dead wife's relatives.

The lawyer was aware that some judges and magistrates took account of tribal law in their sentencing of Aboriginals. He knew that such a procedure was considered experimental and chancy, because it meant the condoning of acts of tribal vengeance, which were, in the strict European sense, felonies under Australian law. Just the same, at the conclusion of the inquest the Pintubi man was released into the care of the Legal Aid lawyer.

The young lawyer himself reflected on the ironies of the two laws as he drove over the red dirt track towards the Pintubi reservation. His client-passenger seemed to have revived, sat forward in the seat of the four-wheel-drive but still had little to say. The lawyer braked the vehicle by the settlement store and went in to ask where the elders were. The composed Pintubi walked among the low bushes across the road, looking sometimes at the ground, like a man choosing a place to start a garden. He seemed to find the place he wanted and stood still there like a well-mannered guest.

Having got directions at the store, the lawyer went looking for the community leaders. It took an hour to track anyone down, convince them of the amazing news that the killer was back. It took another two hours to track down the woman's relatives among the widespread wurleys of the Pintubi camp. Several men of the dead woman's clan, who had been out hunting, turned up towards dusk. They took the news tranquilly. There seemed to be no rush to punish the murderer. They talked among themselves a great deal. Their voices rose only sometimes.

The lawyer grew a little hopeful that perhaps they would do nothing about the man who had killed their blood relative. Then, perhaps at a signal the lawyer couldn't read, all their apparent composure took on a hard edge. There were suddenly a dozen male relatives of the dead woman armed with two or three spears each. There were women too of all ages, crying aloud and keening. They walked off eagerly towards the place the Legal Aid lawyer had last left the Pintubi man. From a distance the lawyer could not see him. But he'd been lying on the ground, and now he rose. The relatives circled him, wailing and chanting. An old man stepped up to him, shouting in accusation. The old man raised a spear, stuck it deftly deep into the meat of the Pintubi's upper leg, then withdrew the point. The Pintubi had not flinched. He stood impassive. Above the noise the relatives were raising the Legal Aid man could not even hear any grunt of shock from the prisoner. He remained upright as another relative stepped up and speared the other leg.

These wounds bled sluggishly, as if among all the yelling a practical knowledge of where the arteries were, and what areas were to be avoided, was being applied. In fact it was. The Pintubi man, by standing silently through most of this, was earning great merit, was earning re-acceptance by his own clan, ultimate re-acceptance by the clan of his dead wife. Even when his savaged legs went and he had to sit in the dust, he remained detached. Fifteen wounds were inflicted in the upper and lower legs before the Pintubi's blood debt was considered paid. As the dead woman's family left, you could almost say that they reverted from their ritual identity to their private selves. Their conversation sounded like normal, daily sort of talk.

The Legal Aid man helped the bleeding Pintubi to the truck. The man tottered but was conscious. At the clinic a little while later he recoiled from the anti-tetanus injection the doctor wanted to give him. But the doctor insisted, and gave him a syringeful of antibiotic as well. As the surgical needles went in, the Pintubi's face became wizened and ancient.

The South Australian magistrate must have known that the Pintubi man would not stay in the Ernabella area. He had to go away, into another country, so that his wife's ghost would not be encouraged by his familiar presence to stay in the Ernabella settlement. The Pintubi travelled north into the Territory, into a troubled and multi-tribal settlement called Papunya. There, months later, the Legal Aid man found him. The South Australian Supreme Court, the lawyer wanted to tell the Pintubi, had issued a *Nulli Prosequi* writ on the charge of murder; that is, the Pintubi would not have to stand trial, the punishments inflicted on him by the relatives would be considered adequate. There would be no trial in the full and baffling legal grandeur of the Adelaide Supreme Court.

The Legal Aid man had been excited by the news, but the Pintubi of course did not understand it, had not understood the inquest, the idea of bail, the idea that there could be further punishment apart from all the expiatory courage of facing the relatives, apart from the year of exile. A few months later he returned to Ernabella, a man fit now to be greeted by his children.

Chapter 8

Alice

The Alice of Alice Springs was named after the wife of the South Australian Postmaster General who had supervised the building of the Overland Telegraph. The *Springs* derives from the spring which rises north of the present town near the Telegraph station itself.

The stone buildings of the Telegraph station with which Alice began are still there, in part a compound, in part a fortress. In the summer of 1872, telegraph station managers travelling north to take over the three plum stations – Barrow Creek, Tennant Creek, Alice Springs – found that the environment would not be easy. One of them died of thirst and two of them survived only by turning back and drinking the blood of their horses.

The town which was founded to the south of the Telegraph station grew very slowly and was for a time called Stuart, in honour of the doughty little Scot who first crossed Australia south to north without any of the grievous drama and death associated with the ill-fated expedition undertaken by Robert O'Hara Burke and William John Wills in 1860. But again it was like Palmerston and Darwin. The title Stuart vanished. The more prosaic name of Alice Springs prevailed. But over what sort of town?

Doris Bradshaw, who first came to Alice in 1899 when her father was appointed manager of the Overland Telegraph station, wrote: 'The villagers at that time were few indeed – perhaps not more than twelve or thirteen. As we passed through the village on our arrival we first saw Mounted Constable Charles Brookes, his wife, and four children at the Police Camp on the southern side of Heavitree Gap. He must have been one of the loneliest policemen in the world, especially as his duties required him to be long distances away from home on horse and camel patrols. Some of my most vivid recollections are of Constable Brookes returning to Alice Springs with lines of Aboriginal prisoners chained by the neck. They never failed to stir in my youthfully democratic breast a deep sense of outrage and revulsion. . . . Only one white woman lived in the township itself. She was Mrs Charles Meyers, whose husband had established a saddlery business.'

It is hard to jump from such beginnings to the fatal manoeuvrings of the Cold War. But in fact the Alice of frontier madmen, rare white women, of bush panache and eccentricity seems to be involved for good or ill more intimately in modern geopolitics than perhaps any other Australian town or city.

PAGE 137 ABOVE:
A former Telegraph station building, Northern Territory. The building of the Overland Telegraph was expensive in lives, and so was the maintenance of the stations. At the Barrow Creek Telegraph station in 1874, for example, the personnel were attacked by natives, and the Stationmaster, Mr Stapleton, his assistant and an Aboriginal servant were all killed. The line, linking with an undersea cable routed through Bali, was joined in August 1972.

PAGE 137 BELOW:
Sunset and moonset simultaneously in the MacDonnell Ranges west of Alice Springs. Within two minutes, the sky will be full of stars of a primeval clarity in which tribal man will read the adventures of his ancestors and which most stockmen can use for navigation.

'An Atom Bomb for Alice' says the cover of a mass market thriller in the bookshop in the Alice Springs Casino. And one of the ironies of Australia's most famous frontier town is that many Australians consider it the most prominent nuclear target in the South West Pacific. The reason is a Joint Defence facility twenty-seven kilometres southwest of the Alice at Pine Gap. Its existence is frankly proclaimed. Anyone can see it from a commercial plane on approach or take-off from Alice Springs. Its white domes sit oddly among the eroded and palpably ancient spines of the MacDonnell Range. But those who attempt to photograph its six domes are turned away by Australian Commonwealth policemen who patrol its security fences.

When Gough Whitlam was engaged in the 1972 campaign which led to his election as Prime Minister of Australia, he promised the electorate that he would make known to them the secret functions of Pine Gap. Having visited the site, however, and been briefed by its directors, he announced that the purpose of Pine Gap was too significant to be disclosed to the Australian people. 'I emphasize they [the facilities at Pine Gap] are not part of weapon systems. They cannot be used to make war on any country . . . we never had a mandate to break the Joint Defence Agreement.' Elsewhere he said: 'We never told the people at the election that we would disclose other people's secrets.'

On a recent visit to Washington, Australian Prime Minister Robert J. Hawke, after meeting the Director of the C.I.A. and the U.S. Defence Secretary, said that he accepted the risk of U.S. defence facilities such as Pine Gap in view of 'global strategic considerations'. (He simultaneously received from the C.I.A. an assurance that, contrary to Australian legend, the Agency had not been involved in the fall of Gough Whitlam in 1975.)

PAGES 138–9 ABOVE:
The Stuart Highway, named after the transcontinental explorer, running north of Alice Springs towards Tennant Creek.

PAGES 138–9 BELOW:
D. D. Smith, who built the road from Alice to Katherine in time for the Allies to face the Japanese threat in 1942. To Smith road-building is a compulsion and in the roads that criss-cross his mind he sees a solution to many of the economic problems of the Territory.

PAGE 140:
Today's generation of sun-bronzed Centralians are likely to come from Calabria or Sicily. This corner coffee bar in Alice combines an Italian family name with that of Undoolya, one of the oldest cattle stations in the Territory.

In the absence of firm news, of any definite statement by the authorities about the function of Pine Gap, rumours abound both among the Australian Press and in Alice itself. One of the more exotic ones, common in Alice Springs pubs and sometimes revamped by the Australian Press, asserts that apart from being a prime nuclear target Pine Gap is a centre for bird smuggling.

Many such fantastic rumours are encouraged in part by the regular arrival at and departure from Alice Springs airport of Globemasters and Galaxies servicing the facility. The Press and the locals have always claimed that the inwards and outwards cargoes of these transports go largely unsupervized by Australian customs officials.

A scenario much favoured by the Australian Press runs like this. We know from the U.S. Senate's enquiry into C.I.A. operations that at the end of the Vietnam war the Southeast Asian division of the Agency was in disarray. In those circumstances, given the genial remoteness of Pine Gap and the complacency of Australian officials, Pine Gap could have provided the Agency with an excellent fall-back position from which some of its unfinished business in Southeast Asia could be finalized.

The Anti-Gap group in Alice, who call themselves 'Concerned Citizens of Alice Springs' are worried both that the base involves a risk

STUART HIGH 280 KULGERA,

UNDOOLYA GAP 29

504 TENNAN 480 AYERS ROCK

1171 MOUNT I. 1712 ADELAIDE

1174 KATHERINE

1451 RUM JUNGLE

1526 DARWIN

This sign post on the Stuart Highway in Alice Springs, almost at the geographical centre of the continent, states clearly the apparent isolation of the Alice. Strangely, the digits on the sign post do not seem to intimidate anyone.

of nuclear attack and that it is a stronghold for an Agency which, as the U.S. Senate enquiry into the C.I.A. shows, has not always been under the firm control of the U.S. government or let its masters know the details of its activities.

Defenders of the Pine Gap installation say that it is a Joint Defence facility, that the Australian Armed Forces benefit in terms of intelligence because of its existence. For the Alice itself, it brings a large infusion of wealthy, intelligent Americans. They participate in local affairs. They are visible at the Henley-on-Todd Regatta and on civic and artistic committees throughout town. Alice has the nation's fifth largest art prize – such style would be impossible without the Pine Gap people. The Art Centre being built at Araluen is so large and well equipped that one would associate it with a place many times the size of the Alice. Under the Joint Defence Agreement, cooks, gardeners, mechanics, maids are all recruited from among the local population. They are briefed at a

Sand has drifted over the graves of these men who died while building the Overland Telegraph near the South Australia–Northern Territory border.

fundamental level on the purpose of the installation and none of them objects, say the defenders, or feels that his national pride has been demeaned. Opponents, of course, say that Australians are involved only on a menial level and that, though Australians make up exactly half of the base's two hundred and fifty employees, in 1981 only sixteen of the Australians were technicians (only eight were scientists). The Gap's defenders further point out that no one knows whether the Russians have a correct or incorrect assessment of what the place is, but that whatever it is, any sensible enemy could knock Pine Gap out with 'a small team of trusted saboteurs with two-inch mortars. That would put it out of action for five years.'

In April 1977, Christopher John Boyce, an employee of an electronics company, TRW Systems Inc., who had C.I.A. clearance, was arrested in Los Angeles and put on trial for selling technical secrets to the Russians. He described some of the information he passed to the Russians in the following terms: 'I agreed to write a statement concerning what I believe to be violations of law against the Australians. I informed them that I worked in a communications room and part of my daily duties was to continue a deception against the Australians. I learned about the way in which we could practise day-to-day deceptions in our transmission to the Australians.'

Boyce never specified during his trial what the day-to-day deceptions against the Australians were, but more recently, on a network current affairs programme in the United States, Boyce mentioned Pine Gap as the key to the deception, and said that the activities of the installation subverted the sovereignty of Australia. The American Senator Daniel Moynihan, however, denied that the Australians were in any way disadvantaged by the existence of Pine Gap. In any case, the Boyce trial, the book he later wrote, and the interviews he gives have all enriched Australian suspicions of the domes at Pine Gap.

According to the Australian press, Pine Gap watches and helps guide satellites which float above the earth at between 30,000 and 40,000 kilometres. This type of high satellite is called the 647. It can pick up by its infra-red telescope the energy emissions of missile exhausts during the early powered stages of flight. It is therefore crucial to America's early warning system, since it can provide pictures of intercontinental ballistic missiles in flight. Pine Gap also helps control the Big Bird and Keyhole spy satellites, which are capable of taking photographs with a resolution of fifteen centimetres from a height of one hundred and fifty kilometres. The Australian press has also claimed that Pine Gap is one of the three keys to the Pyramider communication system of the C.I.A. One satellite is permanently positioned over Pine Gap, another over Redondo Beach in California, a third over C.I.A. headquarters at Langley, Virginia, on the outskirts of Washington. These three satellites enable C.I.A. operatives to plant sensors which monitor nuclear tests throughout the world. In 1978, for example, the C.I.A. placed such a sensor, aimed at China's nuclear installation at Lop Nor in Sinkiang Province, on top of a mountain in the Himalayas. There have been claims that levels of hydrogen fluoride over the MacDonnell Ranges are abnormally high and that this shows that the C.I.A. is illicitly working on chemical laser projects there.

Pravda, in an editorial in 1980, ambiguously warned that the presence of Pine Gap and other American installations endangered the Australian population. Among Australian politicians, the new Australian Prime Minister, Bob Hawke, has taken a different direction in the Pine Gap argument. Yes, he says, it may be a risk, but it is important enough to maintain the base in terms of the U.S. alliance.

Meanwhile, at an Alice level, the American presence seems largely a welcome thing. The American Ambassador graces the shenanigans of Henley-on-Todd with his presence, stands on the fake steamboat called *Pistil Dawn* and goes to the trouble of making a speech to the only partially attentive crowd. The American alliance, which began with MacArthur dropping from the skies onto Batchelor Field and watching a grainy Western in Kilgariff's Cinema in Alice, is consecrated further in

The American Ambassador kisses
the winner of the beauty contest
at the Henley-on-Todd regatta at
Alice Springs. The relationship
between the Alice and the
controversial U.S. installation at
Pine Gap explains his presence at
an event which combines in
equal measure Aussie whimsy and
surrealism.

the dry bed of the Todd on Regatta day. And, as in 1942, no one really knows, except the discreet men of Pine Gap, whether there will be bombs for Alice.

Whatever the purpose of the Pine Gap installation, not all its personnel lightly escape at the end of their tours of duty. Some resign and become devout Centralians. You could think of them as hostages to the sun – there is some appositeness in that image.

The one who is a sun-hostage in the most literal sense is a personable physicist called Bob Collins, a quiet but not shy Southerner. Commentators have remarked on the similarities between Australians and Southerners. *Frontier* still bulks large in the mythology of both races, and certainly a town like Alice would not be as remote from the experience of a man like Collins as it would be from that of a New Yorker. Collins lives with his Australian wife and two young daughters on a low ridge southeast of Alice. It is an area appropriate to experimentation – his next-door neighbour is N. K. Hordern, who, in the face of a lot of rustic scoffing, pioneered vine growing on the slopes here. Between his house and Hordern's place, Bob Collins has dug the largest solar pond to be found outside the Dead Sea area of Israel. It is his prototype, he believes that others exactly like it will be found soon in remote settlements, wherever the cost of trucking diesel fuel is excessive – that is, throughout the Centre, the north and northwest of Australia. In a literal sense, Collins is a servitor of this pool he has dug atop the ridge. When you telephone him from town, his wife will tell you that 'he's down at the pond'. But he receives rewards – the thing delights him. 'It's very satisfying to think of that big elephant sitting there, cruising.'

Filled with salt from the explorer Giles's Lake Amadeus, the pond's water is eight times denser than sea water, and the fence that surrounds Collins's elephant warns the passing traveller of 'Scalding Brine'. The density prevents the sunlight that enters the pond from escaping again. Therefore, though the top layers of water may be less than 20°C, the bottom layer approaches boiling point. The upper stratum is denser than the Dead Sea, says Collins, and so viscid that if, despite the warning signs, a drunken stockman or Aboriginal child fell in, they would penetrate only the more moderate upper layers.

In May 1982 heavy rain fell on the Alice area. Around the pond it penetrated the earth to a depth of only one metre. There it sat, stealing the built-up heat from Collins's great beast. The steady build-up of temperature which had gone on in the bottom layers was reversed. The pond had to be insulated all over again with further layers of plastic sheeting, and throughout mid-1982 the sun struck the bottom of Collins's refilled pond and sat there, beginning to increase the temperature. When it reached 70°C, the water from the bottom of the pond could be pumped into a transformer and used to generate electricity. Governments – the Federal government in Canberra, and the government of Paul Everingham in Darwin, which between them bear the cost of providing generator fuel for every distant clutch of human beings – supported Collins's experiment with capital, and visited his elephant regularly. He had help too from a local aviator, David Frederickson, and from an Adelaide engineering company which adjusted their freon-based transformer for his purposes. It's fascinating, Collins says, how much expertise there is in the Alice.

Collins has had to face a problem to do with solar ponds which the Israelis have not had to confront. The Israeli supply of salt, by courtesy of the Dead Sea, is illimitable. Although salt lakes abound in parts of the Territory, the problems of harvesting are so great that Collins decided to produce a closed-circuit pond, one which once stocked with salt would never have to be stocked again. With Frederickson and others he developed a method of harvesting Lake Amadeus. High-speed, light-weight vehicles were used, a blade attached to their front end. A wafer-thin sheet of salt was cut and deposited in a hopper behind. 'We got into salt in desperation,' says Collins. 'There was no other way to get the quantities we needed.' In the end it took thirty truck-loads of twenty-two tonnes each to saturate the pond.

To match the new harvesting methods, Collins designed a salt recycling process. Water from the salt-heavy upper layers was pumped to a nearby pool, the water being allowed to evaporate and the resultant salt pitched back into the main pond.

To talk to Collins is to talk to a devotee, and his wife and two daughters have that unquestioning acceptance of people who live close to a grand and fruitful obsession. For as much as the sun has captured Collins, Collins has captured the sun, and his life is endowed with a dignity that belongs to those who deal with the major elements of the universe. On the hangover-ridden Sabbaths of Alice there are clear-headed people standing round a great pond outside the town. Wind baffles suspended from wires keep the surface of the water level, and the engineer from Adelaide, Freddo and the physicist from Florida talk engineering, densities, evaporations. One of the Alice's finest inventors is there also. His name is Kurt Johannsen.

Johannsen's father was a Norwegian stonemason who came to the Territory early in the century to build Lutheran mission houses, police stations and cells, and who settled in a log hut at Deep Well, a well provided by the South Australian government for overland travellers, with a tip tray waggon, two horses, twelve cows and a bull. A large part of Johannsen senior's income came from pumping water for travelling stock. He charged one penny a head for cattle, two pence for camels. Camels were rarer visitors. Driven by Afghan handlers, they came through every six months, bringing supplies to the settlements of the Centre and North. Camel mail from Oodnadatta in South Australia to Tennant Creek in the Territory came on the camels of one Hussein Khan. It is in honour of such Afghans that the train from Adelaide to Alice Springs, the one honoured in momentous 1942 by General MacArthur, was named the Ghan.

The Johannsens were a literate and serious-minded family, adaptive, and – by necessity – self-educated. Young Kurt was characterized by a nineteenth-century frontier rectitude and a twentieth-century passion for technology. He remembers his first meeting with an aviator, Francis Birtles, who sent camel teams ahead of his flight path to depot petrol for a south-north flight across the continent in 1921. When Birtles flew over Deep Well and did a victory roll, the Johannsen boy was not cowed by this first sight of the new age, but accepted it as easily as he had accepted the Afghans' camels – as another item of available equipment.

When he was an adolescent in the early 1930s, he began to lead private expeditions as an anthropologist westward to the Petermanns, into the country of the Pitjantjatjara, into the pre-Cambrian hills whose main renown to Europeans was that the legendary gold seeker, Lasseter, had disappeared there. At the age of seventeen, managing a party of ten in trackless country, confident that water could always be found, he met Bob Buck, a bushman and friend of Lasseter's, and the man who would ultimately find Lasseter's bones and bring them to Ly Underdown's pub

Bob Collins (bearded, right), his partners and, behind them, the great Centralian sky trapped at the bottom of their solar pond.

Collins believes the outback will be lit by such ponds, stocked with salt from salt lakes like Amadeus.

Arltunga, in the MacDonnell Ranges west of Alice Springs, was a goldfield discovered in the 1880s and the scene of a 'rush' soon after. But the miners here – digging, cradling and sluicing gravel – did not leave Arltunga rich. Goods cost £60 a tonne to reach the goldfields, and so the goldseeker was priced out of his great quest.

in Alice. According to Lasseter's diary, his tragedy began when near Winter's Glen in the Petermanns his camels fled one evening, taking his water and supplies with them. Johannsen says that the year after Lasseter's disappearance, Buck took him to the undisturbed site where the camels had stampeded. The signs of their panic were legible, only partially blurred by wind, totally untouched by rain. Buck then took Johannsen over a nearby hill and showed him pad marks still visible in a small clearing among mulga trees. The camels, it seems, had pulled up within one and a half kilometres of Lasseter, and the following morning he could have found them by their tracks. Lasseter, said Buck, had died for lack of camels, which had pulled up less than a kilometre from him. According to Johannsen, however, the tracks proved that Lasseter was still alive. No one could die as ineptly as Lasseter had. Johannsen believes, as so many older Territorians do, that Lasseter staged his tragedy in the Petermanns, that he escaped to a new life in America. The bones which Bob Buck would later transport to the Alice failed to convince everyone of Lasseter's passion and death. Survival theories attach themselves to many fabulous figures – to Ned Kelly, Joan of Arc, Jesus Christ,

President Kennedy. In a landscape as enormous and fabled as the Petermanns, it was inevitable that a survival theory for Lasseter should be found.

But as much as Johannsen's mind was exercised by frontier mythology, it was even more exercised by mechanics, by the maintenance of vehicles in remote areas, and then by the twentieth-century question of how to fuel them. During World War II, he designed a wood-burning gas producer for cars. The mechanism was a cylinder, thirty-eight by ninety-one centimetres. On five hundred to seven hundred and fifty grammes of wood per one and a half kilometres, he could cruise at ninety-six and a half to one hundred and four kilometres an hour. There was a slow delivery of power however; the engine took five minutes to start up on Johannsen's burner. Nonetheless, travelling by burner, he covered 64,300 kilometres on the worst tracks in Australia. One of his journeys took him from Brisbane to Alice, and whenever the car stopped he got out and fed it with mulga wood. 'You chopped your wood as you went. A feasible idea in Australia, I thought.'

The fable of Lasseter and of Lasseter's gold reef reclaimed Johannsen in 1950, when a mineral prospector called Jimmie Prince came back from the Petermanns with a bag of rock specimens rich in gold. Prince had nearly perished in the unforgiving country near the Western Australia border. He had developed a well-justified terror of death by thirst. Therefore he did not want to go back to the ore source overland. He approached Johannsen as Johannsen had a Tiger Moth and a truck.

Johannsen and Prince operated from a landing strip at Ilbilba, the same place from which Lasseter's planes had flown to very little good effect twenty years before. One day in 1951, depoting petrol west of Ilbilba in the Tiger Moth, Johannsen and Prince landed on the side of a salt marsh. As they took off again they bogged, nosed over, and broke the propeller. In ten seconds, Prince's fear of thirst took substance. There were only four and a half litres of drinkable water aboard the Tiger Moth. It was September, a month when the temperatures in salt lake areas are building up from the merely harsh to the intolerable.

Johannsen wanted to try to repair the plane and fly out for help, leaving Prince on the salt lake. There was no way the Tiger Moth could carry two men – the propeller was too splintered for that. But Prince feared dying alone on the lake. The four and a half litres of water would last him only three days. Johannsen therefore constructed a condenser by mounting two canisters together, their mouths directly open to each other, and filling the bottom of one with salt brine from a hole he had dug in the salt. Condensation from the brine reached the top of the second can and dripped into a container. The condenser worked well the first night. Prince and Johannsen were both reassured by it.

In the morning, they dragged the Tiger Moth out of its bog, and Johannsen trimmed the propeller with an axe. Then he climbed in and attempted to take off with his motor shrieking at double revolutions. He managed to clear a low dune beyond the lake, but couldn't achieve an altitude of more than fifty feet. Away to his port he noticed some eagles wheeling and steered towards them, knowing that eagles like

The Viking inventor Kurt Johannsen stands by one of his early designs for the self-tracking apparatus which revolutionized the shipment of cattle in the north of Australia.

Stranded on a salt lake far to the west of Alice Springs in 1951, he trimmed the propeller of his Tiger Moth with an axe and managed to bump from thermal to thermal all the way back to town.

His life demonstrates, on a very sophisticated technological level, a bushman's desire to make use of what the Centre offers – sun and rock and mulga wood.

thermals. The updraft he stole from those desert birds lifted the plane, lightened the burden on its motor. Rising and plunging on the uneven air, he reached Hermannsburg Lutheran mission three hundred kilometres away.

It took him three days to fly out from the lake, to get to Alice, to find a new plane. Prince's anguish in those three days need not be described. The plane which had edged over the dune to the east of the lake had not looked like a plane with a future. Johannsen's condenser, however, kept on making sweet water.

The crash, the flight out on the radically doctored propeller, the rescue of Prince by Johannsen in a new plane made national headlines. Here was that elusive Petermann gold reef again, here were crashed planes and the unutterable Centralian thirst. The newspapers did not mention that as well as pursuing Lasseter's reef, Johannsen was also working on an eccentric form of power called solar energy.

He had been designing parabolic panels as collectors, and stored the solar energy in small storage tanks using insulated rock-fill. He approached the board of a power-plant manufacturing company in

Adelaide, but they were not really interested. In those days, says Johannsen, only ten per cent of the cost of electricity was fuel. But now fuel is the major concern, the major expense. Johannsen's panels and rock-filled storage are as feasible, and could be as attractive, as Collins's solar pond. Without using the term loosely, Johannsen is a solar pioneer, and he is often found at Collins's place, consulting with the young physicist around the edges of the brine pond.

Johannsen's solar experiments were treated whimsically by Territorians in the 1950s, as were his experiments with self-tracking trailers capable of transporting herds and transforming the way the cattle industry was run. Just the same, that was what Johannsen did. He changed the beef business overnight, and by invention.

In the late 1940s, Johannsen decided to build a truck that could carry fifty to a hundred head of cattle. A station owner put up £2000

Aboriginal child on bike beside the cross at Hermannsburg mission, a historic Lutheran enterprise now passed into the hands of the Aboriginals themselves.

A road train, descendant of Kurt Johannsen's self-tracking trailer dogs, thunders towards Mataranka from the direction of Queensland.

development money, and Johannsen produced a self-tracking trailer based on a surplus army personnel carrier.

Until then, cattle could only be handled in the winter months – or so went a Northern Territory adage. Further limiting factors on the droving of cattle in the Centre were that stock could not be walked over long distances until they were four or five years old, and that they lost condition on the trail. Yet such was the traditional appeal of overlanding that the cattlemen sat on the fences and watched satirically as Johannsen put together his first big truck shipment, three hundred fat cattle from a number of stations around the Alice, fifty from one, fifty from another, and so on. The prime mover of that first road train was a tank transporter, also bought from the army.

The self-tracking trailers have been refined since then. They can thunder down dirt roads where Johannsen's transports moved at forty-

eight kilometres per hour. But perhaps they are harder on the cattle –
outside every big settlement is a Dead On Arrival pit. The driver of the
cattle train has to go through his cargo, take out the dead stock, pitch it
into the pits. Even so, the wastage is infinitesimal compared to the losses
that occurred on overland cattle drives in the past.

On the day I visited Johannsen, he was in his garage out by the old
Alice Springs Telegraph station working on an attachment which
would utilize the waste heat of automobiles. Automobiles, he explained,
are only eighteen per cent efficient. The box he was designing, fitted
under the bonnet of a vehicle, would harness at least ten per cent of the
wasted heat. To get a ten per cent improvement in heat use would

A Dead On Arrival pit outside
Katherine. Road train drivers
have to go through their cargo of
cattle and drag out the beasts
which have died on the journey
before they can proceed on to the
meat works in town.

produce a fuel saving of thirty per cent. He remembers that the aviator Birtles in 1921 was able to sacrifice two-thirds of his fuel – cans were punctured during the rough camel ride, others leaked and evaporated. Petrol was no problem then. Johannsen, however, has now grown into an age where fuel efficiency is a technological obsession. He is as delighted to see Collins tap the free and copious sun as he is to devise boxes which, by shrinking fuel consumption, shrink the Territory.

The life of Mona Minahan, like the life of Lasseter, shows that the flavour of the nineteenth-century frontier lasted well into the twentieth century in a town like Alice. Mona is now a tough-minded and lively eighty-year-old, married late in life and settled in a bungalow in Alice Springs. In the Old Timers' home through Heavitree Gap, there are old men who will tell you what a spectacular woman she was when she first stepped off the Ghan after a three-and-a-half-day journey from Adelaide in 1932 and began work as a barmaid at Kilgariff's pub. The fable of Mona's beauty spread throughout central Australia in those roaring days. 'A miner bloke came in from prospecting one day, saw Mona, was smitten, and offered her fifty quid to sleep with him. A bugger of a lot of money in those days! So Mona takes him upstairs, and when the poor bugger begins to fondle her, she says, "You gave me fifty quid to sleep with me. Now sleep!" '

In such ways, the rugged, impish virtue of Mona Minahan, Mass-goer and Irish-Australian beauty, has always manifested itself. 'A handful for any bloke,' the old-timers tell you.

When Mona arrived in the Alice there were less than a dozen houses. The population was '250 people, including Abos'. Mona worked for her sister and brother-in-law as a barmaid in what was, then, the town's only pub. The few stores of Alice, however, also kept bars. In those days it was an offence to sell liquor to Aboriginals and so the plentiful liquor of the Alice was consumed by the townspeople, by visiting hunters, prospectors, drovers, explorers, and the occasional thirsty dreamer with some grand scheme to make the desert blossom and grow amenable. Every fortnight, drovers and station people rode in to see the Ghan arrive from Adelaide. The pub would take two hundred pounds on a Ghan day. A rather genteel drink, gin squash, was the favourite, something thirst-quenching but with a kick. In case of unruliness, Mona kept a truncheon under the counter. She did not use it much. She depended on verbal pyrotechnics to arrest the attention of lonely men on sprees.

In those days great dust storms came in out of the desert, red grit pounded against windows and you could be lost in the main street. Sometimes the dust storms were followed by rain. 'It would rain mud,' says Mona Minahan. There was no electricity then – food was kept in a Coolgardie safe, a food cage suspended from the roof and draped in wet hessian. A Spanish windlass was used to pull water to the surface. But even when it rained mud and the meat turned, it was a sweet age. 'Alice has just about reached its limits now,' says Mona. But in those days it was a town of potential. Mona loved the race meetings, when perhaps twenty-five people would band together and race their horses against each other, using Aboriginal part-time jockeys, stockmen who suddenly found themselves wearing gaudy silks and, on the promise of a bonus from the owner, urging their mounts forward among the spinifex, along an eight-furlong course created the day before by dragging a log behind a truck.

Mona was a passionate gambler – she broke into the sessions of *swy* or two-up, a game compounded in equal quantities of Australian informality, love of wagers, and rustic boredom, involving betting on the toss of two coins. It was a male game, a game played in the backyards of pubs after drovers had got their cheques, a game associated with stockmen, prospectors, soldiers. Mona played it furiously and on equal terms. Whenever another player complicated the straightforward passion of the game by falling for Mona, she would carelessly tell him, 'I'm a career girl. What in the hell do I want to get married for?'

The war changed Alice, even before the Japanese became involved. North and south, the road which had till then been nothing but a scrape in the dust was improved to modern standards. Convoys arrived from Adelaide and went on from Alice 1600 kilometres to Darwin. Alice was garrisoned and became a transit camp. The military commander of central Australia was a despotic, but vigorous Australian brigadier, Noel Loutit, a veteran of World War I with the wounds to prove it, a man who, according to the Australian Army history, had reached a further point inland than any other Australian soldier in the bloody and futile landing of Gallipoli. Arriving in Alice now, he fell in love with Mona Minahan. 'All the blokes were keen on me,' says Mona, 'but he really cramped my style. No one else was game to look at me. He was only knee-high to a grasshopper, but because he was strong, he attracted yes men on his staff. *Bullshit Castle* was what the average digger called Loutit's headquarters.'

It was now a town run on curfews. The soldiers could drink in Alice Springs pubs for only one hour a day. Aboriginals had to be out of town every night at 6 p.m. By this stage, Mona owned a small shop in Todd Street. The Aboriginals who came in there were, Mona says, a likeable crowd. They bought 'scenty soap', hair oil and 'rubbin' medicine' (methylated spirits). 'In spite of the "rubbin' medicine" the Alice blacks were better off then,' says Mona. 'Interfering whites have buggered them up. Taken their dignity. That's why you see them hanging round the bed of the Todd.' Into Mona's shop also came young Australian soldiers, on the pretext of getting her to open their two-bottle weekly ration of beer. They would lean on the counter and joke with the general's girl.

In February 1942 the Japanese bombed Darwin, killing hundreds of people. The civil administration moved south to Alice, there to run headlong into the strenuous military authority of Noel Loutit. The brigadier – at once and on his own authority – began expelling people from the Centre. He refused to let civil officials keep their wives with them in Alice. Old Sarah Feeney, who as a child had come to the Territory by waggon train from Port Augusta, gave Loutit trouble. She refused to leave the village of Pine Creek. If you keep pushing me, she told Loutit, I'll go bush, and then you'll never find me. Another woman permitted to stay was, of course, the dazzling Mona Minahan. Apart from Mona and Sarah and a few women of similar calibre, apart from Aboriginal lubras, only a handful of army nurses remained in the Top End and the Centre.

The garrisoning of the Centre was a tedious and dispiriting business for young diggers. In 1942, provoked by the presence of American troops who could drink in the pubs at any time of day, provoked by ennui, poor pay, lack of leave, the soldiers came to town and rioted in Todd Street. One of the windows smashed was Mona's. Mona would thereafter suspend the troops' access to her bottle-opening facilities and to the even more precious device which sealed tops back on half-drunk bottles.

As the rioting soldiers marched through the town, one of them beating a drum, they encountered Brigadier General Loutit, who had rushed to the site of the mutiny. He showed no timidity. He lectured them about what it was like in the trenches in France when he was young, about the lack of leave, the daily misery, the extent of the danger. 'Besides, I haven't had any leave up here,' he said. 'No,' yelled a soldier, 'but you've got Mona.' To his credit, Loutit wasn't offended by such open dialogue. There was a remarkable tradition of that sort of thing in the Australian Army in World War II. The debate proceeded, but at last Loutit was able to persuade them to go back to camp. One of the reasons was that he was a 'game little bugger', and they admired gameness. Nor, after the riots, did he live more circumspectly. He went with Mona for picnics at Glen Helen, a beauty spot forty-eight kilometres from town and out of bounds to all other personnel. Once he took Mona to the Wauchope pub and they played poker all Saturday, Sunday and Monday with the publicans and sundry locals. Perhaps it helped him a little with the troops that he spoke their language, that his vices were the same as theirs. It did not prevent them declaring Mona Queen of the Army and staging a coronation. Mona sat enthroned on a table, and as the brigadier approached her to put the crown on her head, the table collapsed beneath both of them. It was the sort of accident that united Mona, the general, the soldiers, in a common susceptibility to farce.

During the wartime reign of Loutit and Mona Minahan, the most remarkable visitor came to Alice Springs, a defeated and yet already canonized general and presidential hopeful called Douglas MacArthur. MacArthur, his wife Jean and four-year-old son Arthur, had landed in a B-17 at Batchelor Field, southwest of Darwin, in mid-March. The journey had been so frightening and turbulent that Mrs MacArthur swore she would not travel by plane any further. She and MacArthur wanted to journey the 1600 kilometres to Alice Springs by car, but when a doctor indicated that this would not suit the health of their son, they fell back on two commercial DC3s. It was in this way that MacArthur, his family and his staff came to Alice and put up in the hotel. The straggling town, the small garrison, the sparcity of humans in that landscape, must have done little for the morale of the Americans, except of course for the Great Man, whose morale was indomitable. He had come to catch the Ghan to Adelaide, and even though it had gone the day before he was willing to wait for it rather than put his wife and son to the further discomfort of flying. His staff were not as happy as he was with Alice. The way flies covered the back of everyone's shirts avid to drink sweat, appalled them. But MacArthur was sanguine in the Alice. Kilgariff's picture show, open to the sky, attracted him. He watched at least the first feature, a Western from the early thirties, before going back to the hotel to sleep on a camp cot. A plane arrived for MacArthur, and most of his staff caught it. But MacArthur himself stuck to a specially strung-together version of the Ghan, which arrived from South Australia the next day. The locomotive and the two carriages were ancient, straight out of the movie of the night before. But the dining car was set up especially for the comfort of the MacArthurs. As the train chugged south, leaving the bemused town behind, the Generalissimo began to discuss the masses of troops he would demand from the Joint Chiefs of Staff, the build up of men that would occur in this seemingly vacant continent. Douglas MacArthur was no more defeated by the distances, the oddity, the apparent desolation of the Centre than any great explorer, for example John McDouall Stuart, would have been.

Mona broke up with Loutit at the end of the war. She remained in business. For a while, perhaps punitively, the Brigadier opened a business in opposition to her. She pursued her passions for hard work, commerce, horses and gambling. She acquired ownership of the Riverside Hotel. Now she is something of a pillar of Alice. She awards a Minahan Medal for 'the fairest and most brilliant player' in the local Aussie Rules football competition. She enters the Casino and plays a more genteel form of two-up and cards than she knew in the thirties and forties. 'The Casino gets all my hoot,' she says. She married in her seventies. 'Damned housework!' she says. 'At the Riverside, everything was done for me.'

The town is more orderly now, and you can see that she relished the haphazardness of the old town. Sit with her for five minutes, and she will tell you how she burned down the bungalow at the back of Kilgariff's pub because it was a death trap, and because 'blokes came worrying me too much there'. Having set up an alibi, when she was discovered she sat in the middle of the street, laughing, the proper response to being caught in the midst of an act of creative arson on the frontier. She also still remembers with delight the parson who, passing the pub yard and the line full of her lingerie drying in the sun, dragged his hat down over his eyes rather than look too closely at her underwear. 'Thank God I came to Alice,' she says. 'They don't make too many towns like it any more.'

If in other continents you wanted to speak to the men who surveyed and put down the main transcontinental road systems, you would be speaking to Roman engineers, to administrators of the Qin Emperor, or at least to nineteenth-century North American surveyors. If you want to speak to the man who surveyed and built the north-south highway across central Australia, it is a somewhat more feasible business. His

Mona Minahan behind her bar. Coming to the Alice as a girl, she was its great beauty. One of the few women allowed to stay in central Australia during World War II, she saw the defeated Douglas MacArthur pass through town with his wife and son, was declared Queen of the Australian army, ran a store and, in the end her own pub, The Riverside. An unselfconscious feminist, she forced herself into *swy* games and gambled hard among prospectors, cattle men, dingo-shooters and soldiers.

name is D. D. Smith, and he lives on the east side of the Todd River in Alice Springs. Again, he is one of those forerunners you would hardly expect to meet any more in North America. His life and his view of the world were formed by a nineteenth-century-style frontier, yet he has also had the shock of seeing the European development of the frontier foreshortened in the Territory's case. A volume of traffic such as he never envisaged – tourist buses, road trains, family sedans – clogs and creeps through traffic lights at the point where Todd Street turns the corner by the main causeway over the river to become the Stuart Highway of D. D. Smith's devising.

When D. D. Smith was a child and lived in Perth in Western Australia, Sir John Forrest used to come to the Smith household for tea on Sundays. Forrest had begun leading expeditions into the interior of Australia at the age of twenty-two in 1869. He had never been plagued by the darknesses, the doubts about inevitable European progress, that worried Ernest Giles. Significantly, the Gibson Desert, which had killed the Cockney Gibson and gone close to killing Giles himself, was crossed by John Forrest, forthrightly and without fuss, from the west in 1873. By the time he sat D. D. Smith on his knee, he had followed his career in exploration with one in politics, and had been premier of Western Australia. But he brought with him to the tea table not the whiff of the cabinet room but the redolence of the frontier. He was accompanied by his favourite native, 'Big Billy', who sat in a chair a little back from the table, wearing a large brass nameplate on his chest. Forrest spoke to the child not of state treasury matters but of the exquisite red hills of the Centre and the monsoonal country of northwestern Australia. 'The idea of living and working in the back country was instilled in my mind by Sir John', says D. D. Smith, 'when I was still a very small child.' D.D.'s blood lines were right for such an obsession – his father was one of those Scottish railway engineers who laid down track all over the new world, from British Columbia to Tasmania.

When D. D. Smith came to central Australia in the mid-1920s, the only road north of Alice Springs was the track cut out by bullock teams moving north along the line of the Overland Telegraph stations. It was in that respect like the old Roman roads of Britain, defined by wheel-tracks. Every ninety-six and a half kilometres, the government had built a bore from which deep alkaline water could be pumped up. But ninety-six and a half kilometres in those days was a long and perilous remove, because no vehicles other than bullock waggons could move up the rudimentary track. Convoys of bullock and camel teams progressed along it from the direction of South Australia, delivering rations to the Overland Telegraph stations. The bullock teams would leave Port Augusta on Christmas Day of one year, and finish the run at Daly Waters south of Darwin on Christmas Day the following year.

When the Commonwealth Government appointed D.D. as engineer for central Australia, the frontier was still not considered safe for white people. It was certainly not safe for blacks. While D. D. Smith was drawing the plans and laying out the foundations for Alice Springs township in August 1928, a dingo hunter called Fred Brooks was killed by Walpiri tribesmen at Coniston Station. It was a time of drought, and the Walpiri had wandered into Coniston looking for water, and had speared cattle. In reprisal for the killing of Brooks, a mounted constable was sent out with two police trackers. They recruited four white cattlemen, and rode from camp to camp shooting Walpiri. An old Walpiri man still remembers the killing. 'They just draft 'em out like cattle and shot 'em all the men.' On his return to Alice, the policeman unabashedly reported seventeen killings, but it is believed the number may have reached seventy. Later in the year the same policeman, Murray, was despatched again on a punitive expedition and returned reporting that fourteen Aboriginals had been shot. Again, the number may have topped seventy. Strangely two Walpiri arrested for the murder of Brooks and shipped up the long, wheel-rutted track to Darwin for trial, were acquitted.

Such was the nature of many of the dealings between black and white when D. D. Smith became Centralian engineer, his responsibility running from Alice Springs to Daly Waters, over six parallels of latitude, 'a fair bit of dirt, I might tell you'. D.D. began to 'straighten out' the bullock track in 1929. Most of his workers were natives, and most of the formalizing of the track was done with tip drays and long-handled shovels. During the Dry he would work from the Daly Waters end, and during the Wet from the direction of Alice Springs. 'It was a long time between showers in the early days.' And supplies came intermittently. Occasionally camel trains of sixty to eighty camels would arrive and more occasionally a motor vehicle with high-pressure tyres, and rolls of coir matting in the back to be laid down in front of the wheels when sandy patches had to be crossed.

But throughout the thirties, D. D. Smith was permitted to work on the road only intermittently. Because of the Depression, teams of white road workers were sent to the Centre and the 'poor bloody blackfellers were kicked out just as I was getting them used to the discipline and the work. They went bush again and made a damn nuisance of themselves. The whites were good workers, most of them. No other jobs, anyway. They soon learned to be tough.'

In 1935 he was able to persuade the government to give him a road grader, the first road grader in the Territory. For D.D., the public servants in Canberra were always too slow and apprehensive. 'They'd tell me, "That's all right, Smithy, it's only a bloody dirt road in the back of Australia." They reckoned Alice Springs would only be a railhead, but a road? It wasn't necessary.'

D.D. was aware of events in Europe, and in September 1938 went to Darwin to talk to the officer in command there. He was a colonel, soon to become a general, called 'Red Robbie' Robinson, a controversial and rather visionary officer who would get into trouble with both General Blamey, the commander of Land Forces in the South West Pacific Zone during World War II, and with General MacArthur himself. Smith brought Red Robbie down the rough road to Alice Springs, and then accompanied him to military headquarters in Melbourne. As a result of their zealous report, the military asked them to make an assessment of petrol, supplies and equipment needed to put a road between Darwin and Alice Springs.

By the time Hitler invaded Poland, D. D. Smith had supervised the surveying of the road and it was ready for construction. Responsibility for work on the roughest section, the six hundred kilometres from Tennant Creek to Larrimah, was handed out under D. D. Smith's supervision to the road authorities of three states, New South Wales, Queensland and South Australia. The road, which had been envisaged for sixty-seven years, since the linking of the Overland Telegraph, was now built in ninety days. Convoys began to move along it, and after the Japanese entered the war it became the only safe route for the conveying of supplies to Darwin. In 1942 the U.S. 64th Engineers came to Pine Creek to co-operate with Smith. 'They did an excellent job, then got sent to Guadalcanal to get cut to pieces.' They sealed the stretch between Daly Waters and Katherine. By October 1943, the whole Stuart Highway from Alice north was sealed. 'When the road was completed', says D.D., 'we put down the black strip and busted Australia wide open, opened it up and made it safe for people to live here. And never five minutes' industrial trouble with my men. You get in with your workers, and keep an open door to the office.'

There are of course other schemes lying unrealized in the brain of a congenital engineer like D. D. Smith. He wanted to put a railway line through from western Queensland to Darwin, from a place called Dejarra, 'a black stump terminus near Mount Isa. Maps of Queensland show a lot of railways ending in a heap of black stumps. A line from Dejarra would have rationalized all these.' Queenslanders could have sent their stock – cattle and sheep – through to the Barkly Tablelands in the Northern Territory in times of drought, to the best pasturelands in the north. 'But it's like corned beef, they told me. It'll keep.'

When Mark Lang drove out with D. D. Smith towards the old Telegraph station which was the beginning of Alice Springs to take a picture of D.D. on the road he made, motorists on the Stuart Highway, anxious to get the hard dull stretch of five hundred and thirty kilometres to Tennant Creek behind them, honked the old man for driving more slowly than they thought was appropriate for the highway conditions. Their impatience, of course, was based on ignorance. The point is, only D. D. Smith and a few other people know what a miracle seventy kilometres an hour is on that parlous and thirsty bullock waggon trail north of Alice.

Every August, the town fathers of Alice Springs celebrate a regatta in the Todd River. With the sort of surreal whimsicality which characterizes Australians in remote places, they call the event Henley-on-Todd and the whimsy consists in this: that the Todd only flows after rare heavy rain. The regatta is therefore held in the dry sand of the river bed. The organizers yearly take out insurance against rain. To have water in the Todd would spoil the regatta, would send thousands of visitors away, would bring down commercial disaster.

The yachts which compete in Henley-on-Todd have sails but no keels. Squads of brawny central Australians step into them, lift them by means of bars running athwart the vessels, and take off with them, running in unison. The running has to be in time. If those who are carrying a yacht get out of step with each other, the craft will nose-dive into the sand, the runners in the stern will be projected backside over tip through the rigging, perhaps head-first through the mainsail. Paddle races are held too – single sculls to eights. Racing shells have wheels attached and run on rails. The crews project them by digging deep into the sand with paddles. It is all done in great heat and with preposterous energy. Because it is the best sort of joke, it is spitting in the eye of the gods who made the dry, un-European Centre. It is a case of addressing the Australian God of Weather, Hughie, and telling him to stick his bloody rain.

It is, of course, a white celebration. The Aboriginals, who have been living along dry beds since the last Ice Age, cannot be expected to get the point. In 1982, the superb photographer of Africa, Mirella Ricciardi, happened to be in Alice for the event. She was captivated by it, but saw its European significance. 'It's just like Kenya when I was a girl,' she told us.

These days, an area just north of the regatta course is fenced off and labelled as a sacred site. This was as a result of various Aboriginal elders complaining to the Lands Department and identifying the area as a site of importance to people of the caterpillar totem. Though some whites,

The Henley-on-Todd regatta. A yearly event that takes place in the dry river bed of the Todd. Rain would be disastrous to this whimsical event, in which scullers propel their craft by paddling in sand – a joke at the expense of the dry Centre.

given the poor state of relations between the two races in Alice, saw this as merely a black attempt to spoil the fun, the organizers to their credit co-operated in the fencing and protection of the site. The ancestor hero of the caterpillar totem is still there enjoying risky cohabitation with the crazy white rite of Henley-on-Todd.

Opening and closing ceremonies for the Regatta, and all commentary, are carried on from a mock river boat which will never take off on any stream. It is named, in honour of the Centralian thirst, *Pistil Dawn*. A beauty contest is held on board – there are buxom locals and some smooth-tongued American girls from Pine Gap. The American Ambassador makes a speech about kinship between Americans and Australians, and though bikies from Adelaide drinking Four-X lager do not listen, he consecrates the alliance by kissing the winner of the contest. She, is of course, a girl from Melbourne who has decided to settle in Alice. For everyone's interests the home product is the best choice.

Further south along the Todd, its Aboriginal inhabitants stagger in a lost daze which has to do with the death of the ancestor hero, the death of the spirit, the loss of earth, the lust for booze. And on the bank, surrounded by a high fence, the white casino looks down on them. Attached to the casino is an excellent hotel. It is cool in there and elegant. Yet it seems a little embattled – the dry Todd on one side and, behind, an ancient, rust-red Ordovician spur of mountain.

Four out of five of the gamblers in the casino are Australians, either locals or visitors. But like the Darwin casino, it hopes to lock into the Asian and American markets. It has sales offices in Singapore and Los Angeles. Its management boasts that it has one of the best security and corruption-proof systems to be found in gambling anywhere in the world. All cash boxes on the tables are spring-loaded and have dual locks. The gaming manager and an official of the Northern Territory Government must open the boxes together – it is impossible for them to do it away from each other's supervision. The Northern Territory Racing and Gaming Commission officials make the count under the supervision of casino staff in a counting room locked from the outside. All instruments of gaming are handed to the government officials at the end of the day's play and reissued at the start of play the following afternoon. The government issues all playing cards and receives all used cards back. It even weighs the two-up pennies.

Two-up or *swy* (believed to be a corruption of the German *zwei*, two) is a game played since the earliest days of the Australian colonies with two pennies, and is therefore a version of the English pitch-and-toss. It is big in the Alice Springs casino and is played there in the most elegant form that a game of the mining and army camps, of pub backyards and rear alleys has ever achieved. The rite of *swy* is held in a pit surrounded by a large, chest-high wagering table with room for twenty players to place bets on whether pennies, tossed into the air by a Spinner in the pit, will come down heads, the side with the monarch engraved, or tails, the side engraved with the kangaroo. If the coins come down odds – one coin heads, one coin tails – all bets are frozen. It is therefore a game of

Lucio Marzi, manager of the Alice Springs casino, within sight of the empty bed of the ancient Todd. Among the games offered is *swy* (from the German *zwei*) or two-up, the Australian version of 'pitch and toss' played so energetically by itinerant workers in the outback and by Australian soldiers in both world wars.

simple elements, unlike roulette and black-jack. The great appeal it has had historically in Australia is probably based on the fact that it seems to offer the gambler a chance. Any mug can surely make a fair guess about what is going to happen at the next throw through taking a count of what has happened during the last half-dozen.

The Spinner is chosen from among the players. If he can throw three pairs of heads without throwing tails or five consecutive odds, then he picks up 15/2 on his wager. Relationships between the Players and the Spinner are maintained by two officials called Boxers. In the game as it was played in shearing sheds, the Boxers were enormous men dressed in navy-blue singlets and shorts. At the Alice Springs casino they keep order in tangerine tuxedos. The outcome of all the Spinner's throws appears on an electronic board above the entry gate to the pit, so there can be no arguments. The Boxers have to ensure that when the Spinner takes the wooden kip with the two pennies on it in his hand, and obeys their instruction to throw – 'Come in Spinner!' is the traditional formula – the coins rise at least three feet above his head. The coins must spin and are not permitted to touch in the air.

The question of whether a town of 17,000 should be expected to help carry a fully fledged casino is one which the management counters by pointing to what the casino puts back into the community. It pays out over 4 million dollars a year in wages, 2 million dollars a year to local services. It buys local artwork – of high and vivid standard – for its corridors; it uses local legal representation. And as the disproportion of local and overseas users of the gaming tables begins to shorten, the benefits to Alice will be richer still. The rajahs and tycoons of Malaysia, the princes of Beverly Hills may one day leave a bundle on the black-jack tables of the Alice, while the Aussie larrikin and his missus do their dough on a more modest and egalitarian scale at the *swy* pit.

In any case, compared to the question of Pine Gap and of racial anger in Alice, the casino raises few passions, other than the generally modest and honest passions associated with gambling.

At the Old Timers' Home south of Alice, through Heavitree Gap, you can meet the men and women who knew the Alice – as one of them put it – 'when it was itself. Before it became the mess it is today. Before the Federal government buggered the Aboriginals.' If you ask them if that means the days when Aboriginals knew their place and worked on cattle stations for nothing but rations, they will say, 'That's not what I mean. I mean booze. I mean giving them open slather in the pubs.'

Ly Underdown, who arrived in Alice Springs in 1929, opened a drapery store which also sold alcohol, then built the Alice Springs Hotel in 1933 with his Aboriginal side-kick Noony and now resides in the Old Timers' Home. He is a grand source for the oral history of the Territory, and as the nurse leads you down the corridor to his room she has a whimsical smile. 'Everyone who wants to know about Alice in the thirties comes to talk to Ly,' she explains. 'They get an earful, too.'

When Ly stepped off the Ghan with his mother in 1929, Alice had seven houses. When he built his hotel, the population was three hundred. He knew every one of those rather exceptional three hundred. 'Pub owner's like a bloody father confessor.'

Piquant stories of Lycurgus P. Underdown are still told in pubs in the Territory, though now usually by men of Lycurgus's own age. When Bob Buck the bushman found Lasseter's body in the Petermann Ranges, Ly registered the crated remains as a guest in the hotel and gave them a room. Even so, Ly Underdown doubts that they *were* Lasseter's remains. 'Remains of some poor bloody Abo, more likely. Lasseter had debts and a missus. Of course he flitted.' It is no use arguing that Lasseter could perhaps have flitted at somewhat less expense than taking an expedition to the Petermanns. Lasseter lives, O.K.

When Ly Underdown took big winnings in a game of poker with Brigadier Noel Loutit, Loutit attempted to conscript him. 'Had to go to Adelaide and see the Manpower chiefs. Cost me thirty-three quid and a lot of talking. But I talked my way out. I'm the best bloody bush lawyer in the Northern Territory.'

In 1947, Ly Underdown built a new hotel, which still stands and is now called the Telford. He installed in it the first lift in the Northern Territory. He is very proud of it, and after all a lift is a powerful symbol. The frontier is a matter of dirt floors. The first step in the coming of

Lycurgus P. Underdown, publican of Alice. He registered the bones of the explorer Lasseter, packed in a tea chest, as a guest of his hotel. He founded the Red Centre Bar and invented Roof Cricket, a slightly alcoholic version of the real thing which is played beneath the stars on the roof of what is now the Telford Hotel.

European culture to the frontier is floorboards. The second, one could argue, is the stairwell. And a lift? Well, a lift is big city stuff.

To add to the character of the pub Ly invented roof cricket. He built a wire cage up there on the flat roof of the Alice Springs Hotel. There, beneath the Centralian stars, cricket was played at night by teams of men in creams. The pitch was regulation length, there was a sight board behind the bowler. On the onside, a scoring tape began at a height of one metre from the ground at the batsman's end and rose to a height of two and three-quarter metres by the time it reached the bowler's, maintaining the two-and-three-quarter-metres level as it crossed behind the sight board at the batsman's end before returning back up the off.

You scored a run for a hit into the net frame on or under the tape behind the wicket. Similarly a run for a ball hit on or under the one-metre tape. As the tape began to graduate, however, you scored two runs for a ball hit into the net, but once more only if the ball landed beneath the tape. Four runs came off a ball hit under the two-and-three-quarter-metre tape into the sight board behind the bowler. But you were always given out if the ball hit the tape or hit the frame above the tape. You were also out if you didn't strike at two legitimate balls in succession. A key rule reads, 'The first striker to stay in for four consecutive overs purchases refreshments for the five participating teams.'

Running a pub in the sixties became a more complicated matter, a less whimsical affair than the Territory's traditional pub life. The Australian public became passionately interested in the impact of the belated granting of full civil rights to Aboriginals as the result of a Federal referendum. Camera crews came to the Alice, looking for scandals of discrimination, frequently finding them. There was of course resistance from the locals. Lycurgus P. Underdown is famous for having appeared on national television as party to the following exchange:

ABC Interviewer: Excuse me, Mr Underdown, could I have a word with you.

Lycurgus P. Underdown: You can have two. Fuck off!

Ly's profanity was, of course, artfully bleeped when it came up in the living rooms of Australia.

To prove their case on how affairs in the Alice have deteriorated, old-timers like Ly point to the miseries of the Todd bed.

End Note

Just before this book was finished, the Northern Territory government attempted to solve the problem of the Todd by putting a ban on drinking in public within a two-kilometre radius of Alice. Some Aboriginal leaders felt that this would only aggravate violence, but so far it has worked very well, at least in that there are few clashes between police and Aboriginals within Alice now, and there is less aggravation between whites and blacks at the centre of the town. One of the crucial incidents which may have driven the Territory government to impose a two-kilometre ban may have been the murders by poisoning which took place in Alice in March 1981. After dark on a Saturday evening, an Aboriginal found a bottle of Yalumba cream sherry in the grounds of the John Flynn Memorial Church in Alice Springs. It was properly corked and quite full, and looked as though it had come straight from a liquor store or pub. The Aboriginal who found it did not drink it – he took it down to the Todd as a group offering, rather in the way the hunter brings home his catch uneaten.

That night the bottle passed, without being opened, through six hands. It progressed a kilometre and a half down the bed of the Todd to a large encampment of mainly Pitjantjatjara people near the casino. These, with some Aranda and Pintubi, lived in a makeshift camp on the river bed, but in the morning they moved upstream to a 'dinner camp', a place where the large gums which grow in the empty river bed cast good shade.

These Todd bed people were often but not always outcasts of their own community. Elders sometimes encourage trouble-makers in remote reservations to clear out to Alice, where they will have access to the dole and other social benefits. Not all the inhabitants of the river bed of the Todd and the nearby Charles are however a drain on the state. Many of them do not understand the concept of social welfare. Their social welfare has traditionally been the sort of sharing which influenced the man who found the Yalumba sherry to pass it along the Todd in the first place.

Early on the Sunday morning, the sixth 'owner' of the unopened sherry approached a group around a camp-fire. The sherry was opened. David Charlie, a twenty-eight-year-old Pitjantjatjara married to a Pintubi girl, took a mouthful. Nabutta Abbot, a thirty-two-year-old Aboriginal whose husband was away in town, fetching tap water, also took a swig. An Aboriginal called Gorry spat his mouthful out. He preferred Orlando sweet sherry. Six other people took sips.

When Nabutta's husband arrived back with the water, he found his wife convulsing and gasping on the ground beside David Charlie. The six others were also very ill. Nabutta died before any help could be found; Charlie was dead on arrival at Alice Springs Hospital. The six others recovered.

The 2000 Aboriginals who live in Alice in the European manner were horrified by this event. Though the police had not made any comment on the concentration of poison in the sherry, it was now known to be strychnine, and local gossip said that there was half a kilo of strychnine grains dissolved in the bottle. The Europeanized Aboriginals of the Alice feared further attacks on Aboriginal life, since there was someone in the community willing to go to such murderous lengths. There were different kinds of worries in the Todd bed. The six men who had passed the sherry on during the Saturday night now feared retribution at the hands of the kinsmen of those who had drunk the poison. One Aboriginal cut his own leg as a demonstration of sorrow and of his willingness to expiate. Another cleared out to his tribal land in Western Australia.

Some Alice Springs residents, white and black, wondered whether the sherry deaths hadn't been some sort of tribal retaliation anyhow. But most Aboriginals dismissed that proposition. Strychnine was a white man's poison, and tribal vengeance is mainly exacted with traditional weapons rather than adapted European ones. Retribution is also very much a matter of specific victims, whereas the Yalumba sherry was laced for the purpose of bringing about random and widespread death.

In any case, the killer was never found. There is no doubt though that the fear and bitterness of the sherry killings survives.

Chapter 9

By Killarney's Lakes and Dells...

You wonder what homesick Irishman gave Killarney station its name. It sits among low stony hills two hundred kilometres southwest of Katherine, in country where the predominant colour is not Centre-red but instead various subtleties of light brown, blue and grey. The earth has that blue-greyness that suggests it is a continuation of the salt lakes further south and implies bitter earth, hard on the hard-mouthed cattle. Yet it is among the better cattle-lands of the Territory. Once it was a mere outstation of Victoria River Downs, one of the oldest, largest, most prestigious of cattle stations, among whose many owners was the Bovril company of Great Britain, manufacturers of the famed beef extract. (Again, all the glamour and wild labour of the Australian stockmen, white and black, ending up reduced to a banal product in a glass jar.) In grand Territorian style, Killarney is a mere off-cut, 4000 square kilometres in extent, of Victoria River Downs. June Tapp, who is co-owner with her husband, says of it without any self-consciousness that it is just average for around there – she is speaking the mere truth, even though it means that her place is 1000 square kilometres larger than the North Riding of Yorkshire.

Killarney, like most cattle stations, is like nothing so much as a medieval duchy. The forty kilometres of dirt road into the homestead runs through stark and ancient country which makes a mockery of a soft, green name like Killarney. Rubberbush grows everywhere – it is a strong light green shrub introduced to the Territory because it was believed to be a source of high protein. There is still a lot of talk about whether it is really good for cattle or not, but it suits the muted earth very well and makes it look more outlandish still. At the heart of every pastel rubberbush blossom is a perfect inky violet sexagon where all the sweetness lies. But you have to look for that.

Twenty kilometres in from the boundary of Killarney, you pass an earlier abandoned homestead where only the framework and gnarled mulga wood stockyards are left. Once it was a village of sixty people or more, for a homestead is more than just a farmhouse, it is, as we will see, a unique community. The mystery is that social scientists have not yet descended on that peculiar society made up of stockmen, book-keepers, mechanics and cooks, married and unmarried, of black stockmen and their wives and children, who gather around every major homestead, and who work together within a complex set of rivalries, antagonisms, and assumptions.

DRINK MORE BOOZE
A MILLION DRUNKS
CAN'T BE WRONG

3 years
we're going great mate!

SEX APPEAL
GIVE GENEROUSLY

June Tapp, chatelaine of Killarney station. 'Fifteen hundred and sixty-eight square miles we have,' she says, 'which is pretty average for round here.' She is a hearty drinker, helps run a model cattle operation, and is a leader of the Rights for Whites movement.

The Killarney homestead area itself is the size of a small town and is U-shaped around a vast central piazza of trodden grey-brown dust. One arm of the U consists of immense stockyards built of tubular steel. Killarney runs – as well as mere beef on the hoof – a Brahmin stud, a Santa Gertrudis stud, a quarter horse stud. There is a sale ring with a grandstand in which bidders can sit, and an elevated place for the auctioneer. At the base of the U, in a garden watered by artesian bore, is the long brick bungalow which is the Tapp homestead. There are lots of Tapp children – the Tapps will give a fair imitation of not knowing quite how many. His, mine, and ours, says June Tapp, since this is her second marriage. In the second side of the U, running parallel to the stockyards, are offices, single stockmen's quarters, guests' quarters, a schoolhouse, a dining room, a cook house, garages, a meat house, and an open-air recreation area covered with a roof of wire and brush, where station personnel can have their smokos and sit in the evening talking and drinking Carlton Draught. Finally there is a collection of small, corrugated iron huts, the blacks' camp, where the Aboriginal stockmen

live. In all, the population here is just under sixty. Lit with street lights at night, it does have a partially municipal air about it. Petrol for the electric generators and for other purposes costs the Tapps $67,000 a year, a sum which has a municipal heft to it.

The first time we visited Killarney, Bill Tapp did not appear. He had been involved in a helicopter crash while mustering in 1980 – his foot had been hanging out of the door on the passenger side when the craft stalled and dropped to the ground, rolling on his ankle. Occasionally the ankle balloons, the leg swells. 'Might have to call the Flying Doctor,' said June. 'Of course, he's an only child and bungs it on a bit. You know what only children are like.'

She sits on her front verandah, an avid conversationalist, barefooted, smoking passionately. The verandah bookshelves are full of the best stuff – Thomas Mann, Kafka, Patrick White. 'I'd love to meet the old Patrick,' she says. She has read a lot of women writers – Maxine Hong Kingston, Anaïs Nin, Shirley Hazzard's *The Transit of Venus*. She knows

The cook cuts up the breakfast steaks as the sun comes up at Killarney station. Stockmen passing by call to him, 'Cops'll know where you are now, Jack.' Workers on cattle stations like to think of themselves as refugees from justice or the unjust tyranny of alimony. In Jack's case, it was the cramped style of the city of Brisbane that brought him to the outback.

Shirley is a Sydney girl who's made it big in America, marrying a critic called Francis Steegmuller and nabbing the National Book Award, but she thinks the *Transit of Venus* 'a little bit contrived'. Three thousand cattle are just arriving from a mustering camp, you can hear them lowing as the stockmen edge them into the yards, you can smell the dust. 'Feminist books are written for middle-class educated women in the cities,' remarks the chatelaine of Killarney against the noise of incoming cattle.

The second time we come to Killarney, the mustering is going on at a more intense rate, but Bill Tapp is up. He shows us his ankle; it is violet and very swollen. An occupational hazard, he says. Helicopters occur as regularly in his life as they do in Dick Gill's. There is an American called Webb, a Vietnam veteran, who will drop down so low during the mustering that he can nudge recalcitrant cows along with the skids of his machine. Young Billy Tapp tells of travelling over a lagoon with Webb one day and noticing the surface of the water was dimpling with drops of oil leaking from the helicopter. He told Webb, who yelled back, 'It's OK if we crash here. We're close enough to the Top Springs pub.'

But it is not as if the Tapps themselves are lesser in stature or colour than the fabled Webb. The Tapp children have had what must be one of the most extraordinary of upbringings. They attend the classroom on the station – there are still two Tapp children at the station school, a boy of eleven and a girl of nine. The present teacher is a Dutchman called Fritz, a serious young man whose classroom uniform is a singlet and shorts. He says teaching the Tapps and the children of the Aboriginal stockmen is no sinecure. He has all the normal paperwork, as much as a city headmaster has. He is also librarian, counsellor, etcetera. He is a young man who takes educational theory seriously, and says that the Northern Territory, who employ him, are eclectic, choosing the best from a number of state systems. The classroom is well set up with two-way radio, television and video, an extensive library. But Fritz is frustrated. The school population varies between five and thirteen, dependent on which children turn up, dependent on whether the families of Aboriginal stockmen wander away for ceremonies or not. The eleven-year-old Tapp boy, Daniel, is a devout cattleman, and isn't much seen when cattle draughting is in process in the stockyards. At the end of a day of hectic activity, he is likely to fall asleep anywhere, in the Aboriginal stockmen's camp, in the homestead, at a dozen intervening locations. It is a childhood of extraordinary freedom and yet extraordinary toughness. It is the sort of childhood all Daniel's elder brothers and sisters have enjoyed.

When a Tapp child reaches high school age, he or she is sent to one of the best schools in Sydney – Shore for boys, Kambala for girls. Then they come back to Killarney – at least the boys do. They are already expert horsemen; they become flash ringers. June complains that they are not very literary, but they give forth a great certainty. There is nowhere else they would rather be.

The secondary school-age children of the Aboriginal stockmen will attend Yirara College while they go to Alice Springs high schools. The

The chief stockman of Killarney with his children. The children attend the station school, run by a Dutch teacher in shorts and singlet. Later they will leave their small, corrugated iron house and go to an air-conditioned, brick college in Alice Springs.

The youngest Tapp boy, having fled from the school house, watches his brothers and the Aboriginal stockmen mustering cattle at Killarney. The boy is a champion horseman himself and can manage cattle like an adult. At the age of twelve he will go away to a private school in Sydney, before returning to work the rest of his life in the cattle industry.

brick and air-conditioning of Yirara must seem a strange departure from the corrugated iron shacks of the stockmen's camp. Most of them will return – wherever they settle – to more basic housing once their stint at Yirara is over.

June Tapp herself, the duchess of Killarney, drinks with the stockmen and is a great talker. Having attacked me one night for not staying in the city with my kids and writing about that, she got up at 4.30 in the morning, just as the cook was preparing the breakfast steak and eggs and beneath stars of fierce clarity, to apologize. 'Books mean a lot to June,' said Bill Tapp, explaining by implication why we were welcome on

175

Killarney. But the Tapps are used to guests. Up to a thousand people come into Killarney for the quarter horse sales. More honoured guests stay in the guests' quarters, but most bring their swags and camp out. Visitors to these events drink heartily, as do the Tapps themselves. June will go out and, for the amusement of the crowd, throw wild wheelies in the red-grey dust in the four-wheel-drive with its stickers 'Sex Appeal Give Generously' and 'A Million Drunkards Can't be Wrong.' Of Irish descent, she sees no contradiction between these shenanigans and her love of a good sentence, her concern – in that illimitable space – over nuclear armaments, her interest in the characters of Patrick White and Bob Hawke.

The Katherine police send two constables out for the Killarney sales, but the Tapp clan are proud that in 1982 the only ones arrested were two Tapp boys.

A severed hoof lies like the debris of the battle between stockmen and resistant cattle in the station yard of Killarney.

Even taking account of the relaxed Aboriginal attitude towards housing, accommodation for Aboriginal stockmen and their families on cattle stations has always been primitive. 'I'll duck out and clean up the blacks' camp,' said June Tapp when we asked her if we could visit. In fact, the housing on Killarney, the provision of water and so on, is much better than in other places. Certainly better than the conditions described in the *London Observer* as prevailing on Vestey's Gordon Downs station, just over the Western Australia border, in 1979. 'The station provided nine twenty- by twelve-foot one-room tin huts for the Aborigines. There was no piped water. The one pump was broken, and water had to be carried from over two hundred yards away. But the lawn sprinklers were working at the homestead!'

Aboriginal stockmen are certainly astounding horsemen. They wheel open-mouthed in the towers of dust which a moving mob throws up.

Stockman, Killarney station. This man works for the redoubtable Tapp family of Killarney, mustering cattle in an isolated duchy of 2500 square kilometres and living in a village of sixty people which surrounds the Tapp homestead.

Getting cattle into the Killarney stockyards, where there are sprinklers to settle the dust, must be a luxury to them. The normal smothering environment of deep brown grit seems not to touch them. They are different men from the shuffling and beaten inhabitants of the Todd River bed in Alice. Their big point of the year is to go to the Katherine Show and do something flash and clever with horses and cattle in the show ring. In fact, Bill Tapp recruits many of his stockmen from the same show. 'Been working for Tapps since the Katherine Show. Working at Camfield till then, but a no-good head stockman, and we all cleared out.'

The balances, the connections of a society like the one around Killarney homestead would seem adequate to keep a novelist busy for years. Apart from the fascination of the Tapp brood itself and its impressive matriarch June Tapp, there is the relationship between the black and white stockmen, who are peers in the saddle, respected colleagues in the mustering camp, yet who live separate lives in that village around the homestead. But since the society is so small, there are crossings of the barriers. One of the Tapp girls fell in love with an Aboriginal stockman and went to live with him in Katherine. But the girl is welcome back at the homestead for visits, and the grandchild attends Fritz's school in the meantime. 'There's my little black bugger of a grandchild,' June will say, leaning on the school fence and pointing him out among the other children.

At the same time, the Tapps suspect, as nearly all cattlemen do, the Land Rights Act. They see it as window-dressing to enable Canberra politicians to posture as statesmen at the U.N. and before the black nations of the Commonwealth. The Tapps are nervous about claims for Gallery Rock, an old rock-painting site somewhere in the immensity of Killarney. Because June believes land rights and other rights have been given to Aboriginals prematurely and to the peril of both races, she was one of the leaders – along with Les McFarlane, a cattleman himself, Speaker of the House of Assembly in Darwin, much liked by whites, much abominated by blacks – of a march down the long, broad main street of Katherine in favour of Rights for Whites.

The truth is that the situation is too subtle to yield to the sort of easy tags city liberals like to plant on human situations. If you apply a label such as *racist* to an event of this type you are almost begging the question. You may also be, from the safety of a southern city, encouraging the highly developed intransigence of the northern cattleman.

The life of cattle-station people in the Territory, though always harsh and tough in the past, and though harsh and tough now, is in style baronial and, until recently, unfettered. The inroads the Land Rights Act has made on the property and practice of cattlemen are more psychological than a real intrusion. The station owners see Land Rights as a further progression of the campaign that gave Aboriginal stockmen full award wages in the late 1960s. When cattlemen say that Land Rights 'will ruin the cattle industry', they are speaking again perhaps more in psychological terms than in terms of any real damage they themselves

PREVIOUS PAGE:
Young Billy Tapp, flash horseman, musters cattle in temperatures of 45°C and choking dust on his father's cattle station, Killarney.

180

may have suffered, they are clinging to habits of mind, habits of style based on the legend of the cattleman. And so, on a Saturday morning in 1982, the station owners of the Katherine area assembled at the western end of town and marched down the Stuart Highway led by June Tapp of Killarney and Les McFarlane, Speaker of the House.

As well as the stories of the special sort of dynamics that work in a community like Killarney, there are the usual universal tales. The sister-in-law of one of the Aboriginal stockmen comes and stays at Killarney and falls in love with one of the flash stockmen. Soon she is pregnant, but it's OK, the stockman says he loves her. One afternoon, however, a dusty Holden comes in to Killarney – two of the stockman's kinsmen are in it. They want him to go to Western Australia with them, and with that off-the-cuff nomadic manner he does so. The girl is left sitting in the dust in front of her sister's shack and tries to work up the idea that he'll be back in a week or two into something approaching real hope. As well as signifying thus the eternal human fix she's in, she demonstrates her cultural turmoil by playing her small transistorized tape-deck, her one and most obviously precious possession. The tape-deck stands beside her in the shade of a mulga wood, it carries a 'Don't Mess Up the Territory' sticker, and she is playing Fleetwood Mac, and a full cassette of Susie Quatro is on standby. 'Bloody shame,' says June Tapp, 'but the boy's Northern Territory welter-weight champion. No one's going to bring him back.'

End Note

The Tapps had an expensive receiving dish erected in the oasis by their homestead. Now it brings in Australian Broadcasting Commission television transmissions and in the evening, unless there's cattle draughting going on in the stockyards, the Tapps and the stockmen sit down with half a dozen cans apiece and watch concerted bursts of television. From watching ABC current affairs they are better informed on politics, nuclear armaments, the state of the American economy, than most city Australians, who favour the softer pap of commercial television. Throughout 1982, they were also watching *Brideshead Revisited* – the gently camp Charles Ryder, the more outrageous Sebastian Flyte. It is hard to find a frame of reference in the lives that are led on Killarney for the sort of lives those effete members of the English gentry were leading in the twenties and thirties. 'It gets you in, doesn't it,' one of the Tapp boys said. 'But do you think there are really jokers like that?' The question is an index of the fact that ringers see their lives, not as extraordinary, but as sane and central existences. The central life, the only life, is the life of dust and cattle. The dream of cattle, again. Without it, a man could end up toting teddy-bears around. Like that bloody Sebastian Flyte.

Chapter 10

The Paper for this Place

In 1976, before the Northern Territory became self-governing, the Federal government of Australia, despite the resistance of many cattlemen and other white Territorians, introduced an Aboriginal Land Rights Act. The Act created a Land Rights Commission, which could meet anywhere in the Territory, and Aboriginal traditional owners could appear before it and argue their primary responsibility for a particular area of land. Land which had already been alienated to Europeans, land which was held under a pastoral lease (that is, land which was being run as a cattle station under a lease provided by the Territory Government), could not be claimed by Aboriginals. But if there was a sacred site in the midst of a pastoral lease, the traditional tribal owner could appeal to the Land Rights Commission for an *excision*, for title which gave him access to and ownership of that place, whether it be rock, deep spring or cave.

The Land Rights Commissioner, often holding his quasi-judicial hearings in the open air, hears all Aboriginal claims to traditional ownership of country, but cannot himself award any title to the land. He sends his findings to the Minister of Aboriginal Affairs in Canberra ('Never a Territorian!' the Territorians will tell you) who makes the final decision and, if it is positive, hands our freehold title to the traditional owners.

The judge whose enquiries led to the framing of the Land Rights Act, Mr Justice Woodward, said in his report to the Federal government that only the possession of land made possible 'the preservation of a spiritual link . . . which gives each Aboriginal his sense of identity and lies at the heart of his spiritual beliefs'. He quoted the anthropologist Stanner: 'In taking the land from Aboriginals we took what to them meant hearth, home, the source and locus of life and everlastingness of spirit.' 'Can aggression be more absolute?' asked an advocate of Land Rights.

When the Land Rights Act was passed in 1976, there was immediate hostility to the concept of Aboriginals owning perpetual title to land. Pastoralists claimed it would destroy the cattle industry, miners feared it would inhibit the orderly procedure of mineral leases. There were historic precedents which made the miners uneasy. For example, in 1928, Mr Bleakley the Chief Protector of Aboriginals recommended that Arnhem Land be turned into an Aboriginal reserve. 'There should be no obstacle to this as the country is very poor, no one requires it, and those who previously have taken up some of it have abandoned it.' In the

The gorge at the Katherine River. The river flows down from the well-watered and mineral-rich escarpments of Arnhem Land.

182

late 1960s however Arnhem Land began to look more desirable than it had to Bleakley. It was so rich in uranium that even in the Dreaming, ancestors who travelled down 'sore' trails developed weeping ulcers, presumably from radiation, and among the Aboriginals of western Arnhem Land today the 'sore' trails are known and, in most instances, avoided. In any case, Arnhem Land had been granted to the Aboriginals before the value of the 'sore' trails was appreciated. The miners had great problems in convincing traditional owners to permit uranium mining and their negotiations on production methods were strenuously scrutinized by the press and by 'southern liberals'. Now, to grant Aboriginals perpetual title over other 'valueless' land would seem only to invite the same inconvenience and irony to recur.

The Act has never been popular in the Territory and Paul Everingham, the Chief Minister, frankly declared he would like to see the Act amended, but he knew the issue could not be altered simply by making speeches in Darwin or Alice. In the winter of 1982 he came south to present his 'package' of amendments to the Federal politicians in Canberra and to argue his case in front of southern journalists at the Canberra Press Club. Everingham is exactly the sort of politician

The edge of the Arnhem Land escarpment. Below, in the riverine plains, the great art galleries of Obiri Rock and Nourlangie can be found. The escarpment country, written off as useless by the Australian government in 1929 and now Aboriginal freehold, is nonetheless so rich in uranium that the incidence of Downes Syndrome among infants in the North End is four times the national average.

journalists like on sight. He is gutsy, he is tinged with beer flab but very athletic at the same time. He is eloquent, in a forthright, grassroots way, as few of the sanitized politicians of southeast Australia or of the United States can afford to be.

Now he spoke as a reasonable, eloquent populist. Questions over who owned Australia were divisive, he said. Australia was owned by all Australians, but Land Rights were a fact of life in the Northern Territory. Nearly fifty per cent of land in the Northern Territory was either owned by Aboriginal traditional owners or else was under claim waiting to be heard by the Aboriginal Lands Commissioner. This mass of Aboriginal land, claimed and granted, or else under claim, amounted to 672,000 square kilometres. It was land under perpetual title, so that no one could buy or sell it. All mining on Aboriginal land had to be carried on with Aboriginal approval. 'A Miner's Right carries no weight on Aboriginal land,' said Everingham. If the Act is working, Everingham asked, why does the Northern Territory government want to change it? Well, there were a number of Aboriginals who had pastoral leases in the Northern Territory, who ran stations, that is, like any white cattlemen on land not traditionally theirs. They were not protected by the Act in the same way that white leaseholders were. The Aboriginal leaseholder could be turned off land which was not his traditionally by those 'descent groups with a primary spiritual responsibility for the land or site, and who are entitled, by Aboriginal tradition, to forage over the land'.

Another reason for changing the Act was that Aboriginals were making claims to national parks, stock routes and reserves. Most importantly for the cattle industry, pastoral properties could be bought by Aboriginals, then claimed under the Act, and then left unproductive. 'This aspect of the Act could have a devastating effect on the Northern Territory and its ability to support Territorians, regardless of colour.'

Then there was no time limit to the lodging of claims. Claims could be made again and again. Surely there should be a date beyond which claims could no longer be made.

What changes then did Everingham wish to make to the Act? The Northern Territory itself, he said, would pass laws preventing Aboriginals from obtaining freehold title to pastoral leases on land they were working on. They could obtain *perpetual* pastoral leases, but they could *not* have the sort of freehold which entitled them to use the land as they chose, which enabled them to let it lie ungrazed by cattle if that was what they wanted to do. Those Aboriginal cattlemen who owned pastoral leases on land not traditionally theirs would also be protected under Territory law against Land Rights claims.

In return for these changes, Everingham would give Aboriginals title to Uluru or Ayers Rock as long as joint management was carried on between the Pitjantjatjara people and the Conservation Commission. At the same time, the Northern Territory government would want the Commonwealth government to pass amendments to the Act, so that Aboriginals could continue with claims over pastoral properties they already owned, but could make no future claims to freehold title over pastoral properties they took a lease on. They would also not be able to go ahead with claims to national parks, stock routes or public reserves.

Everingham's package of amendments was put forward in so masterly a manner that not everyone understood why there was such an outcry from Aboriginals and white supporters of Land Rights. On the face of it, the package Everingham placed before the southern press at the Canberra Press Club seemed to make straight the crooked ways of the Act. The statistic that nearly fifty per cent of the Territory was owned or under claim by Aboriginals was the sort which powerfully exercised the imaginations even of southeastern Australians with feelings of vague geniality towards the ancient race. In fact, Everingham knew as well as anyone that many such Southerners have baulked when they come against the realities of black ownership. The executive producer of a national current affairs programme wanted to fly into a beach in Arnhem Land with a helicopter and camera crew and film barramundi fishing. When the local Aboriginal council refused him permission, he appealed to Everingham's press secretary. 'You can make them let us in,' he told the press aide. 'No we can't,' said the aide. 'But you're the government of the bloody Northern Territory aren't you?' asked the executive producer. There was a similar surprise when the

Yirrkala people refused Germaine Greer a permit to visit their settlement in 1982. So the fifty per cent figure Everingham quoted appealed to those Australians who felt that, at least in the Northern Territory, the whole Land Rights business had got out of hand.

Everingham's speech in Canberra was backed up by a national advertising campaign, featuring double spreads in magazines and full pages in daily papers. The advertisements appeared over the flag of the Territory, and the inscription 'THE LAND WHERE DREAMS ARE BEING MADE, NOT BROKEN'.

Even at the press conference, Everingham's new package did not go without challenge. One journalist asked him to state the reason the town boundaries of Darwin (population 50,000) and Alice Springs (population 17,000) had been widened to encompass, in each case, an area four times the boundaries of Greater London. Was it to frustrate Aboriginal land claims?

Everingham's deft speech to the Canberra press did, in all good conscience, omit to mention some crucial aspects of his fifty per cent claim. At the moment, Aboriginal people *do* hold title to just over a quarter of the Territory, but much of it is in desert areas, in the Petermann Ranges, the Tanami Desert – land, that is, which is of no use to the cattlemen. Other Aboriginal freehold is wet land and upland scrub – the Arnhem Land area which, in 1928, J. W. Bleakley was so willing to write off. A further eighteen per cent of the Territory is under claim, but most of that, thirteen per cent in fact, is desert or semi-desert – the Simpson Desert, and areas southeast and west of Tennant Creek. Aboriginal people hold only five per cent of the pastoral lease area, so that it is hard to believe that, whatever they did with it, they could drastically affect the cattle industry.

The idea that stock routes should be exempt from Land Right claims was, like the fifty per cent figure, one that appealed to the mythology of white Australians. Australians see the northern cattleman as a battler, whimsical and tough, a figure with the mystique of say the renowned screen actor Jack Thompson; blonde, Aryan, indomitable. The stock routes are the tracks down which he moves his cattle, over hundreds of kilometres, to market. In fact stock routes have not been used for over thirty years; Kurt Johannsen's self-tracking trailers rendered them obsolete. Aboriginals *have* claimed sections of such routes so that at least they can own a little of their ancestral land. Now Everingham, they feared, would abolish their right to do so, without guaranteeing them any chance of obtaining excisions of ancestral land situated in the midst of cattle stations.

The Pitjantjatjara people at Ayers Rock said as much in a letter addressed to the Prime Minister, Malcolm Fraser. They were pleased that they could receive title to Uluru, they'd always wanted it. In fact two traditional owners, Nipper Winmati and Peter Bulla, had earlier failed, for technical reasons, in an attempt to claim Uluru. But now they didn't want Uluru as part of a package which tried to disinherit other people. 'Your government made the Land Rights law in 1976 and now you are going back on your word and trying to change it,' they told

Fraser. 'You are saying, "We are taking rights away from those cattle station mobs (those who seek excisions and stock routes on cattle stations) but we'll give you Pitjantjatjara Uluru instead." We have always wanted the paper for this place, but this way you are shaming us. Aboriginal people don't think that way. Country is sacred to all Aboriginals and we are very sad that you want us to get our country by climbing over those Arandas, Walpiri and others in the North. You are using us and our country against other people.'

To claim an excision under the new package proposed by Chief Minister Everingham, only Aboriginals living on the pastoral lease concerned on 31 March 1981 are eligible. This proposal ignores the nomadic temperament of the Aboriginal people, and it ignores also the events of the late 1960s, when cattlemen, reacting to the granting of award wages to Aboriginal stockmen, forcibly evicted from the stations many Aboriginal families formerly living under the cattleman's patronage on their traditional land. The naming of the gratuitous date caused an outcry from the Tangentyere Council in Alice Springs, who called on a white aide to express their outrage in European terms. (This kind of assistance from Europeans, essential for the understanding of both sides, is often inevitably written off in the Territory as 'communist influence' or 'white stirring'.)

'In most of these areas', the Council stated by way of protest, 'the traditional Aboriginal owners have been forced off their land over the years by one means or another – for example, by mobs of cattle, lack of traditional food and water, restrictions on freedom of movement, poor living conditions, lack of employment, hostility from leaseholders or their management, government removal under the assimilation policy, etc. So they have ended up on other people's country, on settlements, town camps or less hostile stations. The "package" completely ignores these people – the very people who have been most unjustly treated in the past, and who have least hope for the future. It cuts off their chances of ever getting Land Rights.'

Miners and the Northern Territory government have been complaining for some time about the difficulties of going ahead with mineral exploration on Aboriginal land. 'The chances are that if resources are found on Aboriginal land, or land subject to a land claim,' said Everingham in the Northern Territory Assembly in 1979, 'they will take umpteen years to get out.' The Aboriginals replied that they had always co-operated with the mineral seekers, and that they'd reached agreement for the exploration of the Mareenie oil basin and the Palm Valley gas field, and with the Northern Territory government itself for a gas pipeline corridor. To those who felt threatened that they could only come onto Aboriginal land with permission, Aboriginals pointed out the trespass notices, placed by white station owners, in the *Northern Territory News*. 'Any person found trespassing, shooting or camping on Orange Creek Station will be prosecuted. This includes the Hugh River and Rainbow Valley.' In a pamphlet reply to Everingham, a defender of the Land Rights Act as it stands wrote, 'How would Mr Everingham feel if minerals were found in his backyard and the company was happy

PAGE 189 ABOVE:
The gardener at Killarney. He comes from over the border in western Australia, and his rectangular and firm features are characteristic of the coastal tribes of the northwest who resisted the intentions of such wilderness-improvers as Captain Joe Bradshaw.

PAGE 189 BELOW:
The Simpson Desert. This 200,000-square-kilometre wilderness begins to the southeast of Alice Springs and stretches east into Queensland, southeast into a thirsty corner of South Australia.

to leave him in his house while they mined his yard? Wouldn't he demand the right to negotiate the time of entry onto his land, the compensation he should get, the places people couldn't go (e.g. into his lounge room)? So what about Aboriginal people?'

There have also been claims that the Northern Territory government has worked actively against Land Rights claims – by refusing the Northern Aboriginal Land Council access to government papers bearing on the Kenbi land claim over the Cox Peninsula, by extending town boundaries to thwart land claims, as at Borroloola near the Gulf of Carpentaria, and by holding up the land claim appeal to ownership of Bing Bong Station long enough to enable mining interests to snap up the area. And as for the disastrous effect Aboriginals' ownership of cattle land might have on the Aussie battling cattleman, and on the cattle business itself, Aboriginals point out that nearly fifty per cent of all the cattle land is owned by outsiders and foreigners, that properties owned by mineral companies are not being run as cattle stations, that some leaseholders finance their purchase of property by stripping the lease of cattle, that others ruin the land by overgrazing, and that foreign owners from the United States, Britain, Asia dip in and out of the cattle industry as it suits them, taking up and abandoning properties which then take years to restore to their former state, and to be made truly productive.

Gerry Blitner is a Groote Eylandt man and President of the Northern Land Council, which operates from offices above a furniture store in Darwin. How can there be a time limit on Land Rights claims? asks Gerry. To tribal people, the ideas of 'traditional owners', of 'Land Rights' are ones which have no meaning. 'Ownership', an idea which comes easily to Europeans and fuels our passion for real estate, is an idea alien to tribal man and woman. ('It's like trying to explain to a European why he has a right to his own elbow,' a European adviser explained.) For some tribespeople, the whole business of putting in a claim for land, of understanding what are to Aboriginals the fantastic legal fictions of our system, and then arguing in terms of them before a quasi-judicial sitting headed by a European judge assisted by lawyers and anthropologists – all that could take decades. 'With some people, you just can't bowl up and tell them they own land. They don't know what you're talking about. They only know what their country is, that their ancestors made it, that it's part of the same organism as them.'

The problem of preparing traditional owners for ownership of land in the European manner is one which Gerry Blitner's Council, the Central Land Council, the Pitjantjatjara Council and others all have to face. For example, a recent issue of the *Land Rights News* took on the question of fencing in the wild buffalo. 'Buffaloes are worth money to the Aboriginal people and they are good to eat too. But they muck up the land. They break down the banks of the river where other native animals and birds like to live. The rivers get dirty and they don't run like they used to. The birds and animals that used to live there have gone away. Some of these died too because there is no place to live now – nothing to eat. The Councils have white advisers. Richard Ledger knows about

PAGES 190–91 ABOVE:
Desert oaks in the Petermann Ranges. These remarkable trees make central Australia look more hospitable than in fact it is. Their root systems hoard the rare rainfall, and they take a century to grow twenty-five centimetres.

PAGES 190–91 BELOW:
Ghost gum stands, still immaculate on burned ground. The use of fire for hunting purposes is traditional in Aboriginal culture, and is yet another source of grievance between the Aboriginal and the cattleman.

PAGE 192 ABOVE:
The great red sand dunes of the Simpson Desert which, even in the best of seasons, show little herbiage.

PAGE 192 BELOW:
Aboriginal stockmen, according to a government report, 'the backbone of the grazing industry in the Kimberleys and Territory'. After a campaign in the mid-1960s, they won the right to pay on parity with white wages, but their success in the arbitration court was followed by evictions of Aboriginals from cattle stations and a shift to white labour.

animals and how to look after your land. He is called an Agronomist. Gary Garner knows about business and how to make these work properly. He is called a Commercial Analyst.'

A buffalo, hit by a road train, bleaches in the sun.

The *Land Rights News* is full of such instances where European ideas and tribal concepts of land sit oddly side by side. The land claim of the Roper Bar people is a further case. The claim did not come up for hearing until the wet season had started. By then, because of seasonal flooding, no one could get in to the Roper Bar area to inspect this sacred site, and so Gerry Blitner's office sent out people from the Darwin office to get video recordings of the men's secret sites. As the video camera team went off towards the men's site, the women of the clan waited in a neutral zone under an overhang of rock and did not look at that part of the film even when it was shown to the local community to the delight of the tribal men, who now felt they had a video history of their land.

Gerry Blitner himself is at home in both worlds. He is a half-caste, he is not limited – as some of the black leaders of the Centre are – to an Aranda-based station English. In a society based on ceremonial clans, however, on family groups, it was not an easy thing to be a half-caste child. But the advantage is that Gerry understands, from living in both white and black societies, what the earth means both to a European mining engineer and to an Aboriginal from eastern Arnhem Land. He is skilled at directing towards whites the *argumentum ad hominem*; 'Land

194

Roper River Aboriginal, Beswick. The conflict within such a man is best summarized by the life of the Beswick actor, Tommy Lewis, who, at the time this photograph was taken, was far away in Sydney working on a film location. Half his life is thus spent in the European technology of movies, half in the tribal context of Beswick.

Rights', he says, 'have come as a challenge to the white man to make a go of his pastoral leases. To make them viable. To make sure the land isn't eaten out, as it is now, all the lizards gone, and the only grass that's good stolen by the ants for termite mounds.' He has seen old men, returning to their land, weep for it when they see what the hard-hoofed cattle have done to it. But that is exactly the problem – proving your right to land when you don't have any sense of real estate, only a sense of blood and spirits and the dead.

Europeans tend to seek out one or two traditional owners to negotiate with when it comes to matters of land use and mining. But though one man may be leader of a ceremony sect connected with, say, a particular outcrop of ore, it does not mean he can give blanket permission without reference to others. Group unity, says Gerry, breaks down because public servants and miners tend to speak to only one traditional owner of a site, and grow impatient if he wants to speak to all the members of the ceremonial clan who preserve and cherish the site.

The European adviser to the Pitjantjatjara Council, Phillip Toyne, a lawyer from Adelaide, acted for six months for the Walpiri people in their land claim and discovered that the system by which Aboriginals attach themselves to land is far from simple. Your father's country is yours, and therefore all brothers and sisters are equally traditional owners of that. But in addition, your mother's people have country for which you are a trustee. You therefore have interest in two lots of country. Who are really the traditional owners then? Toyne asks. Is it only the traditional owner as defined by the Land Rights Act, or should it also be the mothers and mothers' children, whose duty to the river bed, hill or waterhole in question is best summed up by the European terms, 'trustees' or 'managers'. That is why, says Toyne, the belief of opponents of Land Rights that vexatious and fake claims will be made is unfounded. You cannot have false claims. If a false claim were made, the Aboriginals who did own the land in question would quickly come forward. The 'trustees' and 'managers' are almost as powerfully involved in the land question as are the 'traditional owners'. There are even tribal times and circumstances when the owner can approach the site he owns only in the company of a 'trustee'. In the concept of 'traditional owner' the European law may have found an idea that suits it better than it suits the Aboriginals themselves. Nor do all Europeans understand that the stakes are high. The man who on his own authority gives the earth away will be sung to death by the others.

European Australians – officials, miners, lawyers – are sometimes amazed when their frank offer to negotiate is greeted with silence. They shouldn't be so startled, says Toyne, for what they are really saying to the Aboriginal is, 'I'm trying to help you. All you have to do in return is to reveal your profoundest secrets.' But even when there are no secrets involved, it is naïve of the European to believe that the Aboriginal leader will call together a committee or a community and take a crisply arranged and immediately effective vote. 'We are shamed to talk about some things in front of white people,' said a community leader from Borroloola, Leo Finlay, 'sometimes we want to explain things to our people, we got to go slowly and explain things. We are shamed to do this in front of white people.'

Traditional Aboriginal communities cannot reach a decision by following an agenda and closing the meeting at a given hour. When Paul Everingham visited Ayers Rock to speak to the Pitjantjatjara there, he found the elders disorganized, and accused them 'of ginning around'. He concluded that they did not know what the issues were, that they were being 'stirred' by their white adviser, the lawyer Phillip Toyne. In fact, an hour before the arrival of the government party, Nipper Winmati's sister had died, and her death had had a severe disorientating effect on the community, as most important deaths do. Her body had been removed to the Ayers Rock clinic, so that its presence would not intrude too much on this important meeting. But when Phillip Toyne spoke for the bereaved community, Everingham accused him of manipulating the Aboriginal people and keeping information from them. A Pitjantjatjara elder, Yammi Lester, wrote later, 'Some old people at the Ayers Rock meeting were mixed up, but most of the Aboriginal people know where their freehold land is. Mr Everingham doesn't understand people's feelings in a meeting, and how to give time for others to explain to the old people. The Chief Minister has his advisers. We wonder if *they* are manipulating him to change these laws.'

Chapter 11

Tenny, a Rainbow Serpent

The Kakadu area, beneath the Arnhem Land escarpment, is the traditional country of two tribes – the Gagadju, (from whom Kakadu's name is of course taken) and the Kunwinjku. These peoples have been given freehold title to the Kakadu area, but on condition that it remains a national park. As in other areas of Arnhem Land, anyone who wants to mine there has to come to special arrangements with the tribal council, but what is most likely to change Kakadu is the pressure of white visitors to its rock-painting galleries, its superb wetlands and escarpments.

The East Alligator River (named after a nineteenth-century British survey ship, in no way a misnomer because of the saltwater crocodiles common in its streams and billabongs) flows through the Kakadu land and enters the Timor Sea through a wide estuary. In the flood plain of the river stands the most remarkable of all ancient rock-painting sites, Obiri Rock. Many of the figures at Obiri, though ceremonially restored at various stages, were first painted 20,000 years ago and would therefore seem to be much older than any of the cave paintings of the Dordogne, southwestern France or Spain. They are certainly much more sophisticated than anything Europeans were doing in those remote millennia before the melting of the glaciers. Unlike the early European sites, the figures here are portrayed in a dynamic style. There are yam figures and, in the most extensive gallery of all, a Tasmanian Tiger, now extinct on the mainland, near to extinct in Tasmania itself. The arrival of the dingo on the Australian mainland some 6000 years ago probably contributed to the extinction of the species, in fact not a tiger at all, but a small marsupial, dog-like, marked across its back with brown stripes. After the end of the last Ice Age, about 10,000 years ago, saltwater crocodiles were painted at Obiri, and the X-ray style—the representation of backbone and vitals – was used widely in depictions of fish and animals. There are X-ray paintings of multitudes of small cat fish and of the barramundi, the north's most favoured and succulent fish, a boon which came to the lucky tribes of Kakadu with the great thaw – for which they thank their ancestor spirits – and which they speared, netted and ate in quantity for millennia before the first lucky European was ever served one. As the East Alligator found its estuary – and this could have been as recently as 1000 years ago – human figures began to be portrayed in the X-ray style. Figures with animal heads appeared, and contorted female spirits. There is a spectacular lightning man done as a stick figure and

carrying a fan of magpie geese feathers. Finally there are the paintings of the first Europeans, hatted, holding pipes, lifting aloft rifles as if they were spears. Obiri, it seems, represents a painted history of the Aboriginal occupation of Kakadu, from the recent Dreaming of 20,000 years ago to the arrival of the people from outer space, the Venusians, the Martians, namely nineteenth-century man. As well as the recent disasters which arose from contact with the European way, the origins of everything are shown, the creation itself is recorded. On one of the least favoured sides of the rock complex at Obiri, at a wall subject to water action and erosion, the Rainbow Serpent, the giver of all life, arches in faint yellow ochre. Once it was a large painting, now it is but a glimpse, like the glimpse of a hump of, say, the Loch Ness monster. The serpent is showing us but one of its magic coils. Park officials have put a ridge of silicone above it to try to preserve it from water action. It is probably one of those paintings which have not been touched by Aboriginals since the first cattle and sheep men made their ill-advised attempt to farm the estuary and the Arnhem Land escarpment. It is vanishing, but it is potent.

That is the unavoidable pity of sights like Obiri. The more the whites visit and exploit them, however gently, in whatever good faith, the

A paper bark swamp in the Top End.

more the spirits depart, the less the meaning of the place. The old men who would have cherished and preserved the Serpent are dead. The present Aboriginal management of Kakadu, the Aboriginal rangers, see themselves in part as trustees for those who once knew the layered secrets of Obiri. But in the new world, as whites discover the place by such means even as this book, the chances of the revival of the rock as a centre for ceremonial become more and more remote. The Aboriginals are very genial about it, they are a compliant and forgiving race. But in terms of access, in terms of appreciation, the Venusians are as much the inheritors of the rock as are the Gagadju themselves.

Further south, at a large outcrop called Nourlangie Rock, paintings of women-spirit figures abound, also done in X-ray style, their breasts spread sideways, two-dimensionally. They are perhaps the most beautiful figures of all – they may be the Wawalag sisters, whose wanderings with their brother Djangawul created much of Arnhem Land. On the coat of arms of the Northern Territory, one such female figure is found, flanked on either side by the circle-and-line Dreaming trail maps which are one of the dominant designs of the desert tribes. Having been to awesome Nourlangie and confronted these ancient women, one cannot avoid feeling a little amused or else honestly

horrified at the way these figures are described by the College of Arms, London. 'For Arms, Tenny, representations in the Australian Aboriginal manner of an Arnhem Land rock painting of a woman with stylized internal anatomy between indexed chief and base two symbolic representations of camp sites joined by journey or path markings in the manner of the central Australian Aboriginals, and in sinister chief and base the like all Argent, and for a Crest: Upon a Wreath of the Colours a wedge tailed Eagle (aquila audax) wings elevated grasping with its talons an Australian Aboriginal stone tjurunga proper . . .' It is as if the spirit woman, the Wawalag, has been subsumed into a different sort of tribe and Dreaming, the tribe of Heralds, the Dreaming of Arms.

Nearby, at an outcrop of rock which houses an Aboriginal burial site protected by law, the women are painted in blue ochre. These are really dazzling figures, floating with bent spines across the rock face. Whenever the women are found they are often surrounded by other less definable beings – figures painted for the sake of love magic, for the sake of sorcery, as well as the fishes depicted so exquisitely not for art's sake but for the sake of propagation and fertility. And the spirit women – 'with stylized internal anatomy', as the Herald would have it – done not for art's sake but from respect for their power, their love, the cosmos they made during their travels.

This rock overhang at Obiri features spirit figures, a profusion of kangaroos and fish, and representations of the first amazing white cattlemen and their devil-horses to come into the area. While this particular overhang has probably been painted on since the development of the East Alligator Estuary, other rock surfaces at Obiri carry paintings which date from the last Ice Age.

OPPOSITE:
The Lightning Man of Obiri Rock. He carries a magpie goose feather fan such as are found among contemporary tribes in the East Alligator River area. Therefore he must have been painted only after the development of the East Alligator flood plain brought such water birds to the area.

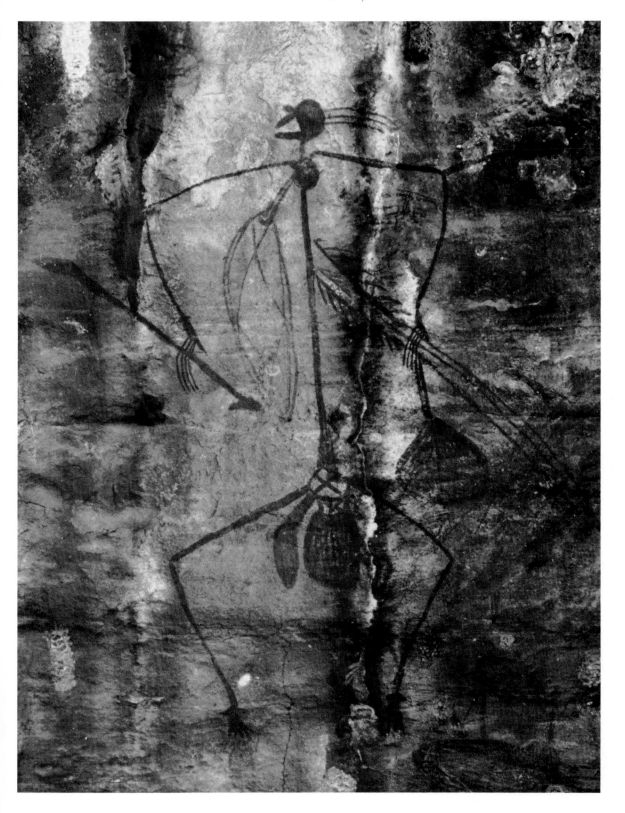

Again, above the blue paintings, someone has put a line of silicone. These too are subject to weathering and rain, as well as algae, fungi and mosses, and insect and animal damage. Against vandalism, mining leases, and the respectful touch of too many Europeans, the line of silicone offers no protection whatever.

On the walls of Nourlangie Rock, proliferating as they do in the estuary of the East Alligator River, are a barramundi, famed for its sweet flesh, a saratoga, and many small catfish.

In the Territory, whites will complain that Aboriginals are being spoiled by mineral royalty money. Whites will tell you passionate stories about Arnhem Land Aboriginals buying four-wheel-drives with royalty cash, driving them until the petrol or oil gives out and abandoning them. They will complain of 'uranium millionaires' – as they like to call some Arnhem Landers – chartering aircraft for flights to remote pubs, where mineral royalty binges are then held. It seems certain that such incidents have occurred. The defenders of royalty payments to Aboriginals point out, however, that if Elizabeth Taylor or Hugh Heffner were to charter an aircraft to go to a party, it would be considered mere panache, even though it would arise from a certain wilfulness in the white megastar rather than from – as is the case with the Aboriginals – a cultural inability to take something as literally disposable as cash with proper seriousness.

Under the Land Rights Act, mining companies which wish to extract uranium, bauxite or other minerals from Aboriginal country have to

Female spirit figures and fish at Nourlangie Rock. For centuries such paintings were retouched by tribal Aboriginals. Since these figures are no longer so maintained, experts are faced with the enormous problem of saving them from weathering, rain-water action, humidity and rock flaking.

negotiate the payment of royalties to the traditional owners. The formula is complicated in each case. For the uranium mining at Jabiru, Ranger Uranium is said by some to have arranged a royalty payment as high as 4.25 per cent of the value of the yellow cake it produces and ships away. At Jabiluka, north of Jabiru, the upfront money paid by Pan-Continental Mining is said to be $9 million, though a large part of that is a loan due to be paid back out of the enterprises the Aboriginals begin with, the capital. Many white Territorians, out of an ignorance they seem to cherish, believe that all of this money goes to the Aboriginal clans of the Jabiluka area. In fact, thirty per cent of it goes to the local tribal council and then to individual Aboriginals. Another thirty per cent goes into a trust fund for the Aboriginal communities of the Territory as a whole, and forty per cent goes to the three Land Councils – the Northern, the Central, the Tangentyere.

The Land Councils employ staffs of lawyers and European experts in all fields – public relations, agronomy, book-keeping. They support financially, in fact they sometimes initiate, Land Rights claims, and of course they administer and oversee royalty payments. The Land Councils, especially the Northern Land Council, whose sphere of influence includes the uranium mines of western Arnhem Land and the bauxite mines of Nhulunbuy on the Gove Peninsula, have attracted a great deal of hostility both from the Australian Mining Council – which

thinks they have too much power and finance concentrated in their hands – as well as from white conservationists who see mining – especially uranium mining – as a threat to mankind and who claim that tribal people do not understand what uranium mining means. A white lawyer at the Northern Land Council, Mr Grant Nieman, defends the body. 'People who say the Aboriginals don't know what is happening are being patronizing. The Aboriginals know very well what is going on. They make a conscious decision. When they agree to negotiate, they decide for the benefit of their community and their children to let part of their sacred lands die.'

In Kakadu – the wonderful parkland which includes Obiri and Nourlangie, their Rainbow Serpents, their Lightning Men, their X-ray kangaroos, their magic Wawalags – the Gagadju association was founded especially by the local tribal council to invest the mineral royalty money. 'We want to invest it, and make returns rather than buy a lot of four-wheel-drive trucks.' The Gagadju Association bought the Border Store, so named because it was on the edge of Arnhem Land near the East Alligator River. Knowing, as the posters say, that booze would destroy their culture, they let the Border Store liquor licence, held by

Uranium miner, wife and child rest in the strangely ideal surroundings of Jabiru mining township beneath the markedly radioactive escarpment of Arnhem Land.

The children of Beswick pose against the fence of the community gathering place. The white children belong to Europeans who work for the tribal council as book-keepers and rating officers.

Europeans for half a century, lapse. Southeast of Nourlangie, they bought the Cooinda pub. It is indeed a very individual pub for the north – white or black, you are permitted to drink only four cans on the premises. You can take half a dozen cans away with you. Ten cans constitutes scarcely more than a pre-dinner drink in the Territory, but again the limitation grows out of a conviction the Gagadju Association has, that booze is the greatest peril.

At the other end of Arnhem Land, where Nabalco mine bauxite and have built an ideal town on the Gove Peninsula, the Aboriginals of Yirrkala have founded Yirrkala Business Enterprises Pty. Limited, a contracting business which collects the garbage in the well-ordered streets of the European town of Nhulunbuy, maintains the pavements and the parks. There are inevitable stories of mismanagement, and Germaine Greer, visiting Gove in 1982 and noting that the bauxite deposits would be exhausted in sixty years, wondered about the future of the Yirrkala community. 'The black community may piss its gains up against the walls, as we say, watch its leadership grow corrupted and alienated and Nhulunbuy sink back into the red earth as scores of Australian settlements have done before.' In all good conscience, that is a risk which will not affect Miss Greer's welfare one whit, nor will it basically affect the welfare of any white Australian. The alternative – of not paying Aboriginals anything for the wealthy minerals taken from their holy earth – is, under any equity, unthinkable.

One of the most positive outcomes of the payment of mineral royalties has been the outstation movement. In the nineteenth and twentieth centuries, missionaries and administrators crammed people of different clans, even of different tribes, together in the one central, more easily supervised place. For only a small number of the settlement people would the ground round about be their traditional country. The outstation movement allows clan groups in Arnhem Land and family groups in the Centre to return to their traditional country. The land councils and the tribal associations provide each outstation with a vehicle, two-way radio and a generator. In the outstation the old connections with the Dreaming can be renewed. At least in part, there is

Explorers such as Charles Sturt were 200 million years out in their suspicion that Australia had a great central sea. This shield shrimp, believed to be capable of lying dormant in dry soaks for years, is a survivor of the corridor of sea and lakes which once stretched across Ordovician Australia.

a return also to the traditional diet – fish, duck, wallaby, snakes, lizards, edible tubers. Psychologically, and certainly in terms of kilometres, the clan is placed at a greater distance from the temptations of booze and welfare. The clan also feels a greater responsibility for its own land, whereas it might have felt little responsibility for 'other fellas'' land in the Yirrkala Mission. A Northern Territory public servant in Nhulunbuy says, 'When you see the difference between the outstations and the central settlements, you realize that the churches and the government went wrong at the very start.' He described an outstation he visited recently. A solar pump provided running water from the creek. There was no visible litter, no booze. An airstrip had been created by hand, after initial rudimentary work using steel bars towed behind a four-wheel-drive. The dwellings were extremely simple, most living was done out of doors. There was no television, so that Charley's Angels could not diminish the Wawalags.

Over in the Yirrkala area, outstations are supplied with water and roads at the expense of the Northern Territory government, but the latter makes appropriate deductions in what it supplies based on the amount of money earned in mineral royalties by the particular community. Much further west in Kakadu, the Gagadju Association puts its own roads and houses into the outstations and when the Northern Territory government declined to put a school in an Aboriginal settlement at Patonga, near the Jim Jim Creek in Kakadu, the Association built one themselves and employed white teachers.

Clearly the outstation movement can only be a partial return to the past. Like motherhood, it is much praised by everyone. Paul Everingham himself believes it is a very hopeful development. It gives Aboriginals a chance to maintain an economic and administrative independence they've rarely had in the past.

How much money a year from mineral royalties gets into the pockets of individual Aboriginals varies from place to place. The Gagadju Association says that the Kakadu Aboriginals are receiving as little as $500 per year each. It is certainly higher than that in other areas. In the Hermannsburg region of central Australia, an annual natural gas royalty paid to the Aranda means that most individuals receive between $3000 and $8000 each. The weekend after the royalty is paid, claim the police at Hermannsburg, much of this money will disappear. Since cash is so visibly meaningless in itself, the Aranda will go to town and buy wrecks of vehicles at four to five times their true value. They will not even have to leave Hermannsburg to be exploited. The police there recently intercepted a South Australian arriving in the area with a car trailer loaded with aged and scarcely pre-cared-for cars worth $600 to $700 which he would sell to the Aranda for $3000 and upwards. The police indicated that the new Land Rights legislation gave powers for the confiscation of his rig if he pushed on into Hermannsburg, and after some argument he departed but pulling away defiantly, shouting as he went, and what he said showed a mercenary insight into the dismissiveness with which money is held by tribal and semi-tribal people. 'I'll bloody well park somewhere legal, and the buggers'll still flock to me.'

In the Territory, the towns that look least ephemeral are the towns built by mining companies. Over on the Gove Peninsula, for example, what looks like an ideal Sydney or Californian suburb has been built in the midst of the tropical bush. There are shopping malls, parks, playing grounds. The electric cables run underground as in an ideal municipality. Residents of this town, which is called Nhulunbuy, are as proud of it as any suburbanites who have recently moved into a new and glamorous housing development. The reality is, however, that you can't really get out of Nhulunbuy except by plane. The only negotiable road on the Gove Peninsula runs between a bauxite mining and refining site through Nhulunbuy to the airport. A spur takes in the Yirrkala Aboriginal settlement. Even there there are restrictions. Europeans are not supposed to enter Yirrkala without a permit, though in practice they are allowed to visit the Aboriginal craft shop. It all adds up in any case to a small toll of repetitive kilometres in which a citizen of Nhulunbuy can move. The town administrator, who is appointed by the mining company Nabalco, admits that people do get depressed here, suffer from 'an isolation complex', especially wives. The men who work at the mine and refining site have the therapy of their long hours, of the exercise of their mining and other skills. The wife is stuck to her air-conditioned hutch, knowing always that she can't drive away to another town. Just the same, says the town administrator, the grand therapy for any such malaise is to be found in the seventy clubs and sporting associations in town. 'We have everything but snow sports here, even a speedway.' For New South Walesmen and Queenslanders, Nhulunbuy provides two brands of rugby. For natives of Victoria, South Australia, Western Australia it offers Aussie Rules, that strange version of 'forcings-back', like Gaelic football except that the ball is shaped differently, and which derived from a game played by nineteenth-century gold miners in the ore-fields of Victoria. Little Athletes train for middle distance on the road between town and the refinery. The sports store in Nhulunbuy is of a size appropriate to a town five times the population of the Gove Peninsula.

Among the 4000 people of Nhulunbuy there are sixty-eight races living together in an equilibrium that does the town credit. In the post office advice on early mailing for Christmas appears in fifteen languages, including Greek, Serbo-Croat, German, Italian, Arabic and Polish. There is occasional strife within one or other national grouping – Croats and Serbs might decide to settle old political and religious scores. There was a recent killing among the Albanians, a homicide based on dark insults between the two parties to the tragedy. Yet Nhulunbuy presents a well-ordered and even Anglo-Saxon face. Even the suburb where the private contractors live, itself called Contractors, a part of town which grew as opposed to being planned, and which therefore has a reputation for architectural anarchy, seems at least as permanent and well arranged as a Darwin suburb.

Mining engineers and technicians, together with public servants from Northern Territory and Federal departments, meet at the Arnhem Club

PAGE 209 ABOVE:
A child takes part in a corroboree performed for whites at Springvale station, one of the earliest Top End cattle spreads.

PAGE 209 BELOW:
Gary Hansen and Tom Keneally in the Olgas.

PAGES 210–11 ABOVE:
Obiri Rock, in the flood plain of the East Alligator River, is one of the most startling Old Stone Age galleries in the world.

PAGES 210–11 BELOW:
Fire at night, Kakadu.

PAGES 212–13 ABOVE:
The Devil's Marbles, the Dreamtime Eggs of the Rainbow Serpent, are six hundred and forty-three kilometres north of Alice Springs.

PAGES 212–13 BELOW:
The Devil's Marbles. It is characteristic of the sacred sites for which Aboriginal Land Rights claims are pending.

in Nhulunbuy, but the atmosphere there is egalitarian rather than exclusive and the prevalent drink is Carlton Draught rather than planter's punch or gin and tonic. A young public servant, drinking his beer there, talks with equal passion about Aboriginal outstations and about the patrolling he does along the Peninsula every weekend as an officer in a Citizen's Military Forces unit. Australia's northern coastline is of course wide open to the smuggling of heroin inwards, and of exotic tropical birds out to Indonesia, Singapore, the Philippines, and from these intermediary ports to the west coast of the United States. As well as that, Taiwanese fishing boats frequently work illegally inside the limits. The local militia patrols the area energetically. Nhulunbuy is a precious node of the Australian good life, and must therefore be protected.

The waters all around this ideal town are practically unswimmable. The sea wasp, the shark, the saltwater crocodile hold the steamy town hostage. Buffaloes come into the suburban streets at night and graze on the lawns. When I was in Nhulunbuy, there were buffalo pats on the steps of the court house, as if the local fauna had wandered into town to leave a reminder to the townspeople of their besieged condition. In spite of the orderliness of Nhulunbuy and the mineral royalties paid to the Aboriginals there is of course always a price to mining. In 1969, the tribal council and the Methodist missionaries of Yirrkala brought a court case to prevent the mining operation from starting up. At that stage there was no Land Rights Act, and the judge who heard the case, though sympathetic, said that the law of Australia did not recognize any communal native title. Justice Blackburn felt he could not therefore issue an injunction against the mining, but he stated his admiration for Aboriginal society, which he described as 'a subtle and elaborate system highly adapted to the country . . . and which provided a stable order of society and was remarkably free from the vagaries of personal whim or influence. If ever a system could be called "a government of laws and not of men", it is that shown in the evidence before me.' The bauxite strip mining proceeded. It affected the off-coast fishing, it killed off the crabs in the mangrove swamps. In *An Aboriginal Children's History of Australia*, published in 1977, we read the following: 'It was at Gove at the place called Nhulunbuy that the white man came and settled down to work. My people thought it was very bad because they came and pulled down our sacred trees that my father's father used for a hunting and dancing place . . . now it is ruined. We only got a few animals, and there are lots of beer cans and grog and it's dusty everywhere.'

But then, as a miner justly remarked, 'While-ever Western man continues to require that his beverages be served in frosted aluminium cans, he is voting for the mining of bauxite, wherever it may occur.'

When the bauxite lease on the Gove Peninsula expires in 2053, the natural life of the area will very likely reassert itself. But the same may not be possible in western Arnhem Land in the country around streams affected by seepage from the uranium mines.

The Aboriginal Northern Lands Council has always taken a different stance towards uranium mine proposals than white conservationists would have liked. It has shown a certain realism, its critics would say a certain fatalism, about its chances of preventing uranium mining, especially when the Federal government, the Northern Territory government, the miners all desire it. It has therefore concerned itself with finding out from the traditional owners what the important Dreaming sites are in a uranium area, in trying to preserve them; and has then gone on to negotiate the best deal possible for the local people. Recently, however, it has been concerned about leakage of radioactive water from the Narbalec mine at Jabiluka into Coopers Creek, and about the low level of water covering radioactive tailing in the tailings dam at Jabiru. Gerry Blitner, the chairman of the Council, is particularly worried that governments will lose interest in safeguarding such places, that radioactive waste will leak out and devastate forever the entire East Alligator River plain. 'Because of these and other problems in the western Arnhem Land area, the Northern Land Council has not been happy with the way the Northern Territory or the Commonwealth governments have been looking after the land and the things that live in it; the thing we call the environment; the thing the Aboriginal people need more than anything else.'

Uranium mining is so sensitive a matter in Australia that it was impossible to get anyone from the Ranger Mine at Jabiru or at Ranger head office to make any comment on or assuage these Aboriginal fears. Even though I assured the people at the mine site that I was seeking to present a balanced picture, I was referred to Ranger's head office, from which I was referred back to Jabiru.

Jabiru township itself is even a more orderly and ideal town than Nhulunbuy. Its shopping malls would do credit to southern California, and it does not have the same limitations as Nhulunbuy. Any day of the week you can drive out westwards on a tarred road a little over two hundred kilometres to Darwin. Again the population is polyglot and highly paid; again there is a proliferation of sporting clubs, including ten basketball teams – Minties and Mixtures, Cazalies and Rebs, Bruisers and Demons, Misfits and Jabiru Globetrotters, etc. When I was there, Jabiru had just walloped Katherine in a one-day cricket match, winning by eight wickets, thereby perhaps rubbing in the lesson that mining and not cattle is the Territory's future. In the Jabiru *Rag*, a miner's wife was advertising for a ballet teacher who might be able to take on her daughter to Grade 2/3 level. The Catholic church offered a marriage encounter weekend, and the local scout troop undertook to look after baby-sitting during the Jabiru Police Ball. 'Responsible adults will be there – there is no question about that. Some people seem to be under the misguided impression that only scouts will be looking after the children. This is definitely not so. We have hired a video and will be showing cartoons and Disney tapes to the children as well as story-telling.'

Whatever doubts the Northern Lands Council might have about tailings dams, the miners are definite that uranium mining will benefit the human race both in the East Alligator River area and in the world in general. In the men's toilet at the South Alligator pub there is a sticker, however, which says that the only trouble with uranium is that you have to wait a quarter of a million years to find out who was right.

End Note

When Malcolm Fraser's Australian Commonwealth government approached the Northern Lands Council and local Aboriginals about uranium mining both at Jabiru and – further north – at Jabiluka, it admitted that it knew that many of the traditional owners would prefer that there was no mining at all. Mining was nonetheless certain to go ahead, and in return the Aboriginals would be given their land back. But there was one further catch. The Kakadu land would have to be for ninety-nine years to come a national park.

In return for coming to terms at Jabiru, the Aboriginals would be given Stage 1 of Kakadu National Park, whose jewel is Nourlangie Rock. In return for Jabiluka they would receive Kakadu Stage 2, at the heart of which lies wondrous Obiri.

In both cases these negotiations attracted the interest of the public, the Press, of Aboriginals from other areas of Australia, of anti-uranium campaigners, of the mining industry. Accusation and rumour multiplied. Miners accused the traditional owners of dragging out the meetings, of being stubborn and evasive. Aboriginals and the anti-uranium lobby accused the miners and the Minister of Aboriginal Affairs of wilfully confusing, pressuring and lying to the traditional owners. In the middle was the Northern Land Council, drawing fire from both sides.

At the time of the negotiations over the Jabiru mine site, the Chairman of the Northern Land Council was a handsome East Arnhem Lander called Galarrwuy Yunupingu, a man of high intelligence but rudimentary English. One has to feel sympathy for Yunupingu's position at that period. The Minister and the miners subjected him to great pressure for a resolution, appealing to his patriotism as an Australian, urging him to produce a quick deal. The traditional owners, however, wanted to settle the matter at their own pace. The Minister had told them that the mining would go ahead with or without their consent. 'The question has always been for you, what are the terms and conditions under which mining can be carried out, not whether Ranger will be mined or not, because that decision was made by the Government in August last year.' But even exercising Hobson's choice, the traditional owners wished to refer back to their communities, to Oenpelli, to Goulburn Island, to Milingimbi. This desire was understandable. They did not *own* the sites – the places where mining was to take place – in their own right but on behalf of all their kin, of all the people who were connected with the Dreaming trail which passed through the country and which now – so said the Government of the nation – would be mined willy-nilly. They *had* to talk to their communities, not least to protect themselves from later vengeance for throwing a Dreaming site away.

The suggestion – originating from the Minister – that they were elected representatives and could speak for their communities without referring back seemed reasonable within European terms, but was inappropriate to the Aboriginal way. Gerry Blitner, the present Council chairman, complained at the time that, 'We as a crowd have got to decide about other people's spiritual land.' The problem now was that all negotiations were made to proceed at a brisk clip, at a European pace rather than an Aboriginal one. In the end, many traditional owners simply wandered away from the proceedings, bewildered, shocked by the speed of events.

Jabiluka was negotiated some years after Jabiru and under Gerry Blitner's chairmanship of the Northern Land Council. It was a big deal – within the next twenty-five years it was expected to yield more than 200,000 tonnes of uranium oxide worth $18 billion. Gerry Blitner was most careful not to be caught in a situation where he found himself making decisions for traditional owners. But again there was the inevitable pressure from the Federal government, from the government of the Northern Territory, from the miners; and again traditional owners stood disoriented, amazed, tragically supine – and all this despite the best efforts of the Northern Land Council.

The case of one traditional owner, who gave his dazed consent to the mining of a Dreaming site for which he had primary responsibility, is particularly but perhaps characteristically tragic. His situation was exactly that outlined above; he was the leader of a ceremonial clan centred in the spirit place the miners now, on the basis of what they genuinely believed to be reasonable negotiations, wanted to crack open. He was the truest *knower* of the place, he was the repository of all its meanings. He held it, that is, on behalf of all his clan.

Immediately upon consenting to the mining agreement his power as an elder diminished. He was avoided by his people. Two other tribal elders sang up his death. The Jabiluka negotiations had occurred in late 1981. By September 1982, he had gone blind. He did not consult any European doctor about his blindness because he believed that there could be no cure from the justifiable, the inevitable singing. At the time of writing he is wasting, his spirit bleeding away. But if its spirit place is broken up for ore, where can the spirit find rest? Perhaps there are other places in the country of his kin to which it may be able to journey. But there is no certainty of that. So it is not just that he is dying; it is that, from within his view of the earth, his soul may be lost forever. Gerry Blitner and others at the Northern Land Council know about and grieve for this man, but know also that no European recourse can help him, that in mineral royalties there are no guarantees for the spirit. The man's grandchildren may have community centres, small industries, four-wheel-drives. The man himself is in hell.

It is not an uncommon story.

Chapter 12

An Account of
a Journey...

The second time we travelled to Ayers Rock for the purposes of this book, it was with the Northern Territory policeman mentioned earlier in this work – Senior Constable Frank Morris. We travelled by way of Curtin Springs, a cattle station five hundred kilometres southwest of Alice on the dirt road to the Rock. The owners started up a road-house here twenty-seven years ago, to catch the Rock trade and as some sort of buffer against the perils of the cattle business. In the first year, they say, they had six people call in for a beer and a meal. Last year, 160,000 watered there. All the tourist buses stopped there, in that desolate country, north of the flat-topped mountain called Conner, southeast of the grand desolation of Lake Amadeus. And with the volume of people, government inspectors are also turning up, making unheard-of demands about fire safety, plumbing, trading hours, waste disposal, the provision of toilets. The family – and this is psychologically under-standable – want to run the tourist side of the station the way they have always run the cattle side, as if the frontier is still a going business, as if in this far reach of the Territory they can make their own arrangements. Bureaucracy is strangulation to them. They do not seem to see it as in any way connected with the surge of pilgrims to the Rock, of visitors to their road-house. To them it is the mark of the urban barbarian.

At the Rock, Mark Lang, who took about sixty per cent of the photo-graphs in this book, asked Toby Naninga to come out to the south side of Uluru and face the sunset for a photograph. (Most of the other photo-graphs in this book, apart from Mark's, were taken by Gary Hansen before his death in a tragic helicopter crash in July 1982, and of this remarkable and much-grieved-for Australian more will be said later.)

Mark Lang uses a Widelux camera which takes three almost simultaneous exposures, the lens sweeping around from left to right, embracing a view fifteen per cent wider than human vision. Each shot takes great preparation and rehearsal however, its composition verified by the taking of a few preparatory Polaroids. Toby Naninga passed the time by working over the desert grevillea bushes in the vicinity, sucking the nectar from their cone-like blossoms. In Yankuntjatjara, he said, the grevillea is called *galling-galling-pa*, in Pitjantjatjara *galling-galling*, a great similarity of sound. That's because the Pitjantjatjara and Yankunt-jatjara are cousins, said Toby.

As well as sucking grevillea with venerable Toby, we also paid respects to Nipper Winmati, the Pitjantjatjara elder and one of the

Rock's traditional owners. He is an old man afflicted with glaucoma, but it was he who organized the search teams on the night of Azaria Chamberlain's disappearance. He still believes the dingo took the baby. 'That woman's not guilty,' he kept saying, seeming to look – as blind people sometimes do – at some more distant and evasive focus of truth than the sighted can quite manage. We asked him if he was going to Darwin to give evidence. No, he said, he never flew. The judge was going to come to him, he said. In fact the judge, the accused Chamberlains, the prosecutor and defendants' council as well as the jury and a tail of press did visit the scene of the child's disappearance and, in the course of the visit, took evidence from Nipper.

Nipper's belief that the dingo killed the Chamberlain infant is not the only source of controversy over the old man. Some of the local whites find fault with Nipper's elegant house. There will be five such houses built for community leaders at the Rock; they are excellently designed by an Alice Springs architect. 'Except when it rains,' a man in one of the Ayers Rock bars complained, 'Nipper uses the place as a bloody cupboard.' A Territory bar has the sort of atmosphere which produces rich aphorisms often based on energetically embraced misinformation. In fact the elders' houses at Ayers Rock are meant to serve not for one man and his wife but for an entire 'family' in the extended, desert sense; that is, for what anthropologists call an entire descent group. If Nipper's place is in any way a cupboard, a rain shelter, it is the cupboard and rain shelter of an entire tribal grouping, and this makes the skill and expense which went into its design absolutely reasonable. The building of such houses is in any case funded in part by mineral royalty and other such payments due to Aboriginal groups.

More rational critics of the Nipper-style house point to the problems associated with the death of important men and women. If the death of a prominent Aboriginal occurs – and may it be many many years yet before this applies to Nipper! – his dwelling place is traditionally burned, and the entire camp moves away. Aboriginals will in fact move entire settlements at the death of an important man or woman. At Warakurna, over the Western Australia–Northern Territory border, the death of an elder caused the entire population to move a kilometre south of the original site. The settlement store and other fixed facilities, placed in relation to the original settlement, are now isolated. To build such permanent structures as these, say the critics, is to fly in the face of the realities of Aboriginal bereavement.

Whatever the truth of all this is, Europeans who expect Aboriginal elders – on being given houses – to treat them like proud suburban householders are bound to be disappointed. The Aboriginal cosmos is full of cyclically replenished items – tools and weapons, animals and plants. Even though Aboriginal painting has become inevitably for whites a matter of aesthetics, their art is not intended for show-casing, and neither is their housing.

To go westward beyond Mount Olga, into the Petermann Ranges Aboriginal Reserve, you require permits from the Central Lands

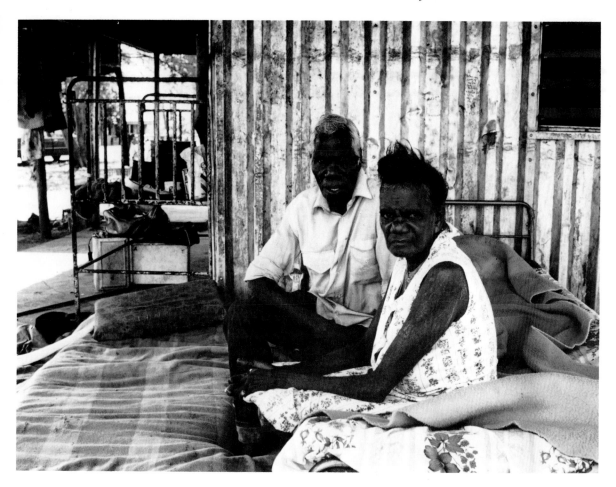

Husband and wife, Beswick. Wide verandahs surround one small room, and therefore the design of this house has some connection with the realities of traditional life.

Council in Alice Springs. The Council gets clearance by speaking to Docker River, the main Petermann settlement, by radio telephone. The clearance given to travellers generally covers only through-travel on the main east–west track. Mark and I had such permits, Frank Morris – being a policeman – didn't need one.

The track into the Petermanns is red dirt, and was made by an engineer called Cartwright by dragging a grading device behind a truck. In rain it is unnegotiable, but the rest of the time it is maintained by a grading machine driven by one of those hermit-graders you meet in the outback, men who, season in and season out, work up and down the same stretch of track and who make do for company out of the conversations of passing travellers and the occasional generosity of Aboriginal women. Their lives are not much different from those led in the early twentieth century by Overland Telegraph linemen.

The grader cuts a road even across the dry beds of the series of creeks and rivers running north–south along Cartwright's track. Scattered along these water courses are Pitjantjatjara outstations, in each of which a patriarch and his family live. At Puta Puta outstation, for example, live an old man, his wife, three sons and their wives, and a number of children. The outstation itself is an expression of a race caught between the Dreaming and technology. Among the wurleys of the families, a four-wheel-drive – *Puta Puta* painted on its side – stands ready for use in hunting or in emergencies. On a nearby pole, a solar panel activates a two-way radio, for use once more in an emergency. A bore has been sunk and a large water tank sits above the tiny arrangement of wurleys. But this is the family's country. Apart from the spiritual irrelevance of water tank and parabolic solar panel, this is the focus of the Dreaming, the earth provided by the Puta Puta ancestors.

Further along the track, in the shade of fine gum trees in the bed of a dry river called the Hull, another patriarch, Harry Bigfoot, sits waiting on the off-chance for a passing traveller. He has tools and weapons for sale – spears, woomeras (which are used to project spears), digging sticks. Harry's name derives from the large artificial foot, circular, made of leather and wood, which he has worn ever since he lost his real foot because of a bone disease. His outstation is off to the north of the Hull, though for reasons which only Harry and his family could explain – reasons to do with death and sorcery – it has been moved away from its supportive water tank. Not so far, however, that the water tank cannot be visited.

There is no denying that visits by Europeans to outstations are a form of intrusion. I must point out therefore that we always sought permission, that Frank Morris went to pains to explain our purpose in being in the Territory, in travelling to Docker River. I am sure that the idea of someone wanting to write a book was no big matter to the Pitjantjatjara. Perhaps Harry Bigfoot and others *did* think it politic to co-operate with the crazy white visitors and with the policeman, but they seemed in no way awed by Frank, there was little of the timidity that is invariably shown towards people and officials they do not already know and trust. We listened to discussion, back-chat and joking, both in Pitjantjatjara and in variable English.

Historically, the Northern Territory police were considered a glamour outfit, rather like the Mounties. In reality, some of its earlier representatives were guilty of massacres which would have done more credit to the SS than to any civilized law enforcement group. These days it demands of its members a wisdom and maturity, a knowledge of both European and Aboriginal cultures, inevitably quite rare among young policemen. Hence there has lately been a large turnover in the force. Like all frontier institutions, it traditionally preferred to cut corners in evidence-gathering, in fitting the crime to the culprit, in presenting the case for trial. Under pressure of modern scrutiny, under pressure of the Aboriginal Legal Aid Service, it has had to become more sophisticated. It is now almost two police forces – the city style force which works in Darwin and Alice, the frontier police force which operates in remote stations. The remote stations of the Centre are now under the supervision of a disarming and literate Irishman, Chief Inspector Michael Gilroy. 'You can't put wallopers out in those remote places these days,' he says. 'They've got to be blokes with a bit of nous and the wisdom of Solomon. If they try to come the heavy too much, they find themselves outnumbered a thousand to one. They can end up with a star-picket through the chest.' In violent settlements like Papunya there is enormous stress at the point of contact between the police and the Aboriginals, especially now that the authority of the elders is starting to decline. Gilroy sees this decline in elder authority as one of the greatest problems his people have to face. 'We've had guys go crazy out there, barricade themselves in the police station. . . .'

When we asked him about travelling on a desert patrol, he said he would match us up with one of the very best, a man called Frank Morris. Frank Morris, he said, consistently evaded promotion because – until 1982 – if you reached the rank of sergeant you had to move into the big towns, and Frank Morris never wanted to serve in there.

Mark Lang and I came to share Gilroy's esteem for Frank Morris. He seems to know every Aboriginal from Ayers Rock west. What is most impressive is the time he will spend talking to people, and this patience and good sense would be demonstrated later in an event which occurred at Docker River. Mark Lang and myself, like most city back-patio liberals ever-watchful for signs of white aggression, were impressed by Morris's unfeigned style. He is tough, he has no doubts about the superiority of Western culture. But he respects and understands the tribal world-view. He understands too, as the old-style policemen perhaps never did, that tribal law is separate, and it is often fruitless for a European peace officer to intrude. He says that once at Yuendumu he stopped a *sorry* ceremony, an exchange of wounds following the death of a prominent tribesman. He explains his motives in a way that would be quite alien to the Territory policeman of the old days. 'It was happening in the creek, just down from the police station. The other copper and I didn't know what in the hell to do. But in the end we decided you can't stand by and watch people assault each other with deadly weapons. We drove between the two lines of combatants and copped half a dozen spears in the back of the Land-Rover for our trouble.' On the other hand, on the Western Australia border, he introduced us to a *kaditja* man who – he said dispassionately – was one of the best in the business. The *kaditja* man is the tribal executioner, who operates on the instructions of the elders. When he travels through the country exacting punishment for wrong-doing – the violation of marriage laws, the utterance of forbidden words and other capital matters – he is replete with spirit power. In European terms he is a murderer, in Aboriginal terms even more than an honourable executioner, a divine instrument. The police have to be philosophic about some killings by *kaditjas* – generally they are quite unprovable in terms of the European law and there is no hope of getting witnesses to come forward. The *kaditja* men have become even more adept under the pressure of the European law. It is believed, for example, that the incineration of an Aboriginal actor on a vacant lot in Darwin was the work of *kaditja* men, though the cause of the fire could not be proven and the victim's blood alcohol level was so high that he could not have roused himself in time to escape even an accidental blaze. Occasionally those who have uttered prohibited words of such seriousness that they must die are pushed off the back of speeding four-wheel-drive vehicles. This too is unprovable. 'He just jumped, Your Honour.' All the available witnesses will testify to the fact that he just jumped.

The police are helpless. The removal of one *kaditja* man will only cause the appointment of another. Frank Morris asked the man we met on the Western Australia border if he would show us his *kaditja* shoes. These are made of eagle feathers and grass, the feathers of course symbolizing magical speed. They are oval in shape, so that the Aboriginal who sees and is galvanized by the footprints of the *kaditja* man cannot tell which way he is going, only that a magical and ubiquitous threat to the wrong-doer has arrived in the locality. The *kaditja* man we encountered understandably pretended not to know what Frank was talking about when the shoes were mentioned. 'OK,' said Frank Morris, the incarnation of European law. 'I just thought these blokes would like to see them, that's all.'

In a sandstone cave by the banks of the Hull, the gold-seeker Lasseter sheltered for twenty-five days at the height of the summer of 1931. Harry Bigfoot was a boy then, but he remembers Lasseter diminishing in that cave.

Harry Bigfoot sits in the dry bed of the Hume River. Head of a small patrilineal group living on its own outstation, in his boyhood he watched Lasseter, fevered and sung by sorcerers, wither to a shadow of a man in a nearby cave.

There is an obsessiveness in the Lasseter story which lifts it above the status of a mere grab for gold. One day in 1908 an Afghan camel driver travelling near the edges of the Gibson Desert discovered the young Lasseter horseless, delirious and clutching a bag of ore samples. He had been looking for rubies in the MacDonnell Ranges, had got lost, had encountered a great reef of gold. Three years after his rescue by the Afghan, Lasseter went out again with Surveyor Harding of the Western Australian government and relocated the reef. But when they returned to Carnarvon, they discovered that their watches were out and that all their bearings were incorrect. Other expeditions attempted to find the reef, but ran into trouble with thirst and Aboriginals. At the beginning of the Depression, the middle-aged Lasseter came to Sydney and spoke to a number of businessmen and even some union officials about his reef. After some investigation of his claims, a Central Australian Gold Exploration Company Limited was founded to devote itself to a final search for the reef.

It is obvious that in those harsh times the idea of a great reef in which the gold nuggets stood out like plums in a pudding was one to which governments and companies took with enthusiasm. Stores and oil were supplied free of charge, government railways transported the expeditionary supplies. The Thornycroft Company donated an enormous truck, and an aircraft was bought with subscribed money.

All the fancy equipment and all the personnel provided in the end came down to this: by December 1930, Lasseter was travelling alone with two camels towards his gold reef. In support of the expedition two planes had crashed, the truck had been bedevilled with mechanical failures, and – without any good reason – Lasseter had become suspicious of the intentions of other expeditionary members, had brawled with Paul Johns, a young dingo shooter and bushman who was to have gone with Lasseter on the final push to the reef. At the end, it seemed, Lasseter was unwilling to share that final sight with any other human being.

And it seems that all alone he did find the gold. The fragments of diary and letters found in Lasseter's cave much later make frequent and garbled reference to it. In letters to his wife, he kept insisting that he had found the reef, and gave details of it.

> Darling I've pegged the reef and marked the exact locality on the map which is buried in my kit on the sandhill where the camels bolted – on the East side . . . of hill and I photographed the datum peg dated 23rd December . . . can't understand . . . relief . . . 28 acre . . . 5 pegs to a block and 8 trenches . . .

A more coherent letter is written on a crumpled strip of paper.

> Rene Darling,
> Don't grieve for me. I've done my best and have pegged the reef, not strictly according to law as the blacks pinched my miner's right and I don't know the number but I photographed the datum post on the Quartz Blow the post is sticking in a waterhole and the photo

The ancient and eroded ridges of the MacDonnell Ranges were named by the explorer Charles Sturt for a fellow Scotsman who happened to be governor of South Australia.

faces north. I made the run in five days but the blacks have a sacred place nearby and will pull the peg up for sure.

I've taken the films and will plant them at Winter's Glen if I can get there the Blight has got me beat.

Take good care of Bobby, Betty, and Joy please, I want Bobby to be a Civil Engineer try and educate him for that.

Darling I do love you so I'm sorry I can't be with you at the last but God's will be done.

Yours ever,
Harry xxxxx

One or two nights after locating the reef, Lasseter's two camels ran away, taking his supplies of water with them. Exactly what happened during his wanderings with the desert Pitjantjatjara, and during his twenty-five days in the cave, is uncertain. He was certainly *sung* by some of the elders, but he scarcely needed sorcery to confirm his desperate position. He hoped he might be able to make it to the Olgas, where an expeditionary depot had earlier been set up. On the long walk he would be dependent on the skills and goodwill of the Aboriginals to find him water, since with his failing health he could manage to carry only 1.7 litres himself. According to local Aboriginal oral history, he did find an

In the MacDonnells. Here, 200 million years ago, the inland sea which the explorer Sturt posited did, in fact, rise.

Aboriginal group to help him even though he was under a curse. He made fifty-five kilometres before collapsing and dying in the spot where later the bushman Bob Buck would find his remains.

It is still supposed to be there, this reef of great nuggets. But if it does exist the mineral boom of the early 1970s, the extensive reconnaissance of central and Western Australia by geologists anxious for a sight of anything geologically promising on which to float a company, failed to discover it.

In a tower of dust beyond Hull River we encountered and overtook a road train. As we drifted by it through a gritty red cloud, we could see the inscription *Big Ernie* on its engine cowl. Once past it, we stopped. It stopped. It was of course someone Frank Morris knew. Perry Morey, a truckie from Alice, was carrying supplies to the Giles weather station across the Western Australia border. Perry speaks gently, after much thought, in a well-modulated and articulate voice. 'Think he was a bloody Q.C.,' Frank Morris says of him in admiration. His rig is called *Big Ernie* in honour of Ernest Giles the explorer, whose two-volume account of expeditions in the Centre, *Australia Twice Traversed*, Perry can discuss endlessly.

The view from the cave where, in 1931, Lewis Lasseter sheltered for twenty-five days before setting out with 1.7 litres of water to try to walk one hundred and forty kilometres to Mount Olga, where he hoped to meet up with his relief party. Assisted by an Aboriginal family, he made the Pottoyu Hills, fifty-five kilometres away, before dying on 28 January 1931.

I travelled with Perry Morey for a time in the high cabin of his road train in the beautiful country west of the Petermanns, country resembling parkland, desert oaks growing beside the track, so tough, so canny with water and – although they take a century to grow thirty centimetres – so tall. They make the country look more forgiving than it is. And Perry expatiated on how in 1874 Giles, returning from the Gibson Desert, having lost the Cockney Gibson – 'That Gibson must have been an awful bushman,' Perry Morey said – followed the line of the mountains to our north, since that was the only way he could find water. 'All this country was far worse in the 1870s,' says Perry Morey. 'It had been dry times then. Last eight seasons have been good in the Centre. It's never looked better.'

Those mountains Giles stuck to, the north of the track we were following, he called the Schwerin Mural Crescent. Two weeks before he encountered them, in the Gibson Desert, his tongue had bloated in his mouth to the size of a frog and now the hellish memory of thirst filled all his sleep; yet the country still delighted him and he remembered all the remote royal patrons of geography. 'The crescent-shaped and wall-like range running from the Weld Pass to Gill's Pinnacle, and beyond it, I named the Schwerin Mural Crescent; and the pass through it I named Vladimar Pass, in honour of Prince Vladimar, son of the Emperor of Russia, married to the Princess of Schwerin.' And he quoted Bunyan. 'Methinks I am as well in this valley as I've been anywhere else in all our journeys; the place methinks suits with my spirit.'

'What a man!' says Perry Morey. 'Beside him, Gosse was just an interloper.'

On his way to Giles, Perry has to cross the dry beds of a number of rivers and creeks – the Hull, the Docker, the Rebecca, Giles Creek. In some of these crossings he will – as a matter of course – bog in the sand. When that happens, he lets the pressure on all his tyres right down, the pressure on the tyres of the dog trailers he is hauling right down too, as low as two hundred and eighty grammes per square centimetre, practically flat even by the standards of a family sedan. So, on the thin layer of air still inside the rubber, he drives *Big Ernie* out, reinflating again on the far bank, hoping for an easier crossing at the next creek.

At one stage, beyond the Western Australia border, an Aboriginal family appeared out of the bush. They wanted motor oil. The Holden they'd bought in Alice had broken down. Perry gave them the oil; the wife had five dollars in her hand. He waved it aside. Another curious thing; they didn't want to try the oil in the engine of their red Holden first, to see if that worked, and if it didn't fetch a ride to Warakurna, their settlement near Giles weather station. They could live out here indefinitely, the mother, the father, the two kids. A broken-down car is an emergency to a European. It is an outrageous hiatus in the maternal care which we believe technology should extend towards us. Mechanical failure orphans us. We look bewildered and outraged as we open the bonnet and peer at the treacherous mechanisms. These people clearly had no such feelings towards the red jalopy they had so unwisely bought in Alice and which now sat mutely by their camp-site in the bush.

At the end of Cartwright's road, where it meets a track gouged by the famed road-maker Len Beadell, Perry stopped again, this time so that we could share a hefty belt of overproof rum softened down with tepid water. Len Beadell's road marker stood there, and once again, like the presence of D. D. Smith in Alice, it proves how close the frontier is. It states the latitude and longitude at which it stands, based on star observations taken on a night in March 1960. It says that Giles is eighteen miles north in one direction, that in the other Kulgara is three hundred and ninety-two miles. On the north road through Giles, it tells us, it is two hundred and thirty-four miles to the Sandy Blight junction and sign.

The Sandy Blight road is an evil track, one of the worst in Australia, weaving north between Lakes Hopkins and MacDonald. On it in 1978 some Aboriginals led Frank Morris to a four-wheel-drive vehicle whose owner had perished inside and been mummified by the sun. Frank had had the job of taking the poor boy's remains back to Alice – the body was that of a young Canadian who had tried the Sandy Blight without letting anyone know where he was going. Clogged with spinifex grass seed, the radiator on his truck had kept boiling, and he had used on it the water he had intended for himself. Understandably enough he had then decided to commit suicide rather than face a frightful death by thirst. He shot himself in the chest, and so died of loss of blood. The finding of the body and the task of conveying it back to Alice had made such an impression on Frank that he went to the trouble of telling Mark and myself how to clear a radiator of spinifex seed. Instead of continuing to feed the thirsty radiator, you fill it once, take off the radiator grille and clear all surplus grass away. Then you start the motor again and get it running at 2000 revs. You saturate a rag in petrol, set it alight and let it fall down the face of the radiator. When the rag burns out, you let the radiator cool. Then you repeat the process until the radiator is again running cool. That is how you proceed when your radiator is taking your life's water.

Late one superb afternoon we got to Docker River settlement. It is a strong Pitjantjatjara centre, though Pintubi live there too. There is a store, a craft centre, a straggle of Pintubi wurleys, some trailers in which the business of the tribal council is carried on. There is a brick clinic, some European-style brick residences for the government nurse, the arts adviser. When one says that Docker River is a centre, it is to an extent just that, since many of the Docker River people live in outstations some kilometres out. It is wonderful country and the light – especially in early morning and late afternoon – has an exhilarating clarity.

From one of the trailers, Roxy Music was playing, as if Docker River were just an extension of a European town, of Alice, for example. We went looking for the president of the tribal council but couldn't find him. That, by the way, is one of the aspects of white behaviour that most seems to bemuse Aboriginals: our expectation that people are findable at any time of the day; the energies we devote to making sure that our comings in and goings out are fully known to friends and colleagues, an

A Pitjantjatjara woman working in the craft centre at Docker River. Such women have declared their influence in tribal society by founding the Pitjantjatjara Women's Council.

urge that reaches its culmination of course in the bleeper. In any case, as we did not know where the president of the tribal council was and as Frank said he was a friend and had been given blanket permission to go anywhere within reason, we travelled through Livingstone Pass into the Kik-in-gura area, and watched the last light go in that magnificent open valley so like a parkland that Giles called it Livingstone Park. We did not during our visit through the Pass approach any burial places or sacred sites.

The next morning when the white community adviser got back from Docker River after doing business in Alice, he came to us where we were parked near the clinic and said that he was distressed to hear that we had gone through the Pass without first speaking to the president of the tribal council and getting his permission. Frank said he had often spoken to the president, and had blanket approval to take friends through Livingstone Pass, that we had Land Council permits anyhow, and that he himself in any case, quite apart from the normal courtesies that existed between the president and himself, needed no permit since police were permitted to travel in tribal land according to their discretion. It has to be said that the president, standing on the edge of the rising dispute between Frank and the community adviser, did not seem much aggrieved. It was true that we'd talked to him earlier in the morning, that he had seemed to speak freely and without any apparent grievance and that he had made no mention of being upset about our going through Livingstone Pass. But of course that was not for us to judge. There could have been some inhibition holding him back. And it was, after all, *his* country, not ours, not Frank's, not the community adviser's. Therefore we apologized to the president as also to the community adviser, and assured them both that we had not lightly and deliberately decided to breach the normal rules and that we would of course be more careful in future. We were both becoming increasingly aware that despite the blare of Roxy Music from the trailer, the landscape retained its ancient importance here.

Our embarrassed apologies did not resolve the matter between Frank and the community adviser, and we became aware that this present argument was based on something that had happened the previous May. There had been rain then and the Docker and Hull had both flooded. The community adviser had believed that a state of emergency existed and had called on the emergency services to make food drops by helicopter to outstations cut off by flood water. Frank Morris had been involved in the food drop, and it was his opinion, from what he had seen of conditions in the outstations, that the people there were perfectly set up for sitting out the flood waters, that they had had thousands of years' experience at this sort of thing and that the expense of drops of supplies had therefore been quite unnecessary. Frank had said so in his official report. Whether he was right, or whether the community adviser had done the right thing in calling in the emergency services, was something certainly beyond our competence to decide, but the dispute over our going into Kik-in-gura seemed at least in part therefore another round in a debate fascinating to the outsider if painful to the two honest men

The community president, Beswick (right), and friend. The community president is elected and holds a position equivalent to that of mayor. He is not always the traditional owner or the most powerful elder, but is nonetheless a man respected by the various clan groups.

involved. One felt that this was not the last time that a pretext would be seized on to raise old grievances. The community adviser spoke of Frank's 'normal bombastic ways', ways with which we ourselves were certainly not familiar from having travelled with him. Frank hurled a few similar accusations at the community adviser. Mark and I went on making our speeches and saying that if the tribal president was upset, then we were both extremely sorry. Only the tribal president was silent through all this. Perhaps that says something about the two races.

A West Country woman called Pat Kemp is the government nurse at Docker River. Her clinic is a three-bed hospital. There is an operating room in case women choose to have their babies in the Western manner, and in case the Flying Doctor, arriving to collect a case, believes he must operate on the spot. The most common complaints she treats are mild malnutrition in children, runny ears, incipient glaucoma. Recently, she called in the Flying Doctor for a child bitten by a western brown snake, and although the Flying Doctor broke down on the Docker River strip, the child recovered through a dosage of antihistamines. She is aware that there is an alternative medicine of the type described earlier in this book. She is aware of the animist world, the world of spirits in which the Docker River Aboriginals subsist. On a bookshelf which includes photographs of her parents' green and leafy home in Dorset sits a series of photographic albums depicting her life at Docker River. Frequently, following the death of an Aboriginal, people enter her flat while she is at the clinic and remove any photographs of the deceased. Even on the night she was leafing through the albums in our presence she came across blank spaces which she had never noticed before. A photograph is exactly the sort of object on which a confused spirit might seize, on which it might depend to give itself substance, to which it might cling as a pretext for staying on in the settlement and not returning to its spirit place.

You would think that a life in Docker River, among all these mysteries, would be a lonely one. Even among the Europeans, Pat Kemp stands a little apart. The others are more 'ideological' than she is, she says. But the life is obviously an addictive one. She does not see any future for herself beyond that of working as a government health sister in remote settlements.

In the small flat next door to Pat Kemp lives a white artistic adviser to the Pitjantjatjara women. Her name is Kathie Walters, and she has introduced the women to the technique of batik. She in no sense teaches them design – she says they have no need of that, since with these women design is a matter of instinct and comes naturally. She says there is a great difference between working with Pitjantjatjara women and working with white women in the cities.

When you ask whites to go and tear cloth on which to make a design, they begin by tearing a small square. They are intimidated, that is, by the blankness of cloth. Yet though the technique of batik was until recently entirely unknown to the Pitjantjatjara women, they tear away great swathes of fabric. They are confident of the symbols they have, of the symbols they will apply to the white space. For that reason batik has become a popular art form among Aboriginal women both in the Top End and the Centre, and a few metres of good batik will sell for hundreds of dollars. The Docker River batik enterprise is still in its developmental stage, and although the technical quality of the work is variable, the competence and design skill is richly apparent. The women sell their work to the occasional traveller, but hope that soon they will be shipping large quantities of it to Aboriginal craft shops in Alice or the major southern cities.

In this distant reach of the Territory, you encounter in unexpected quantity abandoned cars, some doorless, some wheel-less, some tipped on their hoods, some standing on their sides. Even at Warakurna in Western Australia, a settlement which has voted not to have European-style housing, there is a sizeable automobile dump. The wrecks stand as testimony to the fact that smart dealers in town are always willing to rip off the Aboriginal purchaser, and also signal the relaxed attitudes of tribal Aboriginals towards money and possessions. Aboriginals who break down on the road between Alice and their settlement will – if they suspect the problem has to do with the manifold, the universal tail shaft, the exhaust – roll the vehicle on its side and work on it standing up. Such a method can of course cause acid to spill from the battery, further complicating the already weak mechanics of the vehicle they have been sold. At Warakurna we saw the red Holden, whose owners had earlier asked Perry Morey for oil, join the settlement's detritus. A dozen Aboriginal males were pushing it, trying to give it a jump start. Aboriginal kids sat on the bonnet and leaned out of the broken windscreen, waving at those who were putting so much muscle into a futile cause. At last the young family who were the registered owners under the white law walked away from it, as did the pushers, as did everyone. At least it means that the Dreaming can still be rather dismissive of General Motors.

But the cars lying abandoned around settlements contribute to a totally unexpected social disorder, the prevalence of petrol sniffing by Aboriginal children. Everyone in the Territory is worried about petrol sniffing – the elders, the community advisers, the police. One day in 1979 an eleven-year-old boy at Docker River climbed into an abandoned car with a large peach tin full of petrol he'd syphoned off from the tank of the wreck. Inhaling the stuff he passed out, his nose and mouth jammed into the mouth of the can. Frank had had the task of placing this child's body in a green plastic bag and driving it into Alice for a post mortem. One morning, by accident the morning the community adviser returned to Docker River, a number of children in the area were found wandering dazed and with dilated pupils. In the absence of the community adviser, the council appealed to Frank. The council president, Frank, and an Aboriginal police aide wearing a U.S. airforce sergeant's shirt, drove off in four-wheel-drives to collect the spaced-out children. A council meeting was instantly called. It did not immediately gather. Gathering is a gradual business. People at outstations have to have a chance to get in. People wandered in and out of the clearing in which the meeting was to be held, they talked with each other and laughed, but in a manner as if they were waiting for some communal decision to coalesce and begin the meeting.

Among those who turned up was a tribalized white called Salty, a refugee from the suburb of Northcote in Melbourne. He was not feeling well, he said. He had followed a rock wallaby all day the day before, had shot it, and had carried it back to his outstation. He said that it had really buggered him, carrying the thing all that way. He was certainly pale and shaking. He didn't like rock wallaby anyhow, he claimed. Kangaroo was juicier and softer. In any case the hunter didn't get the best cuts, only

Constable Frank Morris discusses a petrol-sniffing incident with the tribal council at Docker River. It is no use sending the guilty children to a home in Alice Springs, says Morris. The problem has to be solved at Docker River itself. He suggests the culprits be hit on the

the head and shoulders. The man who did the cooking got the tail. Various of his wife's relatives got the rest. All were provided for in the cutting up of a kangaroo. It was always done the same way. One day Salty's sons or even sons-in-law would hunt for him, and he would receive with honour the best cuts.

Salty had originally been a bikie from Melbourne. He had come up here to the Territory and married an Aboriginal girl, later divorcing her. Then he had moved to Docker River and married his present wife. He'd been through initiation, but all he would say about it was that it was very tough, that it went on for weeks and 'took a lot out of you', that there were tests on your body and tests on your soul. 'You wouldn't believe how tough. I didn't know just what I was letting myself in for.'

His name had once been Johnny, an innocuous European name, but when a prominent man of the same name died, both his Aboriginal name and European soubriqet became equally *kuminata*, forbidden to be uttered, in case the spirit, hearing the name, answered to it. While I spoke to Salty, the young petrol sniffers sat in a group, apparently shame-faced, certainly exhausted, demoralized, washed-out.

At last it seemed that everyone was in place. Most of the conversation was in Pitjantjatjara, but with Frank saying in English that petrol sniffing was a problem at Docker River, that had to be solved there. It couldn't be solved in Alice Springs and it couldn't be solved by him. The elders had to do something about it there. He urged that a European-style punishment be inflicted. The elders should appoint someone to hit each petrol sniffer – not hard, Frank kept saying, but definitely, on the backside. This suggestion kept on being politely evaded. The assistant community adviser, who spoke Pitjantjatjara and who had been translating from English, said that the problem was who would do the hitting. For in a society where relationships are so complicated, where degrees of relationship are so formalized, where some contacts are prohibited and where there is always retribution for physical assault, the public slapping of a delinquent is not a simple process. The Pitjantjatjara police aide, brought in from beyond the South Australian border to work at Docker River precisely because he was not closely related to anyone there, was also wary of Frank's suggestion. Frank could sense this and so gave up pushing his proposal. What happened in the end, after some hours of discussion, was that the petrol sniffers were brought into the centre of the meeting. The elders spoke to them, brandishing at them the hose piping the children had used the evening before to syphon the fuel. The elders brought the tubing hard down on the palms of their own hands to show what would happen – next time – to children who went sniffing. To a Western eye, it has to be said, their manner seemed more whimsical than firmly disciplinary. The police aide brought out his handcuffs, shaking them, and made a long speech to the children. The children hung their heads. The meeting ended with Frank urging the elders again with the idea that they had to deal with this business in their own community, that petrol sniffing could stop a kid's heart dead. That there had to be firm action, and only they could take it. The elders listened with patience, but everyone there seemed to know that the

backside, more to shame them than to hurt them. But even such light punishment is hard to arrange in a society traditionally gentle with children and riven with family and tribal grievances.

An alternative is the showing of such instruments of the European law as handcuffs.

business of the day had not been truly resolved, that the possibilities were horrifying, that there would be other outbreaks once the shame of the morning's public event passed, and that for complex reasons – cultural, social, historical – most parties to the tragedy were powerless.

At Giles weather station, they had run out of beer, and so Perry Morey's arrival, hauling a container-load of supplies, was very welcome to the four weather officers, the mechanic, the cook, who occupied the meteorological station on its desolate ridge on the edge of the Gibson Desert. The heartiness of the greeting of Perry Morey is an echo of the feverish welcome which must have been extended, up into modern times, to the yearly camel trains. The weather station is a straggle of tin huts which look as dominated by the absolute landscape as does an Antarctic base. In fact, most of the men who serve here have done stints in Antarctica. In Giles it is an ideally uncomplicated and, in its way, monastic life. Every morning the boys mix up their own hydrogen and send up a weather balloon, tracking it with radar during the day, monitoring the data it sends back. The day is passed in radar shifts.

The police aide shows handcuffs to the young petrol-sniffers. The aide has been employed by the community, and comes from South Australia. He is less likely to be constrained by family and tribal prohibitions than a local man would be. The decision about what to do with the petrol-sniffers took three hours, much debate between community leaders, elders, policeman and European community adviser.

Evenings are spent in the bar-dining room dedicated to Ernest Giles.

Robyn Davidson spent some time at Giles preparing for the most dangerous part of her 1977 camel journey from Alice Springs to the Indian Ocean. She travelled with four camels and a dog and her journey was as much an exploration of the Gibson, as an exploration of herself. She was therefore in a solitary mood when she came here, and took some offence at the gaucheries of male society at Giles.

Not far from the weather station is the Aboriginal settlement of Warakurna. 'These are very traditional people,' said Frank Morris, 'very traditional.' 'They are of course in limbo,' said their community adviser, Ron Sanden. A girl sitting outside the community store

The bar of the weather station at Giles in Western Australia. Here the name of Ernest Giles is much respected and honoured by toasts. From Giles, Robyn Davidson set out on her remarkable camel journey across the Gibson Desert, the trek is commemorated in the book *Tracks*.

encapsulated limbo. She chewed *pituri* and picked up Dolly Parton, transmitted from a radio station in Laverton, on her transistor radio. Landscape was nonetheless a very important matter in Warakurna as it had been in Docker River. Before photographs were taken, Frank got the permission of Ivan Shepard, the president of the tribal council. It was said that Ivan had gone through his initiation very well, as through the subsequent processes by which a man increases in knowledge and power. Every photograph taken was negotiated with him and with the subjects of the shot. We thought that people might be uneasy about posing, given what we had heard about photographs and death from Pat Kemp in Docker River. But since the book was being published far away those issues did not seem to concern the Warakurna people. Whether certain mountains and ridges were in a shot – that seemed to be the major consideration. The people being photographed would, after long discussion with Ivan, move themselves around until certain features of the landscape no longer appeared through the view-finder. Through all this, the *kaditja* man mentioned earlier leaned on the hood of a Holden, occasionally making his own comments, sometimes laughing.

Though the Warakurna people are so traditional, Ron Sanden says that when he became community adviser and inherited the management of the settlement store he spent a year winning the population away from Coca-Cola and onto fruit juice, and also away from white bread and sugar onto the brown varieties. There is guilt for a community adviser in managing a store. You are selling the people alien elements all the time. Yet a totally traditional life is no longer possible, and besides, the people demand certain things, such as playing cards. Aboriginals are enthusiastic card players. 'Cards cause almost as much trouble as grog,' says Ron Sanden. The hardest task, with a store, he says, is to convey the idea of credit, its limitations, why it cannot be endlessly given.

As a community adviser, Sanden says that he has pushed the idea that the people should have confidence when faced by whites, that they should not be too submissive and go against their true desires when a European presents them with concepts of housing, health, law, which he may think are entirely appropriate but which they know to be futile. That is why there is no housing in Warakurna. To a European the only question would be, 'What sort of housing would you like?' The idea that people might not want any is beyond the European terms of reference.

The other complication, says Ron Sanden, and nearly everyone else faced with that problem, is the difficulty of explaining the concept of Land Rights – it is a problem in the sense that when you see the earth as an extension of your body, the concept that you should go through a bewildering white legal process to show that what *is* organic to you belongs to you is beyond the grasp of most traditional people.

Behind the settlement, a compound is devoted to the orderly stacking of wrecked and abandoned vehicles. It is like a tide-mark of the mechanical world, the world of artificial organisms, the world of another legalism. Houses will ultimately come to Warakurna, and so will a legal understanding of Land Rights. But by that time the Dreaming and the special meanings of the earth may have withered.

Ron Sanden, community adviser at Warakurna in Western Australia. The community here is so traditional that they moved three-quarters of a kilometre down the road when an important man died near the store. Yet contradictorily it took Sanden a year to wean the Warakurna people off cola and onto fruit juice. The people are in limbo, he says.

PREVIOUS PAGE:
Perry, the scholarly truckie, taking supplies to Giles meteorological station in *Big Ernie*, named after Ernest Giles, the explorer. *Big Ernie* is likely to bog regularly in the sandy beds of dry rivers, and to get it out Perry has to reduce the pressure on all tyres to the point of flatness. Once across, he reinflates and drives on. He says there's a positive joy in delivering goods in country like this. Your arrival is always welcome.

OPPOSITE:
Pitjantjatjara family, Warakurna. The taking of this photograph required considerable discussion between community elders until a background was found which did not include important Dreaming sites.

End Note

We were to return to Alice by way of a road that swung down from Giles across the northwest of South Australia. This area was Pitjantjat-jara country too, in fact the South Australian government had given title over their section of this country to the Pitjantjatjaras themselves. Frank radioed ahead, however, using the portable two-way radio which you connect to the terminals of the battery in your vehicle, and found out that there were Red-Ochre ceremonies in progress near Amata in South Australia, and that the road would therefore be blocked. 'I could insist on going through,' said Frank, 'but it wouldn't be polite.'

The Red-Ochre men are a powerful lodge or free masonry which operates all through the Western Desert areas regardless of state boundaries – a disciplinary and ceremonial organization. They meet up periodically in one place for major ceremonies, called by their leaders according to criteria which are a mystery. They may even be a trans-tribal lodge – at Ayers Rock the Yankuntjatjara seem to be involved as well as the Pitjantjatjara. Each group of Red-Ochre men has specific responsibility for a given area. Like the *kaditja* man, when they travel through the country carrying the symbols of their authority, the Red-Ochre men move and operate with magical power, with the power of spirits. No white we spoke to seemed to be certain about the division of authority between Red-Ochre men and the *kaditja* man, what juris-diction belonged to each. Red-Ochre men though are always on the move in some part of the desert. When they get to the end of their zone, they meet up with the Red-Ochre men from the next area of authority and ceremonially hand on the emblems of their power. Derek Roff, the ranger of the Rock, says that he has never seen men so relieved as those who return to their normal lives after a stint as Red-Ochre men. The punishments they have exacted from wrong-doers, the ceremonies they have taken part in, have been an enormous ordeal, and it seems that the Red-Ochre man is under threat himself from the very spirits from which he takes his power. The fact that the Red-Ochre men would turn up in four-wheel-drives for their Amata meeting does not seem to have lessened in any obvious way the awe in which they are held.

Heading back east therefore in the late afternoon, having given up the idea of going back through South Australia, we left the road without warning, our vehicle careering off out of control southeast among the spinifex grass. A steering rod had snapped, which meant that one of the front wheels was travelling in any direction it chose. When Frank finally managed to stop, we pushed the vehicle back to the side of the road and made a camp. We radioed the Alice Springs police, who then radioed the Adelaide meteorological bureau, who then radioed Giles weather station.

Later that night we heard a truck on the road. It was three of the men from Giles, among them the mechanic. They had brought beer with them to last the journey and still had some left. 'They're all good practical men,' Perry Morey had said in his judicious manner, 'the men at Giles.' 'When we got the radio call,' the mechanic said, 'we were hoping it was three sheilas from Western Australia broken down out here and anxious for company. As it turns out, all it is is a bloody mug copper, a Pommie photographer and a poofter writer.' (To many Australians, anyone who has anything to do with the arts is referred to by the honorific 'poofter'. It is a futile answer to produce pictures of your children.)

After some more introductory talk, the Giles truck was turned headlights on to our headlights, and it took the six of us to jack up the front of the police vehicle in the soft red sand, an operation in which the good practical men of Giles showed a lot more aptitude than the Pommie photographer and the poofter writer.

For those who live in lonely weather stations, even something as mechanical as a steering rod can serve as an erotic symbol. It took nearly an hour and a lot of solidly earthy imagery to detach the steering rod from the front end of the police vehicle. Then the mechanic put on his goggles and welded the break. He talked non-stop throughout the welding; the pleasure he took in his expertise, in his capacity to fix us up for the road, in getting a copper, a photographer, a writer on their way again, was palpable. When he had finished, he considered the white hot mend. 'Well,' he said, 'in the absence of a Nubian slave to leak on it, we're going to have to exercise blackfeller's patience and bury it in the sand for an hour while it anneals.'

So, while everyone drank tea, the steering rod was buried, later disinterred, and screwed back in place. Again the lonely weather men and mechanic of Giles missed out on none of the possible metaphors.

The welded steering rod lasted throughout the long tough road back to Alice.

Final Note

Most of the pictures for this book were taken by two professional photographers. But before I speak of them I must thank my wife, Judith Keneally, for the pictures she herself contributed and for her skill in research and in preparing the groundwork for many of the contacts recorded in this book. The historic shots which appeared herein came from the Northern Territory Tourist Commission, from a devout Territorian called Chris Torlach. The photograph of the Australian Minister for Aboriginal Affairs* handing title to land at Hermannsburg over to Arunta people, as also the photograph of Cyclone Tracy's devastation, come from the Australian Information Service.

* The Minister in the photograph is, incidentally, not the one involved in the Jabiru negotiations mentioned earlier.

PREVIOUS PAGE:
Mates, Beswick. Later, the enormous gulf of values between the two races will itself put stress on such friendships.

The Australian Minister for Aboriginal Affairs hands over title deeds to traditional owners in the Hermannsburg area.

An expatriate English photographer called Mark Lang took over the photographing of this book after the death of Gary Hansen. Mark Lang is rake-lean, a goon, a grand enthusiast. With his tripod and his silver case of equipment he would vault the flames of bushfires to get a shot from the epicentre of the blaze. He is the type of man who constructs each photograph; he did not shoot from the hip and in great quantity as the effusive Gary Hansen did. I believe the styles of both men, based on differences of temperament but on equal expertise, complement each other very well in these pages.

Gary Hansen began the book and shot – on our initial reconnaissance of northern Australia – something like thirty per cent of the photographic material needed for the work. He knew the outback intimately,

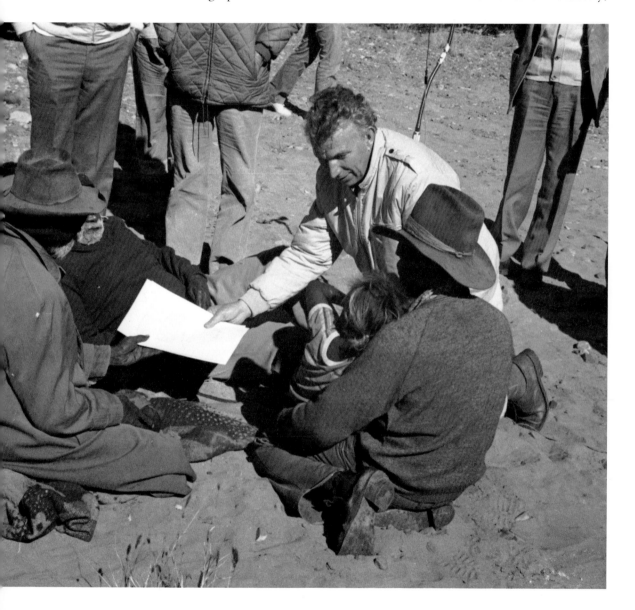

drove like a rally driver on its dubious tracks and was constantly vivified by it. Physically he was large, curly haired, beak-nosed. He threw himself like a large and zealous bird around a landscape he loved.

The late and revered Gary Hansen on top of Ayers Rock, two weeks before his death.

As a cinematographer he had worked on a number of Australian movies, but he had also produced a book of stills called *Australia – Impressions of a Continent*. He had been cameraman with Lord Snowdon on the Bourke and Wills segment of *The Explorers* for BBC television. More recently he had worked as director of cinematography on *We of the Never-Never*.

In Katherine one day we met three former Northern Territory cops who had served as omni-providers on the production of *We of the Never-Never*, which was to be Gary Hansen's last feature film. 'Anything the director wanted, we got,' they boasted. 'Even broke into Elder's three times for him.' Gary had previously spoken to me about these three. His favourite story about them was that one evening the director had asked them to provide three speared bullocks for the next day's shoot, and at dawn the next morning the bullocks were delivered to the set (the film was shot on the Elsey itself) each with a discreet bullet-hole behind its ear and studded with spears. 'I mean, ordinary people ought to work on a picture once in their lifetime, just for the experience,' said one of the three. 'That film crew – there they were, living out at Mataranka on the fat of the land, feeding like stud bloody bulls, and the bastards were whingeing. I said to one of them, what would you be doing if you were in Sydney now? I'll tell you what. You'd be eating some Greek rubbish and getting run over by taxis.'

The truth was that the film crew and actors had gone stir crazy in Mataranka on a steady diet of hard work, isolation and chicken supreme. To the three former coppers though, life on the set had been plush times. 'I'll never forget when I was stirring up what was supposed to be the Ferguson River, for when Jeanie Gunn crossed it by flying fox. They paid me twenty dollars an hour and one hundred and fifty dollars for the use of my power boat. And all I did all day was drive in circles, making waves, one hand on the wheel, a can of Carlton in the other. If I can just find someone silly enough to offer me work like that for the rest of my life!' But though these three Territorians may not have respected all of those 'city poofters', their respect for Gary Hansen was obvious.

My journeys with Gary in the Territory featured a recurrent scene which reminded me always – since Gary was a cinematographer – of the brilliant well scene in David Leen's *Lawrence of Arabia*, the scene in which a dot on the horizon, wavering in heat haze, ultimately becomes a human figure who suddenly solidifies, arrives, makes a statement. In the case of the scene in *Lawrence*, the statement was that the arriving Arab shot the one who stood beside Lawrence himself.

The outcome was never so violent in our case, but always we would see a wavering dot in the distance, and it would turn into a horseman, riding through the apparent lakes of heat haze and arriving and solidifying with the question, called over a distance of perhaps fifty metres, 'G'day, you great hairy bastard! When's that bloody picture goin' to be on?' For half the Katherine area seemed to have been involved as extras, as horsemen or helpers, on the production of *We of the Never-Never*.

The cinematography of the film is dazzling, and though Gary won posthumously the Australian Film Industry award for it, the prize was no sentimental gesture – he would have won it in any case. Nothing expresses the Territory better than the opening sequence. It is a helicopter shot of an immensity of tall grass. We move at grass-top level in a landscape vast as Siberia, and we see nothing human. Just as the scope of this ancient and beautiful earth begins to oppress us we catch sight of a small feature, a horseman galloping among the grass, a figure reduced to insignificance by the earth, yet not in the least aware of that, a man on an errand, a man with purposes that dominate distance.

Between journeys to the Territory, Gary was working on similar shots, but in more dangerous terrain, for the New South Wales Tourist Commission. He always hated helicopter shoots, the machines alarmed him, and given the number of accidents that result from filming by helicopter he had good statistical grounds to be wary of the machines. He was filming mountain horsemen above an alpine meadow in the Snowy Mountains when the helicopter from which he was working struck power lines. The pilot was thrown clear, but Gary, his assistant, his director were all killed.

This book is heartily dedicated to his memory.

Illustration
Acknowledgments

The photographs on pages 10, 12, 13, 14, 17, 18, 20–21, 25, 27, 28–9 *above*, 29 *below*, 34, 36, 38, 43, 44, 45, 64, 88, 89, 91, 98, 102, 103, 110, 111, 114, 116, 117, 118–19, 120, 123, 126, 137, 142, 143, 152, 153, 154, 171, 176, 177, 183, 189 *below*, 192 *above*, 194, 202, 203, 206, 209, 216 *above*, 228, 229 and 250 were taken specially for this book by the late Gary Hansen and those on pages 15, 16, 19, 28 *below*, 30–31, 32–3, 39, 40–41, 46, 48, 52, 57, 65, 68, 78, 100–101, 113, 122, 124, 125, 130–31, 138–9, 145, 148, 151, 159, 163, 165, 167, 172–3, 174, 174–5, 178–9, 184–5, 189 *above*, 190–91, 192 *below*, 195, 198–9, 201, 204, 205, 210–11, 212–13, 214 *above*, 214–15 *below*, 215 *above*, 223, 226, 230, 233, 234, 238, 240, 241, 242, 244, 245 and 246 by Mark Lang.

The author and publishers of this book are also grateful to the following for permission to reproduce the photographs on the pages indicated. The Australian Information Service for the photographs on pages 74–5 and 249; the Bradshaw Collection by courtesy of the Conservation Commission of the Northern Territory for the photographs on pages 82–3; the Conservation Commission of the Northern Territory for the photographs on pages 60, 84–5 and 149; Judy Keneally for the photographs on pages 105, 140 and 200; Peter Kingston, courtesy of the Northern Territory Trust Commission for the photograph on page 216 *below*; the National Trust of Australia (Northern Territory) for the photographs on pages 70–71 and 104–5; the Wutke Collection by courtesy of the Conservation Commission of the Northern Territory for the photographs on pages 83 and 86–7.

Index